The Quotable Lawyer

David S. Shrager
and
Elizabeth Frost

A New England Publishing Associates Book

Facts On File
New York

The Quotable Lawyer

Copyright © 1986 by New England Publishing Associates, Inc.

Facts On File, Inc.
460 Park Avenue South
New York NY 10016

Library of Congress Cataloging in Publication Data
Main entry under title:

The Quotable lawyer.

"A New England Publishing Associates book."
Bibliography: p.
Includes index.
1. Law—Quotations. I. Shrager, David S.
II. Frost, Elizabeth.
K58.Q86 1986   340'.02   85-10380
ISBN 0-8160-1184-2 (hc)
ISBN 0-8160-2058-2 (pb)

A British CIP catalog record for this book is available from the British Library.

Facts On File books are available at special discounts when purchased in bulk
quantities for businesses, associations, institutions or sales promotions. Please call
our Special Sales Department in New York at 212/683-2244 or 800/322-8755.

Cover design by Ron Monteleone
Manufactured by the Maple-Vail Book Manufacturing Group
Printed in the United States of America

10 9 8 7 6 5

CONTENTS

CONTENTS

*Elizabeth Frost would like to dedicate this book
to her mother, Lorena*

INTRODUCTION

From the time of the ancient Greeks, law has been the bedrock of civilized society. The Ten Commandments, the Code of Justinian, the Magna Carta and the United States Constitution represent a common thread of basic rules of conduct which govern the relationships among individuals and with their rulers or governments.

As society grew more complex and rule by dictatorial fiat or royal decree became intolerable, lawyers and jurists became necessary to interpret and apply the law, and to protect individual rights and liberties. As lawyers became advocates for a partisan viewpoint, whether before a court or jury, their success came to be determined by the skill and art of their persuasive communication. Lawyers and judges have become "word merchants" in the best sense. The successful advocate should be able to synthesize a complex legal precedent in a few pithy sentences and articulate a point of view within the sweep of a compelling sentence.

Lawyers and jurists have been among the most articulate professionals. Louis Brandeis, William Seward, Felix Frankfurter, Oliver Wendell Holmes, Jr., Learned Hand and William O. Douglas are just a few of the many brilliant and quotable attorneys and jurists, whose names are now well etched in American jurisprudence. There is surely no subject for a book of quotations more deserving and appropriate than the law.

But the law has not been the object of discussion or quotation only by members of the judiciary and bar. Not surprisingly, the legal system has been the focus of comment by every sector of society. Lawyers as partisans and the sometime purveyors of ill tidings have been subjected to criticism over the ages. "First, let's kill all the lawyers" was simply the Shakespearean articulation of the practice of the ancient Greeks who first received the message from the bearer of ill tidings and then proceeded to kill the bearer. "The law's delay" may be seen as a pejorative reference to the predictable reaction of the citizen who perceives that his or her case is not being expeditiously handled by the legal system.

The Quotable Lawyer brings together nearly 2,600 of the best quotes concerning the law, made not only by jurists and lawyers, but also by priests, poets, playwrights, prophets, politicians, humorists, actors and activists. In this respect, the book for the first time gathers within one volume the best in the written and spoken word from a wide variety of sources, so long as the quotes serve the common theme of comments relating to the legal arena.

In another departure from earlier works, *The Quotable Lawyer* cites several hundred quotations by women. Other volumes, limiting themselves largely to comments by members of the legal profession, have omitted quotations by women. Although it is only in recent years that women have entered the law in large numbers, already including prestigious practitioners and jurists within their ranks, they have not been silent on the law, whether as writers, thinkers or activists. Their observations, from the 16th century on, will be found here.

Since there has not been a legal quotation book published in the United States for more than 15 years, the editors have attempted to incorporate as many quotations as possible from the past decade. There is no geographic preference as to source, though most recent citations tend to be from this side of the Atlantic.

The quotations have been organized in chapters in a topical fashion, and arranged chronologically within each chapter. Anonymous comments, Biblical and Talmudic quotes, maxims, proverbs and folk sayings will all be found at the beginning of the chapters. Following each quotation, its author, source and approximate date are given. In the event the precise date of the quote could not reasonably be established, the biographical dates of the author are identified.

As a practical matter, the editors have not identified those men and women listed in the biographical section of *Webster's Ninth New Collegiate Dictionary*. Nor have they identified well-known contemporary figures, such as popular writers, entertainers and the like. Career descriptions have been supplied for obscure figures and those who are perhaps not widely known outside their field. In some instances, a career description is followed by a job description, which indicates the position held by the author at the time of the quotation, e.g., Donald Cressey, American educator; professor, University of California, Santa Barbara; Bernard Segal, American lawyer; president, American Bar Association; Frank Hague, American politician; mayor, Jersey City, New Jersey.

The Quotable Lawyer also contains an Index of Authors and an Index of Subjects, in which the quotations are topically arranged along with their entry numbers. This index also contains cross-references to other subjects under which related quotations can be located.

No edited work of this sort could have been completed without reference to the many collections that have come before. The volumes that have been particularly helpful are listed in the selective bibliography at the end of the book. Other sources are cited throughout the text.

The editors would like to express their sincere appreciation to the following people for their generous help:

John Thornton, Joe Reilly, Eleanor Wedge and Adrienne Saich for their invaluable editorial advice and assistance

Elizabeth Clifford and Sarah Claudine Kurian for their help in researching, compiling and typing the quotations

Mark Carson, John Guinther and William Packard for contributing their favorite sayings

David Shrager
Elizabeth Frost

A

1. ACCOMPLICES

1.1 How near to guilt without actual guilt.
> Latin proverb
> W. Gurney Benham, *Putnam's Complete Book of Quotations, Proverbs and Household Words,* 1927

1.2 He who helps the guilty shares the crime.
> Publilius Syrus, Latin writer
> *Sententiae,* c.43 B.C.

1.3 He who profits by a crime commits it.
> Seneca, *4 B.C. ?– A.D. 65*
> *Medea,* 1st century

1.4 He who does not prevent a crime when he can encourages it.
> Seneca, *4 B.C. ?–A.D. 65*
> *Troades,* 1st century

1.5 No one shall be a thief with me as his helper.
> Juvenal
> *Satires,* c.120

1.6 Those who consent to the act and those who do it shall be equally punished.
> Sir Edward Coke, *1552–1634*
> W. Gurney Benham, *Putnam's Complete Book of Quotations, Proverbs and Household Words,* 1927

2. ACCUSATIONS

2.1 Trust me, no tortures which the poets feign,
Can match the fierce, the unutterable pain,
He feels, who night and day, devoid of rest,
Carries his own accuser in his breast.
Juvenal
Satires, c.120

2.2 Let your accusations be few in number, even if they be just.
Xystus I, pope
The Ring, c.120

2.3 It warms the very sickness in my heart,
That I shall live and tell him to his teeth,
"Thus diddest thou."
Shakespeare
Hamlet, IV, 7, 1600–1601

2.4 Like a rough orator, that brings more truth
Than rhetoric, to make good his accusation.
Philip Massinger
Great Duke of Florence, 1627

2.5 The best apology against false accusers is silence and sufferance, and honest deeds set against dishonest words.
John Milton
Apology for Smectymnuus, 1642

2.6 Believe not each accusing tongue,
As most weak persons do;
But still believe that story wrong,
Which ought not to be true.
Attributed to Richard Brinsley
Sheridan, *1751–1816*
W. Gurney Benham, *Putnam's
Complete Book of Quotations, Proverbs
and Household Words,* 1927

2.7 In all criminal proceedings, the accused shall enjoy the right . . . to be informed of the nature and cause of the accusations, [and] to be confronted with the witnesses against him.
Constitution of the United States,
Sixth Amendment, 1791

2.8 The breath
Of accusation kills an innocent name,
And leaves for lame acquittal the poor life,
Which is a mask without it.
Percy Bysshe Shelley
The Cenci, 1819

2.9 The law does not expect a man to be prepared to defend every act of his life which may be suddenly and without notice alleged against him.
John Marshall, *1755–1835*
Albert J. Beveridge, III, *Life of
Marshall,* 1919

2.10 It is not uncommon for ignorant and corrupt men to falsely charge others with doing what they imagine that they themselves, in their narrow minds and experience, would have done under the circumstances. . . .
John H. Clarke, American jurist
Valdez v. United States, 244 U.S. 432, 450 (1917)

2.11 Lady Helen: To accuse is so easy that it is infamous to do so where proof is impossible!
Zoë Akins, American writer
Déclassé, 1919

2.12 The Constitution . . . speaks not only of the freedom of speech but also of trial by jury instead of trial by accusation.
Margaret Chase Smith
Newsweek, June 12, 1950

2.13 When a man points a finger at someone else, he should remember that four of his fingers are pointing at himself.
Louis Nizer
My Life in Court, 1960

2.14 Ours is an accusatorial and not an inquisitorial system—a system in which the state must establish guilt by evidence independently and freely secured and may not by coercion prove its charge against an accused out of his own mouth.
Felix Frankfurter
In majority opinion that confessions extracted by police coercion may not be used in evidence, March 26, 1961

3. ACTS

3.1 Those who do a thing are consenting parties.
Latin proverb

3.2 Overlook our deeds, since you know that crime was absent from our inclination.
Ovid
Fasti, c.8

3.3 Good laws are begot by bad actions.
Macrobius
Saturnalia, c.400

3.4 Do as we say, and not as we do.
Giovanni Boccaccio
Decameron, 1348–1353

3.5 The best way to keep good acts in memory is to refresh them with new.
Francis Bacon
Apophthagmes, 1625

3.6 Laws undertake to punish only overt acts.
de Montesquieu
The Spirit of Laws, 1748

3.7   A man wants no protection when his conduct is strictly right.
William Murray, 1st earl of
Mansfield, English jurist; chief justice
Bird v. Gunston (1785), 3 Doug. 275

3.8   Never do today what you can do as well tomorrow; because something may occur to make you regret your premature action.
Aaron Burr,   *1756–1836*
Marshall Brown, *Wit and Humor of Bench and Bar,* 1899

3.9   Our deeds determine us, as much as we determine our deeds.
George Eliot
Adam Bede, 1859

3.10   But the character of every act depends upon the circumstances in which it is done.
Oliver Wendell Holmes
Schenck v. United States, 249 U.S. 47, 52 (1919)

3.11   We cannot think first and act afterwards. From the moment of birth we are immersed in action, and can only fitfully guide it by taking thought.
Alfred North Whitehead,   *1816–1947*
Franklin Pierce Adams, *F.P.A. Book of Quotations,* 1952

3.12   Inaction without more is not tantamount to choice.
Benjamin N. Cardozo
Richard v. Credit Suisse, 242 N.Y. 346, 351 (1926)

3.13   Action . . . stimulates hope.
Louis Nizer
My Life in Court, 1960

4.   ADVERSARY PROCESS

4.1   . . . my desire is . . . that mine adversary had written a book.
Old Testament, *Job* 31:35

4.2   And do as adversaries do in law—
Strive mightily, but eat and drink as friends.
Shakespeare
The Taming of the Shrew, I, 2, 1593–1594

4.3   In case of defence 'tis best to weigh
The enemy more mighty than he seems.
Shakespeare
Henry V, II, 4, 1598–1599

4.4   My prayer to God is a very short one: "O Lord, make my enemies very ridiculous!"
Voltaire
Letter to M. Damilaville, May 1767

4.5 Treating your adversary with respect is giving him an advantage to which he is not entitled.
Samuel Johnson
James Boswell, *The Life of Samuel Johnson,* 1791

4.6 When a man voluntarily engages in an important controversy, he is to do all he can to lessen his antagonist, because authority from personal respect has much weight with most people, and often more than reasoning. . . .
Adams: You would not jostle a chimney-sweeper.
Johnson: Yes, Sir, if it were necessary to jostle him *down.*
Samuel Johnson
James Boswell, *The Life of Samuel Johnson,* 1791

4.7 A man cannot be too careful in the choice of his enemies.
Oscar Wilde
The Picture of Dorian Gray, 1891

4.8 It's not my enemies I worry about. It's my friends.
Warren Harding, *1865–1923*
New York Times, July 9, 1984

4.9 [A farmer], before sunrise on a cold and misty morning, saw a huge beast on a distant hill. He seized his rifle and walked cautiously toward the ogre to head off an attack on his family. When he got nearer, he was relieved to find that the beast was only a small bear. He approached more confidently and when he was within a few hundred yards the distorting haze had lifted sufficiently so that he could recognize the figure as only that of a man. Lowering his rifle, he walked toward the stranger and discovered he was his brother.
Louis Nizer
My Life in Court, 1960

4.10 . . . the advocacy system has become a means of exploiting the weaknesses of our system . . . using the legitimate safeguards built into our system to prevent it from functioning effectively.
Ronald Reagan
Address, State Bar Association of California, November 15, 1972

4.11 The business of the advocate, simply stated, is to win if possible without violating the law.
Marvin E. Frankel, American jurist; judge, U.S. District Court
National Observer, November 1, 1975

4.12 In most cases, both sides have much to gain by accommodating and very much to lose by litigating. But in many situations, the lawyers, following their professional attachment to strict adversary loyalties, find themselves obstructing the way toward mutual compromise.
Robert Coulson, president, American Arbitration Association
Address, American Bar Association, reported in the *Los Angeles Times,* August 30, 1976

4.13 . . . trials by the adversarial contest must in time go the way of the ancient trial by battle and blood.
Warren Burger
Speech, American Bar Association, Las Vegas, February 12, 1984

5. ADVICE

5.1   If the old dog barks, he gives counsel.
German proverb
W. Gurney Benham, *Putnam's Complete Book of Quotations,* 1927

5.2   Counsel is as welcome to him as a Shoulder of Mutton to a sick Horse.
Proverb
Thomas Fuller, *Gnomologia,* 1732

5.3   Advice is judged by results, not by intentions.
Cicero
Ad Atticum, c.66 B.C.

5.4   Who cannot give good counsel? 'Tis cheap, it costs them nothing.
Robert Burton
Anatomy of Melancholy, 1621

5.5   If any whimsical notions are put into you by some enthusiastic counsel, the Court is not to take notice of their crotchets.
George Jeffreys
Hayes' Case (1684), 13 How. St. Tr. 134

5.6   Better counsel comes overnight.
Gotthold Ephraim Lessing
Emilia Galotti, 1772

5.7   We ask advice, but we mean approbation.
Charles Caleb Colton
Lacon, 1820

5.8   Extremely foolish advice is likely to be uttered by those who are looking at the laboring vessel from the land.
Sir Arthur Helps, English historian and writer
Friends in Council, 1847–1859

5.9   A lawyer's advice is his stock in trade.
Attributed to Abraham Lincoln, *1809–1865*
M. Francis McNamara, *Ragbag of Legal Quotations,* 1960

5.10   The fact that a lawyer advised such foolish conduct, does not relieve it of its foolishness. . . .
Lucilius A. Emery, American jurist
Hanscom v. Marson, 82 Me. 288, 298 (1890)

5.11   It is always a silly thing to give advice, but to give good advice is absolutely fatal.
Oscar Wilde
Portrait of Mr. W. H., 1890

5.12 He had only one vanity; he thought he could give advice better than any other person.
Mark Twain
The Man That Corrupted Halleyburg,
1900

5.13 [*Advice*:] The smallest current coin.
Ambrose Bierce
The Devil's Dictionary, 1906

5.14 The advice of the elders to young men is very apt to be as unreal as a list of the hundred best books.
Oliver Wendell Holmes
"The Path of the Law," *Collected Legal Papers,* 1921

5.15 [When business people want] creative legal opinion, [lawyers] often give business advice, which is as good as my legal opinion. . . . They tell us "this is the law," when the truth and what they should be saying is, "this is our opinion of the law."
Donald P. Kelly, American business executive; president, Esmark Corporation
Address, American Bar Association, Chicago, reported in the *San Francisco Examiner & Chronicle,* August 14, 1977

6. AGREEMENTS

6.1 Agreement makes law.
Latin legal maxim
W. Gurney Benham, *Putnam's Complete Book of Quotations, Proverbs and Household Words,* 1927

6.2 A lean agreement is better than a fat judgment.
Proverb
Rosalind Fergusson, *The Facts On File Dictionary of Proverbs,* 1983

6.3 They two agreed like two cats in a gutter.
Proverb
John Heywood, *Proverbs,* 1546

6.4 Men keep agreements when it is to the advantage of neither to break them.
Ascribed to Solon, *c.630–c.560 B.C.*

6.5 The main object of conciliation lies in reaching a solution to a case based upon morals and with a warm heart.
Confucius
Analects, c.500 B.C.

6.6 We seldom attribute common sense except to those who agree with us.
La Rochefoucauld
Maximes, 1665

6.7 It is evident that many great and useful objects can be attained in this world only by cooperation. It is equally evident that there cannot be efficient co-operation if men proceed on the principle that they must not cooperate for one object unless they agree about other objects.

Thomas Babington Macaulay
Gladstone on Church and State, 1839

6.8 Ah! don't say you agree with me. When people agree with me I always feel that I must be wrong.

Oscar Wilde
The Critic as Artist, 1891

7. ALIBIS

7.1 Poor men's reasons are not heard.
German proverb
W. Gurney Benham, *Putnam's Complete Book of Quotations, Proverbs and Household Words,* 1927

7.2 [*Alibi:*] a lie by which criminals escape punishment.
Dublin barrister
Marshall Brown, *Wit and Wisdom of Bench and Bar,* 1899

7.3 Better a bad excuse than none.
Nicholas Udall
Ralph Roister Doister, c.1553

7.4 And, oftentimes, excusing of a fault
Doth make the fault worse by the excuse.
Shakespeare
King John, I, 1, 1596–1597

7.5 I know'd what 'ud come o' this here mode o' doin bisness. Oh Sammy, Sammy, vy worn't there a alleybi!
Charles Dickens
Pickwick Papers, 1836–1837

7.6 If your governor don't prove a alleybi, he'll be what the Italians call reg'larly flummoxed.
Charles Dickens
Pickwick Papers, 1836–37

7.7 He always has an alibi, and one or two to spare:
At whatever time the deed took place—
Macavity wasn't there.
T.S. Eliot, *1888–1965*
Macavity: The Mystery Cat

8. APPEALS

8.1   Once a lawyer was arguing a case before three lord justices in the court of appeal, dealing with an elementary point of law at inordinate length. Finally, the master of the rolls, who was presiding, intervened: "Really," he protested, "do give this court credit for some intelligence." Quick as a flash came the reply: "That is the mistake I made in the court below, my lord."
> Anonymous
> Archibald Edgar Bowker,
> *A Lifetime with the Law,* 1961

8.2   It is needless to enter into many reasons for quashing the conviction, when one alone is fully sufficient.
> William Murray, 1st earl of
> Mansfield, English jurist; chief justice
> *Rex v. Jarvis* (1756), 1 Burr. Part IV,
> p. 152

8.3   The point appears here in its virgin state, wearing all its maiden blushes, and is therefore out of place.
> Logan E. Bleckley, American jurist
> *Cleveland v. Chambliss,* 64 Ga. 352,
> 359 (1879)

8.4   If no appeal were possible . . . this would not be a desirable country to live in. . . .
> Charles Bowen, English jurist; lord
> justice
> *The Queen v. Justices of County of
> London* (1893), L.R. 2 Q.B. 492

8.5   [*Appeal*:] In law, to put the dice into the box for another throw.
> Ambrose Bierce
> *The Devil's Dictionary,* 1906

8.6   An appeal, Hinnissy, is where ye ask wan coort to show its contempt f'r another coort.
> Finley Peter Dunne
> *Mr. Dooley Says: The Big Fine,* 1906

8.7   In this Court dissents have gradually become majority opinions.
> Felix Frankfurter
> *Graves v. New York ex rel. O'Keefe*
> 306 U.S. 466; 83 L.Ed. 927; 59 Sup.
> Ct. 595 (1939)

8.8   We granted certiorari, and in this Court the parties changed positions as nimbly as if dancing a quadrille.
> Robert H. Jackson
> *Orloff v. Willoughby,* 345 U.S. 83, 87
> (1953)

8.9   Appeal must be to an informed, civically militant electorate.
Felix Frankfurter
Baker v. Carr, 369 U.S. 186, 82 S. Ct. 691, 7 L.Ed.2d 663 (1962)

8.10   "[Dissents are] appeals to the brooding spirit of the law, to the intelligence of another day."
Charles Evans Hughes, *1930–1941*
Irving Kaufman, "Keeping Politics out of the Court," *New York Times,* December 9, 1984

9. ARGUMENTS

9.1   A lawyer's primer: If you don't have the law, you argue the facts; if you don't have the facts, you argue the law; if you have neither the facts nor the law, then you argue the Constitution.
Anonymous

9.2   He opens the door with an ax.
English proverb
John Ray, *English Proverbs,* 1678

9.3   The sergeant pleads with face on fire,
And all the court may rue it;
His purple garments come from Tyre;
His arguments go to it.
Epigram
Marshall Brown, *Wit and Humor of Bench and Bar,* 1899

9.4   Prepare your proof before you argue.
Jewish folk saying
Joseph L. Baron, *A Treasury of Jewish Quotations,* 1956

9.5   An argument derived from the abuse of a thing does not hold good against its use.
Latin legal phrase
W. Gurney Benham, *Putnam's Complete Book of Quotations, Proverbs and Household Words,* 1927

9.6   There is no arguing with one who denies first principles.
Latin legal phrase
W. Gurney Benham, *Putnam's Complete Book of Quotations, Proverbs and Household Words,* 1927

9.7   A legal decision depends not on the teacher's age, but on the force of his argument.
Talmud, *Bava Batra*

9.8   Do not attempt to confute a lion after he's dead.
Talmud, *Gittin*

9.9   No honest man will argue on every side.
Sophocles
Oedipus at Colonus, c.408 B.C.

9.10 In a just cause it is right to be confident.
Sophocles, *496?–406 B.C.*
W. Gurney Benham, *Putnam's Complete Book of Quotations, Proverbs and Household Words*, 1927

9.11 Arguments derived from probabilities are idle.
Plato
Phaedo, c. late 4th century B.C.

9.12 We must make a personal attack when there is no argumentative basis for our speech.
Cicero
Pro Flacco, c.58 B.C.

9.13 In a heated argument we lose sight of the truth.
Publilius Syrus, Latin writer
Sententiae, c.43 B.C.

9.14 Who over-refines his argument brings himself to grief.
Petrarch
Vita di Madonna Laura, c.1350

9.15 He draweth out the thread of his verbosity finer than the staple of his argument.
Shakespeare
Love's Labour's Lost, V, 1, 1594–1595

9.16 Be calm in arguing; for fierceness makes
Error a fault, and truth discourtesy.
George Herbert
"The Church Porch," *The Temple,* 1633

9.17 Bluster, sputter, question, cavil; but be sure your argument be intricate enough to confound the court.
William Wycherley
The Plain Dealer, 1677

9.18 He'd undertake to prove, by force
Of argument, a man's no horse.
He'd prove a buzzard is no fowl,
And that a Lord may be an owl,
A calf an Alderman, a goose a Justice,
And rooks, Committee-men or Trustees.
Samuel Butler
Hudibras, 1663–1678

9.19 First settle what the case is, before you argue it.
Lord Chief Justice Howe
Trial of the Seven Bishops (1688), 12 How. St. Tr. 342

9.20 I know you lawyers can, with ease,
Twist words and meanings as you please.
John Gay
Fables, 1727

9.21 Heat is in proportion to the want of true knowledge.
Laurence Sterne
Tristram Shandy, 1760

9.22 It seems to me that the defendant's counsel blows hot and cold at the same time.
Justice Buller
I'Anson v. Stuart (1787), 1 T.R. 753

9.23 [Johnson said] . . . striking his foot with mighty force against a large stone, till he rebounded from it, "I refute it thus."
Samuel Johnson
James Boswell, *The Life of Samuel Johnson,* 1791

9.24 He is an ingenious council who has made the most of his cause; he is not obliged to join it.
Samuel Johnson
James Boswell, *The Life of Samuel Johnson,* 1791

9.25   This is the last hair in the tail of procrastination.
> Sir Lloyd Kenyon, English jurist; lord chief justice; sitting in the Rolls Court, indignant at one of the parties, late 18th century
> Marshall Brown, *Wit and Humor of Bench and Bar,* 1899

9.26   Be brief, be pointed, let your matter stand
Lucid in order, solid and at hand;
Spend not your words on trifles but condense;
Strike with the mass of thought, not drops of sense;
Press to the close with vigor, once begun,
And leave—how hard the task!—leave off when done.
> Joseph Story
> *Advice to a Young Lawyer,* 1835

9.27   I was with you, Mr. Scott [Lord Eldon]—until I heard your argument.
> Edward Thurlow, English jurist; lord chancellor, *1731–1806*
> Sir Travers Twiss, *Life of Lord Eldon,* 1844

9.28   The gentleman puts me in mind of an old hen which persists in setting after her eggs are taken away.
> Fisher Ames, American lawyer, *1758–1808,* referring to opposing counsel
> Theophilus Parsons, *Memoirs of Theophilus Parsons,* 1859

9.29   The last point is perfectly new, and it is so startling that I do not apprehend it will ever become old.
> Sir William Henry Maule, English jurist
> *Whitaker v. Wisbey* (1852), 12 C.B. 44, 58

9.30   Once, when he [Lord Mackay] was counsel in a case the presiding judge asked him whether he estimated it would be possible to start the next case after lunch time the next day: "Oh yes, my Lord," replied Mackay. "I'll certainly have finished my argument by then." "Yes, Mr. Mackay," said the judge, "I know you'll have finished, but will you stop?"
> Lord Mackay, Scottish jurist
> Francis Cowper, "London Letter," *New York Law Journal,* April 8, 1963

9.31   The weapon of the advocate is the sword of the soldier, not the dagger of the assassin.
> Ascribed to Sir Alexander Cockburn, British jurist; lord chief justice, *1802–1880*
> H. L. Mencken, *A New Dictionary of Quotations,* 1946

9.32   When facts were weak, his native cheek
Brought him serenely through.
> Charles H. Spurgeon, English devine *1834–1892,* commenting on an eminent lawyer
> W. Gurney Benham, *Putnam's Complete Book of Legal Quotations, Proverbs and Household Words,* 1927

9.33   No mistake is so commonly made by clever people as that of assuming a cause to be bad because the arguments of its supporters are, to a great extent, nonsensical.
> Thomas H. Huxley
> *Science and Education—Essays,* 1897

9.34   "You are old," said the youth, "and your jaws are too weak
For anything tougher than suet;
Yet you finished the goose, with the bones and the beak.
Pray, how did you manage to do it?"

"In my youth," said his father, "I took to the law,
And argued each case with my wife,

And the muscular strength which it gave to my jaw
Has lasted the rest of my life."
Lewis Carroll, *1832-1898*
"You Are Old, Father William"

9.35 If the court please, I am about to illustrate it by diagrams, and I hope to make it so plain that the audience and perhaps the court will understand it.
James T. Brown, American lawyer, addressing a circuit court judge in Indiana
Marshall Brown, *Wit and Humor of Bench and Bar*, 1899

9.36 If the court will listen, the court will learn.
John A. Campbell, American jurist
Marshall Brown, *Wit and Humor of Bench and Bar*, 1899

9.37 But to generalize is to omit. . . .
Oliver Wendell Holmes
Donnell v. Herring–Hall–Marvin Safe Co., 208 U.S. 267, 273 (1908)

9.38 We see what you are driving at, but you have not said it, and therefore we shall go on as before.
Oliver Wendell Holmes
Johnson v. United States, 163 Fed. 30, 31 (1908)

9.39 One has to try to strike the jugular and let the rest go.
Oliver Wendell Holmes
Speeches, 1913

9.40 Lawyers earn their bread in the sweat of their browbeating.
James Huneker
Painted Veils, 1920

9.41 To be brief is almost a condition of being inspired.
George Santayana
Little Essays, 1920

9.42 The obvious is better than obvious avoidance of it.
H. W. Fowler
A Dictionary of Modern English Usage, 1926

9.43 To get the sympathy of the Tribunal for himself ought always to be one of the first objects of the advocate.
Richard Burdon Haldane
An Autobiography, 1929

9.44 The elaborate argument . . . does not need an elaborate answer.
Oliver Wendell Holmes
United States v. Wurzbach, 280 U.S. 396, 399 (1930)

9.45 A judge of the Massachusetts Supreme Judicial Court found the long-winded speeches of lawyers especially trying and advised them to take a course of reading risque books that they might learn to say things by innuendo.
Attributed to a judge of the Massachusetts Supreme Judicial Court
Ed Bander, *Justice Holmes ex Cathedra*, 1966

9.46 The brilliant, ruthless F. E. Smith, afterwards Lord Chancellor Birkenhead, was a master of the unanswerable *riposte*. Once when he was starting his opening speech for a plaintiff an impatient judge interrupted him saying: "I've read the pleadings in this matter and I don't think much of your case." "Oh, I'm very sorry to hear that, my lord" replied Smith smoothly, "but you'll find that the more you hear of it the more it will grow on you." On another occasion a judge unwisely said to Smith who was opening a complicated case: "I've listened to you for an hour and I'm none the wiser." "None the wiser, perhaps,

my lord," said Smith, "but certainly better informed."
Frederick Edwin Smith, English jurist; lord chancellor *1872–1930* Francis Cowper "London Letter," *New York Law Journal,* August 28, 1961

9.47 Expediency may tip the scales when arguments are nicely balanced.
Benjamin N. Cardozo *Woolford Realty Co. v. Rose,* 286 U.S. 319, 330, 76 L.Ed. 1128, 52 S. Ct. 568 (1932)

9.48 A doctrine capable of being stated only in obscure and involved terms is open to reasonable suspicion of being either crude or erroneous.
Sir Frederick Pollock, *1845–1937* Mark De Wolfe Howe, *Holmes-Pollock Letters,* 1946

9.49 The picture cannot be painted if the significant and the insignificant are given equal prominence. One must know how to select.
Benjamin N. Cardozo, *1870–1938* "Law and Literature," *Selected Writings of Benjamin Nathan Cardozo,* edited by Margaret E. Hall, 1947

9.50 Or, supposing fishes had the gift of speech, who would listen to a fisherman's weary discourse on flycasting, the shape and color of the fly, the size of the tackle, the length of the line, the merit of different rod makers and all the other tiresome stuff that fishermen talk about, if the fish himself could be induced to give his views on the most effective methods of approach? For it is the fish that the angler is after, and all his recondite learning is but the hopeful means to that end.
John W. Davis Association of the Bar of the City of New York, *The Argument of an Appeal,* October 1940

9.51 Judicious omission is preferable to correct superfluity.
Walter Kidde Foreword, *We Give You Walter Kidde,* 1940

9.52 A phrase begins life as a literary expression; its felicity leads to its lazy repetition; and repetition soon establishes it as a legal formula, undiscriminatingly used to express different and sometimes contradictory ideas.
Felix Frankfurter *Tiller, Executor v. Atlantic Coast Line Railroad Co.,* 318 U.S. 54, 68 (1943)

9.53 Moderation is power.
George W. Keeton, ed. *Harris's Hints on Advocacy,* 1943

9.54 It is pretty hard to make the tail wag the dog.
Sidney Post Simpson, American educator; professor, Harvard Law School *1934–1945* Eugene C. Gerhart, *Quote It!* 1969

9.55 . . . answers are not obtained by putting the wrong question and thereby begging the real one.
Felix Frankfurter *Priebe and Sons v. United States,* 332 U.S. 407, 420 (1947)

9.56 I give up. Now I realize fully what Mark Twain meant when he said, "The more you explain it, the more I don't understand it."
Robert H. Jackson *Securities Commission v. Chenery Corporation,* 332 U.S. 194, 214 (1947)

9.57 Counsel searching for authority for lack of argument.
N. R. Jessel Arthur Goodhart, *Five Jewish Lawyers,* 1949

9.58   The petitioner's problem is to avoid Scylla without being drawn into Charybdis.
> Robert H. Jackson
> *Montana-Dakota Utility Co. v.*
> *Northwestern Public Service Co.,* 341
> U.S. 246, 250 (1951)

9.59   It is one thing, though, to recognize and properly apply a sound principle. It is quite another to run that same sound principle into the ground. It is one thing for a dog to have a tail. It is quite another for the tail to wag the dog.
> Joseph C. Hutcheson, Jr., American
> jurist
> *Deal v. Morrow,* 197 F.2d 821 (1952)

9.60   If you want to win a case, paint the Judge a *picture* and keep it simple.
> John W. Davis
> Annual meeting of Scribes, August
> 21, 1955

9.61   Proceed. You have my biased attention.
> Learned Hand, *1872–1961,* speaking
> to a counsel who demanded the right
> to reargue a motion already heard
> M. Frances McNamara, *2000 Famous*
> *Legal Quotations,* 1967

9.62   The best way to win an argument is to begin by being right. . . .
> Jill Ruckelshaus, American
> government official
> Frederic A. Birmingham, "Jill
> Ruckelshaus: Lady of Liberty,"
> *Saturday Evening Post,* March 3, 1973

9.63   Things in law tend to be black and white. But we all know that some people are a little bit guilty, while other people are guilty as hell. . . . However, once you get into the courtroom, you are doomed to do battle; then it becomes yes or no, guilty or not guilty. You cannot bring in a verdict that the defendant is a little bit guilty.
> Donald R. Cressey, American
> educator; Professor, University of
> California, Santa Barbara
> *Center Magazine,* May–June, 1978

9.64   Among attorneys in Tennessee the saying is: When you have the facts on your side, argue the facts. When you have the law on your side, argue the law. When you have neither, holler.
> Albert Gore, Jr.
> *Washington Post,* July 23, 1982

9.65   In determining the outcome of a given case, a lawyer's flamboyance plays a part. His or her performance in the courtroom is responsible for about 25% of the outcome; the remaining 75% depends on the facts. Those who criticize flamboyant lawyers are just envious.
> Melvin Belli
> *U.S. News & World Report,*
> September 20, 1982

9.66   In saying what is obvious, never choose cunning, yelling works better.
> Cynthia Ozick, *1928–*

10. ASSASSINATION

10.1   Believe me, a thousand friends suffice thee not;
In a single enemy thou hast more than enough.
Ali Ibn-Abi-Tālib,   *c.600–661,*
Arabian religious leader and victim of assassination
Franklin Pierce Adams, *F.P.A. Book of Quotations,* 1952

10.2   Though Cato lived, though Tully spoke,
Though Brutus dealt the godlike stroke,
Yet perished fated Rome.
Robert Craggs Nugent, English politician and poet
Ode to William Pulteney, 1739

10.3   Despotism tempered by assassination, that is our Magna Charta.
Russian noble
Message to Count Münster on the assassination of Paul I, emperor of Russia, 1800

10.4   Assassination has never changed the history of the world.
Benjamin Disraeli
Speech, May 1865

10.5   Assassination is the extreme form of censorship.
George Bernard Shaw
The Rejected Statement, 1903

10.6   America is the place where you cannot kill your government by killing the men who conduct it.
Woodrow Wilson
Address, in Helena, Montana, September 11, 1919

10.7   Is it too much to hope that the martyrdom of our beloved President might even soften the hearts of those who would themselves recoil from assassination, but who do not shrink from spreading the venom which kindles thoughts of it in others?
Earl Warren
Eulogy, on the death of President John F. Kennedy, November 24, 1963

11. AUTHORITY

11.1 Fear God, and offend not the Prince nor his laws,
And keep thyself out of the Magistrate's claws.
Anonymous
Hundred Points of Good Husbandry,
1557

11.2 Great men in judicial places will never want authority.
Proverb
Sir Edward Coke, *Institutes of the Lawes of England,* vol. 2, 1628–1641

11.3 There is no king where there is no law.
Proverb
E. Gordon Duff, ed., *Salomon and Marcolphus,* 1892

11.4 Laws should have authority over men, not men over laws. [when asked why it was not permitted to change any of the ancient laws].
Pausanius, king of Sparta,   *c.400 B.C.*
Burton Stevenson, *Home Book of Proverbs, Maxims and Familiar Phrases,* 1948.

11.5 He who lies hid in remote places is a law unto himself.
Publilius Syrus, Latin writer
Sententiae, c.43 B.C.

11.6 She made what pleased her lawful.
Dante
The Divine Comedy: Inferno,
c.1310–1312

11.7 Who to himself is law, no law doth need, offends no law, and is a king indeed.
George Chapman
Bussy D'Ambois, 1607

11.8 His [Cardinal Wolsey's] own opinion was his law.
Shakespeare
Henry VIII, IV, 2, 1612–1613

11.9 It is not wisdom but Authority that makes a law.
Thomas Hobbes
Dialogue of the Common Laws, c.1670

11.10 . . . there is nothing too absurd but what authority can be found for it.
Sir Henry Manistry, English jurist
Henderson v. Preston (1888), 4 T.L.R. 632, 633

11.11 The passing of an unjust law is the suicide of authority.
Pastoral letter of the American Roman Catholic hierarchy, February 1920

11.12 The young are too apt to believe what a great man says, especially if he be an authority in the profession they follow.
> George W. Keeton, ed. *Harris's Hints on Advocacy,* 1943

11.13 Decisions of this Court do not have intrinsic authority.
> Felix Frankfurter
> *Adamson v. California,* 332 U.S. 46, 59 (1947)

11.14 The decision finally rests not upon appeals to past authority, but upon *what people want.*
> S. I. Hayakawa
> Laurence J. Peter, *Peter's Quotations,* 1977

B

12. BAR

12.1 O lady, lady, all interruption and no
      sense between us, as
      if we were lawyers at the bar! but I
      had forgot, Apollo
      and Littleton never lodge in a head
      together.*
      Anonymous
      William Andrews, ed., *The Lawyer in
      History, Literature, and Humour,* 1896

12.2   I will for ever, at all hazards, assert
      the dignity, independence, and integ-
      rity of the English bar; without which,
      impartial justice, the most valuable
      part of the English constitution, can
      have no existence.
      Thomas Erskine
      Trial of Thomas Paine (1792), 22
      How. St. Tr. 358, 412

12.3 I think of times when far
      Aloof cold envy stood,
      And brethren of the Bar
      Professed good brotherhood—
      No soulless etiquette,
      But friendship warm and true—
      With heart and hand we met
      When this old wig was new.

*i.e., law and letters do not flourish together

No greedy hand was then
Projected for a fee;
We held no servile pen
To any lordly he;
And none of us demurred
The poor man's cause to sue,
For honour was the word
When this old wig was new.
      George Outram, *1805–1856*
      "When This Old Wig Was New"

12.4   Shall I ask what a court would be,
      unaided? The law is made by the Bar,
      even more than by the Bench.
      Oliver Wendell Holmes
      "The Law," *Speeches,* 1913

12.5   Membership in the bar is a privilege
      burdened with conditions.
      Benjamin N. Cardozo
      In re Rouss, 221 N.Y. 81, 84 (1917)

12.6   The unique advantage of the Bar as
      a profession is that it offers in later
      years to those who have succeeded in
      it the sanctuary of the Bench. . . .
      Harold Macmillan
      A Man of Law's Tale, 1953

12.7   The Senate no longer need bother about confirmation of Justices but ought to confirm the appointment of law clerks.
>   Robert H. Jackson, *1892–1954*
>   John P. Frank, *Serving Justice,* 1974

13.   BILL OF RIGHTS

13.1   Congress shall make no law respecting an establishment of religion, or prohibiting the free exercise thereof; or abridging the freedom of speech, or of the press; or the right of the people peaceably to assemble, and to petition the Government for a redress of grievances.
>   Constitution of the United States,
>   First Amendment, 1791

13.2   The right of the people to be secure in their persons, houses, papers, and effects, against unreasonable searches and seizures, shall not be violated. . . .
>   Constitution of the United States,
>   Fourth Amendment, 1791

13.3   No person shall be held to answer for a capital, or otherwise infamous crime, unless on a presentment or indictment of a Grand Jury, . . . nor shall any person be subject for the same offence to be twice put in jeopardy of life or limb; nor shall be compelled in any Criminal Case to be a witness against himself, nor be deprived of life, liberty, or property, without due process of law; nor shall private property be taken for public use, without just compensation.
>   Constitution of the United States,
>   Fifth Amendment, 1791

13.4   In all criminal prosecutions, the accused shall enjoy the right to a speedy and public trial. . . .
>   Constitution of the United States,
>   Sixth Amendment, 1791

13.5   What seems fair enough against a squalid huckster of bad liquor may take on a different face, if used by a government determined to suppress political opposition under the guise of sedition.
>   Learned Hand
>   *United States v. Kirschenblatt,* 1926

13.6   Bills of rights give assurance to the individual of the preservation of his liberty. They do not define the liberty they promise.
>   Benjamin N. Cardozo
>   "Paradoxes of Legal Science," in
>   *Selected Writings of Benjamin Nathan Cardozo,* edited by Margaret E. Hall, 1928

13.7 Thoughts, emotions, and sensations [demand] legal recognition.
Louis D. Brandeis
The Curse of Bigness: Miscellaneous Papers of Louis D. Brandeis, 1935

13.8 Civil liberties had their origin and must find their ultimate guaranty in the faith of the people.
Robert H. Jackson
Douglas v. Jeannette, 319 U.S. 157, 182 (1943)

13.9 If there is any fixed star in our constitutional constellation, it is that no official, high or petty, can prescribe what shall be orthodox in politics, nationalism, religion, or other matters of opinion or force citizens to confess by word or act their faith therein.
Robert H. Jackson
West Virginia State Board of Education v. Barnette, 319 U.S. 624, 638 (1943)

13.10 The very purpose of a Bill of Rights was to withdraw certain subjects from the vicissitudes of political controversy, to place them beyond the reach of majorities and officials and to establish them as legal principles to be applied by the courts. One's right to life, liberty, and property, to free speech, a free press, freedom of worship and assembly, and other fundamental rights may not be submitted to vote; they depend on the outcome of no elections.
Robert H. Jackson
West Virginia State Board of Education v. Barnette, 319 U.S. 624, 638 (1943)

13.11 We set up government by consent of the governed, and the Bill of Rights denies those in power any legal opportunity to coerce that consent. Authority here is to be controlled by public opinion, not public opinion by authority.
Robert H. Jackson
West Virginia State Board of Education v. Barnette, 319 U.S. 624, 641 (1943)

13.12 It is not only under Nazi rule that police excesses are inimical to freedom. It is easy to make light of insistence on scrupulous regard for the safeguards of civil liberties when invoked on behalf of the unworthy.... History bears testimony that by such disregard are the rights of liberty extinguished, heedlessly, at first, then stealthily, and brazenly in the end.
Felix Frankfurter
Davis v. United States, 328 U.S. 582, 66 S. Ct. 1256, 90 L.Ed. 1453 (1946)

13.13 Of course I know how illusory would be the belief that my vote determined anything; but nevertheless when I go to the polls I have a satisfaction in the sense that we are all engaged in a common venture. If you retort that a sheep in the flock may feel something like it; I reply, following Saint Francis, "My brother, the Sheep."
Learned Hand
The Bill of Rights, 1958

13.14 It seems as if the Department [of Justice] sees the value of the Bill of Rights as no more than obstacles to be overcome.
Sanford H. Kadish, American educator; professor, University of California, Berkeley
Los Angeles Times, July 25, 1969

14. BRIBERY

14.1   He that buyeth magistracy will seek justice.
  English proverb
  John Ray, *English Proverbs,* 1678

14.2   Bribes throw Dust into cunning Men's eyes.
  Proverb
  Thomas Fuller, *Gnomologia,* 1732

14.3   Death's boatman takes no bribe. . . .
  Horace
  Odes, 23 B.C.

14.4   And if thou freely wilt, in bribes thy coyne bestowe,
  Both judge, and jurie will bee prest, all favour thee to showe:
  Yea Gods from heaven will hither come, all honour thee to doe.
  Stefano Guazzo
  Civile Conversation, 1574

14.5   Honesty stands at the gate and knocks,
  and bribery enters in.
  Barnabe Rich, English writer and soldier *1542-1617*
  The Irish Hubbub, c.1617

14.6   Though the bribe be small, yet the fault is great.
  Sir Edward Coke
  Institutes of the Lawes of England,
  vol. 3, 1628-1641

14.7   Where many a Client Verdict miss'd, For want of Greazing in the fist.
  Thomas D'Urfey
  Collins's Walk Through London, 1690

14.8   Every man has his price, I will bribe left and right.
  Edward Robert Bulwer-Lytton, 1st earl of Lytton
  Walpole, 1875

14.9   When their lordships asked Bacon
  How many bribes he had taken
  He had at least the grace
  To get very red in the face.
  Edmund C. Bentley, English journalist and poet
  Baseless Biography, 1939

14.10   [It is] very much better to bribe a person than kill him. . . .
  Sir Winston S. Churchill
  F. B. Czarnomski, ed., *The Wisdom of Winston Churchill,* 1956

15. BUSINESS

15.1   The man of law who never saw
The wayes to buy and sell,
Wenyng to rise by merchandize,
I pray God speed him well.
> Attributed to Sir John Fortescue,
> English jurist; chief justice,
> c.1385-1479
> W. Gurney Benham, *Putnam's
> Complete Book of Quotations, Proverbs
> and Household Words,* 1927

15.2   Corporations cannot commit treason, nor be outlawed, nor excommunicated, for they have no souls.
> Sir Edward Coke
> *Case of Sutton's Hospital* (1612), 5
> Rep. 303; 10 Rep. 326

15.3   Trade is the mother of money.
> Thomas Draxe, *?-1618*
> *Bibliotheca*

15.4   ...everyone thirsteth after gaine...
> Sir Edward Coke
> *Institutes of the Lawes of England,*
> vol. 3, 1628-1641

15.5   Did you expect a corporation to have a conscience, when it has no soul to be damned and no body to be kicked?
> Edward Thurlow, English jurist; lord
> chancellor, *1731-1806*
> Wilberforce, *Life of Thurlow,* 1775

15.6   A corporation cannot blush. It is a body, it is true; has certainly a head— a new one every year; arms it has and very long ones, for it can reach at anything; . . . a throat to swallow the rights of the community, and a stomach to digest them! But who ever yet discovered, in the anatomy of any corporation, either bowels or a heart?
> Howell Walsh
> Speech, Tralee assizes, c.1825

15.7   The selfish spirit of commerce knows no country, and feels no passion of principle but that of gain.
> Thomas Jefferson, *1743-1826*
> Letter to Larkin Smith

15.8   The rule of my life is to make business a pleasure, and pleasure my business.
> Aaron Burr, *1756-1836*
> Letter to Pichon, secretary of the
> French Legation at Washington, D.C.

15.9   I think that there is nothing, not even crime, more opposed to poetry, to philosophy, ay, to life itself, than this incessant business.
> Henry David Thoreau
> *Life Without Principle,* 1854

15.10 The ways by which you may get money almost without exception lead downward.
Henry David Thoreau
Life Without Principle, 1854

15.11 It must be remembered that all trade is and must be in a sense selfish. . . .
John Duke Coleridge, English jurist;
lord chief justice
Mogul Steamship Co. v. McGregor, Gow & Co. (1888), L.R. 21 Q.B.D. 553

15.12 The director is really a watch-dog, and the watch-dog has no right, without the knowledge of his master, to take a sop from a possible wolf.
Timothy Bower, English jurist
In re North Australian Territory Co., 1892

15.13 Don't steal; thou'lt never thus compete successfully in business. Cheat.
Ambrose Bierce
The Devil's Dictionary, 1906

15.14 The gambling known as business looks with austere disfavor upon the business known as gambling.
Ambrose Bierce
The Devil's Dictionary, 1906

15.15 . . . the most enlightened judicial policy is to let people manage their own business in their own way.
Oliver Wendell Holmes
Dr. Miles Medical Co. v. Park & Sons Co., 220 U.S. 373, 411 (1911)

15.16 . . . mere money-making cannot be regarded as the legitimate end [of business] since with the conduct of business human happiness or misery is inextricably interwoven.
Louis D. Brandeis
Address, Brown University, 1912

15.17 . . . while I should be the last to say that the making of a profit was not in itself a pleasure, I hope I should also be one of those to agree that there were other pleasures than making a profit.
Learned Hand
Thacher et al. v. Lowe, 288 Fed. 994, 995 (1922)

15.18 . . . the notion that a business is clothed with a public interest and has been devoted to the public use is little more than a fiction intended to beautify what is disagreeable to the sufferers.
Oliver Wendell Holmes
Tyson and Brother v. Banton, 273 U.S. 418, 446 (1927)

15.19 To say that only those businesses affected with a public interest may be regulated is but another way of stating that all those businesses which may be regulated are affected with a public interest.
Harlan Fiske Stone
Tyson and Brother v. Banton, 273 U.S. 418, 451 (1927)

15.20 The business of America is business.
Calvin Coolidge, *1872–1933*
Franklin Pierce Adams, *F.P.A. Book of Quotations,* 1952

15.21 Strong responsible unions are essential to industrial fair play. Without them the labor bargain is wholly one-sided.
Louis D. Brandeis
The Curse of Bigness: Miscellaneous Papers of Louis D. Brandeis, 1935

15.22 When . . . you increase your business to a very great extent . . . the man at the head has a diminishing knowledge of the facts, and . . . a

diminishing opportunity of exercising a careful judgment upon them.
Louis D. Brandeis, *1856–1941*
Alpheus Thomas Mason, *Brandeis: A Free Man's Life,* 1946

15.23 What to an outsider will be no more than the vigorous presentation of a conviction, to an employee may be the manisfestation of a determination which it is not safe to thwart.
Learned Hand
National Labor Relations Board v. Federbush Co., Inc., 121 F.2d 954, 957 (1941)

15.24 When I hear artists and authors making fun of business men I think of a regiment in which the band makes fun of the cooks.
H. L. Mencken
A New Dictionary of Quotations, 1946

15.25 Of course there's a different law for the rich and the poor; otherwise who would go into business?
E. Ralph Stewart
Laurence J. Peter, *Peter's Quotations,* 1977

15.26 The legal system is in part responsible for the very size and growth [of big business and big government]. And too often when the individual finds himself in conflict with these forces, the legal system sides with the giant institution, not the small businessman or private citizen.
Edward M. Kennedy
Address, American Bar Association, New York, reported in the *Washington Post,* August 8, 1978

C

16. CASES

16.1 It's better to measure ten times and cut once, than measure once and cut ten times.
Jewish folk saying
Joseph L. Baron, *A Treasury of Jewish Quotations,* 1956

16.2 The laws are adapted to those cases which most frequently occur.
Legal maxim

16.3 A rotten case abides no handling.
Shakespeare
2 *Henry IV,* IV, 1, 1597–1598

16.4 I have betrayed myself with my own tongue;
The case is altered.
Ben Jonson
The Case Is Altered, 1598

16.5 Decided cases are the anchors of the law, as laws are of the state.
Francis Bacon
De Augmentis Scientiarum, 1623

16.6 Every case stands upon its own bottom.
Sir Francis Pemberton, English jurist; chief justice
Fitzharris' Case (1681), 8 How. St. Tr. 280

16.7 I accede to the authority of that case, although I think it is a very strong decision. It does not convince me; it overcomes me.
Sir Edward Hall Alderson, English barrister
Mearing v. Hellings (1845), 14 M&W 711, 712

16.8 Hard cases, it is said, make bad law.
John Campbell, British jurist; lord chief justice
Ex parte Long (1854), 3 W.R. 19

16.9 This case reminds me of one in which I likened the Plaintiff's case to a colander, because it was so full of holes.
Sir George Jessel, English jurist
Ex parte Hall (1882), 19 Ch. D. 580, 584

16.10 My wonder is really boundless,
That among the queer cases we try,
A land-case should often be groundless,
And a water-case always be dry.
John G. Saxe, American lawyer and poet, *1816–1887*
Marshall Brown, *Wit and Humor of Bench and Bar,* 1899

16.11 The mere advocate, however brilliant, will lose the most cases, though he may win the most verdicts.
> B. F. Butler, American general and politician
> *Autobiography and Personal Reminiscences,* 1892

16.12 A case is only an authority for what it actually decides. I entirely deny it can be quoted for a proposition that may seem to follow logically from it. Such a mode of reasoning assumes that the law is necessarily a logical code, whereas every lawyer must acknowledge that the law is not always logical at all.
> Hardinge Stanley Giffard, 1st Earl Halsbury, English jurist; lord chancellor
> *Quinn v. Leathem* (1901), A.C. 495, 506

16.13 Great cases like hard cases make bad law. For great cases are called great, not by reason of their real importance in shaping the law of the future, but because of some accident of immediate overwhelming interest which appeals to the feelings and distorts the judgment.
> Oliver Wendell Holmes
> *Northern Securities Co. v. United States,* 193 U.S. 197, 400–401 (1904)

16.14 General propositions do not decide concrete cases.
> Oliver Wendell Holmes
> *Lochner v. New York* 198 U.S. 45, 76, 49 L. Ed. (1905)

16.15 Cases were decided in the chambers of a six-shooter instead of a supreme court.
> O. Henry, *1862–1910*
> *Law and Order*

16.16 No two cases are exactly alike. A young attorney found two opinions in the New York Reports where the facts seemed identical although the law was in conflict, but an older and more experienced attorney pointed out to him that the names of the parties were different.
> Cuthbert W. Pound, American jurist
> "American Law Institute Speech of Judge Pound," 5 *New York State Bar Association Bulletin* 265, 267 (1933)

16.17 I long have said there is no such thing as a hard case. I am frightened weekly but always when you walk up to the lion and lay hold the hide comes off and the same old donkey of a question of law is underneath.
> Oliver Wendell Holmes, *1841–1935*
> Mark De Wolfe Howe, *Holmes-Pollock Letters,* 1946

16.18 There is an old and somewhat foolish saying that "Hard cases make bad law," and therefore the law must be left as it is. It would be equally true to say, "Bad law makes hard cases," and therefore the law must be amended. The real truth lies somewhere between. Mere freaks of fortune should not be made an excuse for weakening a law which is sound. But a law which is seen to multiply hard cases . . . is not worth preserving, for the law was made for man, not man for the law.
> A. P. Herbert, *1890–1971*
> *Uncommon Law,* 1936

16.19 The law itself is on trial in every case as well as the cause before it.
> Harlan F. Stone, *1872–1946*
> Laurence J. Peter, *Peter's Quotations,* 1977

16.20 Law students are trained in the case method, and to the lawyer everything in life looks like a case. His first thought in the morning is

how to handle the case of the ringing alarm clock.
> Edward B. Packard, Jr.
> *Columbia Forum,* Spring 1967

16.21 You don't approach a case with the philosophy of applying abstract justice—you go in to win.
> Percy Foreman
> *Newsweek,* February 3, 1969

16.22 I'm sick and tired of hearing about the number of cases disposed of when we discuss the judicial system. The chief justice should know that the job of the courts is not to dispose of cases but to decide them justly.

Doesn't he know that the business of courts is justice?
> Jim R. Carrigan, American jurist; justice, Supreme Court of Colorado, *Los Angeles Herald-Examiner,* August 3, 1977

16.23 Of every hundred cases, ninety win themselves, three are won by advocacy, and seven are lost by advocacy.
> A. Fountain
> *Wit of Wig,* 1980

16.24 We're approaching space-age technology with Model-T statutes and cases.
> Lori B. Andrews, American lawyer, describing infertility cases and the law
> *New York Times,* June 27, 1984

17. CERTAINTY

17.1 Too much subtlety in law is condemned, and so much exactitude destroys exactness.
> Latin legal phrase
> W. Gurney Benham, *Putnam's Complete Book of Quotations, Proverbs and Household Words,* 1927

17.2 That is sufficiently certain which can be made certain.
> Legal maxim

17.3 Better an ounce from the ground than a pound from the roof.
> Talmud, *Yevamot*

17.4 Doubt cannot override a certainty.
> Talmud, *Yevamot*

17.5 It is better the law should be certain, than that every Judge should speculate upon improvements in it.
> John Scott, Lord Eldon
> *Sheldon v. Goodrich* (1803), 8 Ves 481, 497

17.6 The power of the lawyer is in the uncertainty of the law.
> Jeremy Bentham
> Letter to Sir James Macintosh, 1808

17.7   The glorious uncertainty of the law was a thing well known and complained of, by all ignorant people, but all learned gentlemen considered it as its greatest excellency.
Richard Brinsley Sheridan
Parliamentary History, 1820

17.8   Being a lawyer, I don't like to advise parties to go to law. I know the glorious uncertainty of it, as it is called.
Horace Mayhew, English journalist
The Image of His Father, 1848

17.9   . . . it is always probable that something improbable will happen.
Logan E. Bleckley, American jurist
Warren v. Purtell, 63 Ga. 428, 430 (1879)

17.10   Our life is wrought of dreams and waking, fused
Of truth and lies. There lives no certitude.
Arthur Schnitzler
Paracelsus, 1899

17.11   Delusive exactness is a source of fallacy throughout the law.
Oliver Wendell Holmes
Truax v. Corrigan, 257 U.S. 312, 342 (1921)

17.12   We must distinguish between the sound certainty and the sham . . . and then, when certainty is attained, we must remember that it is not the only good that we can buy at too high a price.
Benjamin N. Cardozo
Growth of the Law, 1924

17.13   They do things better with logarithms.
Benjamin N. Cardozo
Paradoxes of Legal Science, 1928

17.14   The law is not a series of calculating machines where definitions and answers come tumbling out when the right levers are pushed.
William O. Douglas
"The Dissent, A Safeguard of Democracy," 32 *Journal of The American Judicial Society,* 105 (1948)

18.   CHANGE

18.1   Every innovation occasions more harm and derangement of order by its novelty, than benefit by its abstract utility.
Legal maxim

18.2   Can an Ethiopian change his skin, or a leopard his spots?
Old Testament, *Jeremiah* 13:23

18.3   The laws of a state change with the changing times.
Aeschylus
Seven Against Thebes, 467 B.C.

18.4   Ancient laws remain in force long after the people have the power to change them.
Aristotle
Politics, c.322 B.C.

18.5   That which is a law today is none tomorrow.
Robert Burton, English clergyman and writer
The Anatomy of Melancholy, 1621

18.6   The law is like apparel, which alters with the time.
John Dodderidge, English jurist
Jones v. Powell (1628), Palm. 536, 538

18.7   The law is not the same morning and night.
George Herbert
Jacula Prudentum, 1651

18.8   When I hear any man talk of an unalterable law, the only effect it produces upon me is to convince me that he is an unalterable fool.
Sydney Smith, English essayist
Peter Plymley's Letters, 1807

18.9   Laws and institutions must go hand in hand with the progress of the human mind.
Thomas Jefferson, *1743–1826*
Laurence J. Peter, *Peter's Quotations,* 1977

18.10   I do not allow myself to suppose that either the convention or the League have concluded to decide that I am either the greatest or the best man in America, but rather they have concluded it is not best to swap horses while crossing the river, and have further concluded that they might not make a botch of it in trying to swap.
Abraham Lincoln
Address to a delegation from the National Union League, June 9, 1864

18.11   If truth were not often suggested by error, if old implements could not be adjusted to new uses, human progress would be slow.
Oliver Wendell Holmes
The Common Law, 1881

18.12   In law . . . the evil of lax definitions . . . has not been without compensation. Men are very ready to accept new ideas, provided they bear old names.
John Chipman Gray, American jurist
"Some Definitions and Questions in Jurisprudence," 6 *Harvard Law Review* 21 (1893)

18.13   . . . it is a step for further advance to see what has been won from chaos already.
John Chipman Gray, American jurist
"Some Definitions and Questions in Jurisprudence," 6 *Harvard Law Review* 21 (1893)

18.14   Law is merely the expression of the will of the strongest for the time being, and therefore laws have no fixity, but shift from generation to generation.
Brooks Adams, American historian
The Law of Civilization and Decay, 1896

18.15   After all, that is what laws are for, to be made and unmade.
Emma Goldman
"The Social Aspects of Birth Control," *Mother Earth,* April 1916

18.16   Our course of advance, therefore, is neither a straight line nor a curve. It is a series of dots and dashes.
Benjamin N. Cardozo
The Paradoxes of Legal Science, 1928

18.17   The law is a living growth, not a changeless code.
Inscription carved over the entrance to the Yale Law School, 1929–1931

18.18   A year ago, if I had $100 in gold in my pocket, I was a law-abiding citizen; if I perchance had a pint of whiskey I was a criminal. Today, if I have the whiskey, I am a law-abiding citizen; but if I have the gold, I am a criminal violating the law.
Lester Jesse Dickinson, American politician
Speech, Cleveland, Ohio, January 5, 1934

18.19   Just because we cannot see clearly the end of the road, that is no reason for not setting out on the essential journey. On the contrary, great change dominates the world, and unless we move with change we will become its victims.
Robert F. Kennedy
Farewell statement, Warsaw, Poland, reported in the *New York Times,* July 2, 1964

18.20   Law must be stable, and yet it cannot stand still.
Roscoe Pound, *1870–1964*
Kenneth Redden, *Modern Legal Glossary,* 1983

18.21   Change just for the sake of change is not necessarily good. But, change to adapt to the situation is *survival.*
"Adapt—or Lose!" *Ohio State Bar Association Report,* vol. XL, no. 21 (May 22, 1967)

18.22   Law must become the principal instrument of social change but it must move faster and in a more responsive way to social needs. In the question of racial integration, for example, if we were to move at the same rate as the first nine years since the Supreme Court decision, it would take us another nine centuries to do the job effectively.
Ramsey Clark
New York Times, December 14, 1969

18.23   Had Rip Van Winkle gone away and come back today . . . and if he went into the courts, the principal changes he would have observed would have been the wearing apparel, the increased number of judges and the air conditioning. Most of the rest would be the same as when he began his legendary exile in the Catskill Mountains.
Warren E. Burger
Address to the Economic Club, New York, reported in the *Wall Street Journal,* March 15, 1974

18.24   That man is a creature who needs order yet yearns for change is the creative contradiction at the heart of the laws which structure his conformity and define his deviancy.
Freda Adler, American educator
Sisters in Crime, 1975

19. CHARACTER

19.1   Man's advocates are repentance and good deeds.
Talmud, *Shabbat*

19.2   Our characters are the result of our conduct.
Aristotle
Nicomachean Ethics, c.335 B.C.

19.3   Character is habit long continued.
Plutarch
Moralia: Education of Children, c.95

19.4   Confidence in others' honesty is no light testimony of one's own integrity.
Michel de Montaigne
Essais, 1588

19.5   Good sense is, of all things among men, the most equally distributed; for every one thinks himself so abundantly provided with it, that those even who are the most difficult to satisfy in everything else, do not usually desire a larger measure of this quality than they already possess.
Descartes
Discourse of the Method of Rightly Conducting the Reason and Seeking Truth in the Sciences, 1637

19.6   Humility is a Vertue all preach, none practise, and yet every body is content to hear.
John Selden   *1584–1654*
Table-Talk, 1689

19.7   Every single Act either *weakeneth* or *improveth* our Credit with other Men; and as an habit of being *just* to our Word will *confirm*, so an habit of too freely *dispensing* with it must necessarily *destroy* it.
George Savile, 1st marquess of Halifax, English politician, *1633–1695*
The Complete Works of George Savile, First Marquess of Halifax, 1912

19.8   He that leaveth nothing to Chance will do few things ill, but he will do very few things.
George Savile, 1st marquess of Halifax, English politician, *1633–1695*
The Complete Works of George Savile, First Marquess of Halifax, 1912

19.9   It is a general Mistake to think the Men we like are good for every thing, and those we do not, good for nothing.
George Savile, 1st marquess of Halifax, English politician, *1633–1695*
The Complete Works of George Savile, First Marquess of Halifax, 1912

19.10   It is the nature of all greatness not to be exact. . . .
Edmund Burke
"Speech on American Taxation," April 19, 1774

19.11   Character is much easier kept than recovered.
Thomas Paine
The Crisis, 1776–1783

19.12   You, my lord, are a judge; I am the supposed culprit. I am a man; you are a man also. By a revolution of power we might change places, though we could never change characters.
Robert Emmet, *1778–1803*
Speech to judge when on trial for treason

19.13   Character is like a tree and reputation like its shadow. The shadow is what we think of, the tree is the real thing.
Abraham Lincoln, *1809–1865*
Franklin Pierce Adams, *FPA Book of Quotations,* 1952

19.14   In my opinion the best character is generally that which is the least talked about.
Sir William Erle, English jurist; chief justice
The Queen v. Rowton (1865), 34 L.J.M.C. 63

19.15   I think there should be no occasion on which it is absolutely, as a point or rule of law, impossible for a man to redeem his character.
John Duke Coleridge, English jurist; lord chief justice
In re Brandreth (1891), L.J. 60 Q.B.D. 504

19.16   If you will think about what you ought to do for other people, your character will take care of itself.
Woodrow Wilson
Address at Pittsburgh 1914

19.17   I don't say embrace trouble. That's as bad as treating it as an enemy. But I do say meet it as a friend, for you'll see a lot of it and had better be on speaking terms with it.
Oliver Wendell Holmes, *1841–1935*
Eugene C. Gerhart, *Quote It!* 1969

19.18   . . . it cannot be said that by common experience the character of most people indicted by a grand jury is good.
Oliver Wendell Holmes
Greer v. United States, 245 U.S. 559, 561 (1918)

19.19   If I were dying my last words would be: Have faith and pursue the unknown end.
Oliver Wendell Holmes, *1841–1935*
Catherine Drinker Bowen, *Yankee from Olympus,* 1944

19.20   . . . to be civilized is to be potentially master of all possible ideas, and that means that one has got beyond being shocked, although one preserves one's own moral and aesthetic preferences.
Oliver Wendell Holmes, *1841–1935*
Mark De Wolfe Howe, *Holmes-Pollock Letters,* 1946

19.21   We can forgive a man the defects of his qualities, if only he has the qualities of his defects.
Oliver Wendell Holmes, *1841–1935*
Irving Dilliard, *The Spirit of Liberty,* 1960

19.22   The heroic hours of life do not announce their presence by drum and trumpet, challenging us to be true to ourselves by appeals to the martial spirit that keeps the blood at heat. Some little, unassuming, unobtrusive choice presents itself before us slyly and craftily, glib and insinuating, in the modest garb of innocence. . . . Then it is that you will be summoned to show the courage of adventurous youth.

Benjamin N. Cardozo,   *1870–1938*
"Law and Literature," in *Selected Writings of Benjamin Nathan Cardozo,* edited by Margaret E. Hall, 1947

19.23   . . . one of my best French quotations "On ne régne sur les âmes que par le calme." He was never in a hurry, never anxious to make an effect or sensation. He sat still and men came to him.

Sir Winston S. Churchill
A Roving Commission, 1941

19.24   Absolute discretion is a ruthless master. It is more destructive of freedom than any of man's other inventions.

William O. Douglas
United States v. Wunderlich, 342 U.S. 98, 101 (1951)

19.25   We need be bold and adventuresome in our thinking to survive.

William O. Douglas
Adler v. Board of Education, 342 U.S. 485, 511 (1952)

19.26   Of those qualities on which civilization depends, next after courage, it seems to me, comes an open mind,

and, indeed, the highest courage is, as Holmes used to say, to stake your all upon a conclusion which you are aware tomorrow may prove false.

Learned Hand
Irving Dilliard, *The Spirit of Liberty,* 1960

19.27   Still, I know of no higher fortitude than stubbornness in the face of overwhelming odds.

Louis Nizer
My Life in Court, 1960

19.28   . . . there is more respect to be won in the opinion of this world by a resolute and courageous liquidation of unsound positions than by the most stubborn pursuit of extravagant or unpromising objectives.

George W. Kennan
"Kennan on Vietnam," *New Republic,* February 26, 1966

19.29   Courage in the courtroom is more important than brains. If I were hiring a lawyer and had to choose between one that was all brains and one that was all guts, I would take the guts.

Percy Foreman
Los Angeles Times, May 16, 1976

20. CHEATING

20.1   Feather by feather the goose is plucked.
Scottish proverb
W. Gurney Bentham, *Putnam's Complete Book of Quotations, Proverbs and Household Words*, 1927

20.2   A false balance is an abomination to the Lord.
Old Testament, *Proverbs* 11:1

20.3   My revenue is the silly cheat.
Shakespeare
The Winter's Tale, IV, 2, 1610–1611

20.4   He is not cheated who knows he is being cheated.
Sir Edward Coke
Institutes of the Lawes of England, vol. 1, 1628–1641

20.5   Many men *swallow* the being cheated, but no man can ever endure to chew it.
George Savile, 1st marquess of Halifax, English politician
Maxims, 1693

20.6   'Tis no sin to cheat the devil.
Daniel Defoe
History of the Devil, 1726

20.7   To cheat a man is nothing; but the woman must have fine parts, indeed, who cheats a woman.
John Gay
The Beggar's Opera, 1728.

20.8   He'll cheat without scruple, who can without fear.
Benjamin Franklin
Poor Richard's Almanack, 1743

20.9   Thou shalt not steal; an empty feat, When it's so lucrative to cheat.
Arthur Hugh Clough
The Latest Decalogue, c.1849

20.10   It's heads Law wins, tails they lose.
William De Morgan
It Can Never Happen Again, 1909

21. CHILDREN

21.1 The unwise man and the forweaned [spoiled] child have but one law.
English proverb
Richard Morris, ed., *Trinity College Homilies: Old English Homilies of the Twelfth Century,* 1873

21.2 Let children support their parents or be imprisoned.
Roman law

21.3 Let nothing which is disgraceful to be spoken of, or to be seen, approach this place where a child is.
Juvenal
Satires, c.120

21.4 Infants have no privilege to cheat men.
Peter King, English jurist; lord chancellor
Evroy v. Nicholas (1733), 2 Eq. Ca. Ab. 489

21.5 The law of grab is the primal law of infancy.
Antoinette Brown Blackwell, American feminist and writer
The Sexes Throughout Nature, 1875

21.6 It is said that famous men are usually the product of unhappy childhood. The stern compression of circumstances, the twinges of adversity, the spur of slights and taunts in early years, are needed to evoke that ruthless fixity of purpose and tenacious mother-wit without which great actions are seldom accomplished.
Sir Winston S. Churchill
Marlborough, His Life and Times, 1933–1938

21.7 I've been struck by the upside-down priorities of the juvenile-justice system. We are willing to spend the least amount of money to keep a kid at home, more to put him in a foster home, and the most to institutionalize him.
Marian Wright Edelman, American lawyer
Margie Casady, "Society's Pushed–Out Children," *Psychology Today,* June 1975

22. CITIZENSHIP

22.1   The crowd of changeable citizens.
Horace
Odes, 23 B.C.

22.2   If a man be gracious and courteous to strangers, it shows he is a citizen of the world.
Francis Bacon
Essays, 1612

22.3   Before Man made us citizens, great Nature made us men.
James Russell Lowell, *1819–1891*
"On the Capture of Certain Fugitive Slaves."

22.4   Every citizen or subject of another country, while domiciled here, is within the allegiance and the protection, and consequently subject to the jurisdiction, of the United States. . . .
Horace Gray, American jurist; judge, U.S. supreme court
United States v. Wong Kim, Ark., 169 U.S. 649, 42 L.Ed. 890, 18 Sup. Ct. 456 (1898)

22.5   If cats were born in an oven would they be biscuits?
Finley Peter Dunne, *1867–1936,* in reference to *United States v. Wong Kim, Ark.,* 1898, which held that all Chinese born in the United States were citizens
M. Frances McNamara, *2,000 Famous Legal Quotations,* 1967

22.6   The power of citizenship as a shield against oppression was widely known from the example of Paul's Roman citizenship, which sent the centurion scurrying to his higher-ups with the message: "Take heed what thou doest: for this man is a Roman."
Robert H. Jackson
Edwards v. California, 314 U.S. 160, 182 (1941)

22.7   As citizens of this democracy, you are the rulers and the ruled, the law-givers and the law-abiding, the beginning and the end.
Adlai E. Stevenson
Speech, Chicago, September 29, 1952

23.   CIVIL DISOBEDIENCE

23.1   Men of most renowned virtue have sometimes by transgressing most truly kept the law.
John Milton
Tetrachordon, 1644–1645

23.2   If a law commands me to *sin I will break it;* if it calls me to *suffer,* I will let it take its course *unresistingly.* The doctrine of blind obedience and unqualified submission to any human power, whether civil or ecclesiastical, is the doctrine of despotism, and ought to have no place 'mong Republicans and Christians.
Angelina Grimké, American abolitionist
"Appeal to the Christian Women of the South," *Anti-Slavery Examiner,* September 1836

23.3   All men recognize the right of revolution.
Henry David Thoreau
Civil Disobedience, 1849

23.4   Must the citizen ever for a moment, or in the least degree, resign his conscience to the legislator? I think that we should be men first, and subjects afterward.
Henry David Thoreau
Civil Disobedience, 1849

23.5   The only obligation which I have a right to assume is to do at any time what I think right.
Henry David Thoreau
Civil Disobedience, 1849

23.6   Under a government which imprisons any unjustly, the true place for a just man is also a prison.
Henry David Thoreau
Civil Disobedience, 1849

23.7   Unjust laws exist: shall we be content to obey them. . . .
Henry David Thoreau
Civil Disobedience, 1849

23.8   I will have no laws. I will acknowledge none. I protest against every law which an authority calling itself necessary imposes upon my free will.
Pierre Joseph Proudhon
Idée générale de la révolution, 1851

23.9   I submit that an individual who breaks a law that conscience tells him is unjust, and who willingly accepts the penalty of imprisonment in order to arouse the conscience of the community over its injustice, is in reality expressing the highest respect for the law.
Martin Luther King, Jr.
Why We Can't Wait, 1964

23.10　The right to defy an unconstitutional statute is basic in our scheme. Even when an ordinance requires a permit to make a speech, to deliver a sermon, to picket, to parade, or to assemble, it need not be honored when it is invalid on its face.
> Potter Stewart
> *Walker v. Birmingham,* 388 U.S. 307,
> 87 S. Ct. 1824, 18 L.Ed.2d 1210
> (1967)

23.11　One can say categorically that there is no constitutional right of civil disobedience to a valid law.
> Archibald Cox
> Mark De Wolfe Howe and J. R.
> Wiggins, *Civil Rights, The Constitution and The Courts,* 1967

23.12　Social protest and even civil disobedience serve the law's need for growth. . . .
> Archibald Cox
> Mark De Wolfe Howe and J. R.
> Wiggins, *Civil Rights, The Constitution and The Courts,* 1967

23.13　The core of the evil in true civil disobedience is that it weakens the bonds of law and compels the state to resort to power.
> Archibald Cox
> Mark De Wolfe Howe and J. R.
> Wiggins, *Civil Rights, The Constitution and The Courts,* 1967

23.14　. . . those whose conscience demands that they defy authority in some ways that involve great consequences must be willing to accept some penalty. . . .
> Joseph Wood Krutch
> "If You Don't Mind My Saying So
> . . .," *American Scholar,* Winter
> 1967–1968

23.15　While the State may respectfully require obedience on many matters, it cannot violate the moral nature of a man, convert him into a serviceable criminal, and expect his loyalty and devotion.
> Liane Norman, American educator
> "Selective Conscientious Objection,"
> *Center Magazine,* May/June, 1972

23.16　The defiance of established authority, religious and secular, social and political, as a world-wide phenomenon may well one day be accounted the outstanding event of the last decade.
> Hannah Arendt
> "Civil Disobedience," *Crises of the Republic,* 1972

23.17　Disobedience is the worst of evils. This it is that ruins a nation.
> Jean Anouilh, *1910–*
> Laurence J. Peter, *Peter's Quotations,* 1977

24.   CIVIL RIGHTS

24.1   The law, in our case, seems to make the right; and the very reverse ought to be done—the right should make the law.
Maria Edgeworth, Irish novelist
The Grateful Negro, 1802

24.2   No man is good enough to govern another man without that other's consent.
Abraham Lincoln
Speech, Peoria, October 16, 1854

24.3   . . . in view of the Constitution, in the eye of the law, there is in this country no superior, dominant, ruling class of citizens. There is no caste here. Our Constitution is color-blind, and neither knows nor tolerates classes among citizens . . .
John Marshall Harlan
Plessy v. Ferguson, 163 U.S. 537, 559–560 (1896)

24.4   In respect of civil rights, all citizens are equal before the law. The humblest is the peer of the most powerful.
John Marshall Harlan
Plessy v. Ferguson, 163 U.S. 537, 559 (1896)

24.5   . . . most people, no doubt, when they espouse human rights, make their own mental reservations about the proper application of the word "human."
Suzanne LaFollette, American feminist and writer
"The Beginnings of Emancipation," *Concerning Women,* 1926

24.6   The Fourteenth Amendment . . . nollifies sophisticated as well as simple-minded modes of discrimination.
Felix Frankfurter
Lane v. Wilson, 307 U.S. 268, 275 (1939)

24.7   Distinctions between citizens solely because of their ancestry are by their very nature odious to a free people whose institutions are founded upon the doctrine of equality.
Harlan Stone
Hirabayashi v. United States, 320 U.S. 81 (1943)

24.8   A license cannot be revoked because a man is red-headed or because he was divorced, except for a calling, if such there be, for which red-headedness or an unbroken marriage may have some rational bearing.
Felix Frankfurter
Barsky v. Board of Regents, 347 U.S. 442, 470 (1954)

24.9   . . . in the field of public education the doctrine of "separate but equal"

has no place. Separate educational fa-
cilities are inherently unequal.

Earl Warren
Brown v. Board of Education of
Topeka, 347 U.S. 483, 74 S. Ct. 686,
98 L.Ed. 873 (1954)

24.10   We come then to the question presented: Does segregation of children
in public schools solely on the basis
of race, even though the physical fa-
cilities and other "tangible" factors
may be equal, deprive the children of
the minority group of equal educational opportunities? We believe that
it does.

Earl Warren
Brown v. Board of Education of
Topeka, 347 U.S. 483, 74 S. Ct. 686,
98 L.Ed. 873 (1954)

24.11   It may be true that the law cannot
make a man love me. But it can keep
him from lynching me, and I think
that's pretty important.

Martin Luther King, Jr.
Wall Street Journal, November 13,
1962

24.12   I don't want to be told that I must
love a woman or a man because of
their color, any more than I want to
be told that I must hate them because of their color. I love and hate
only a few, and their color may have
as little or as much to do with it as
their height or the color of their hair
or the way they walk. It is for themselves in their totality that I am
drawn to them or recoil from them—
for their totality and their humanity.

Max Lerner
"Notable & Quotable," *Wall Street*
Journal, March 29, 1963

24.13   . . . a century after the Emancipation Proclamation, no American
should have to demonstrate in the

streets in order to be admitted to a
hotel or to eat at a lunch counter or
to see a motion picture.

Editorial, "The Civil Rights
Message," *New York Times,* June 20,
1963

24.14   I have a dream that one day on the
red hills of Georgia, the sons of former slaves and the sons of former
slave-owners will be able to sit together at the table of brother-
hood. . . . That one day even the state
of Mississippi, a state sweltering with
the heat of oppression, will be trans-
formed into an oasis of freedom and
justice. . . . That my four little children will one day live in a nation
where they will not be judged by the
color of their skin but by the content
of their character.

Martin Luther King, Jr.
Address, Lincoln Memorial, during
the National March on Washington,
August 28, 1963

24.15   . . . there is no constitutional right
for any race to be preferred . . . If
discrimination based on race is constitutionally permissible when those
who hold the reins can come up with
"compelling" reasons to justify it,
then constitutional guarantees acquire an accordion-like quality . . .

William O. Douglas
De Funis v. Odegaarde, 416 U.S. 312
(1974)

24.16   The law changes and flows like
water, and . . . the stream of women's
rights law has become a sudden rush-
ing torrent.

Shana Alexander
State-by-State Guide to Women's
Legal Rights, 1975

24.17   Preferring members of any one
group for no reason other than race

or ethnic origin is discrimination for its own sake. This the Constitution forbids. . . .
Lewis F. Powell, Jr.
University of California v. Bakke, 438 U.S. 265, S. Ct. 2733, 57 L.Ed.2d 750 (1978)

25. CLIENTS

25.1   Who lied to me about his case,
And said we'd have an easy race,
And did it all with solemn face?
It was my client.
Anonymous
Jacob M. Braude, *Lifetime Speaker's Encyclopedia,* 1962

25.2   A client twixt his attorney and counsellor is like a goose twixt two foxes.
Proverb
Rosalind Fergusson, *The Facts On File Dictionary of Proverbs,* 1983

25.3   He that is his own lawyer has a fool for a client.
Proverb
Rosalind Fergusson, *The Facts On File Dictionary of Proverbs,* 1983

25.4   Lawyers' gowns are lined with the willfulness of their clients.
Proverb
Rosalind Fergusson, *The Facts On File Dictionary of Proverbs,* 1983

25.5   Fools and stubborn men make wealthy lawyers.
Spanish proverb
H. L. Mencken, *A New Dictionary of Quotations,* 1946

25.6   From your confessor, lawyer and physician,
Hide not your case on no condition.
Sir John Harington, English writer
Metamorphosis of Ajax, 1596

25.7   Good counsellors lack no clients.
Shakespeare
Measure for Measure, I, 2, 1604–1605

25.8   Never fear the want of business. A man who qualifies himself well for his calling, never fails of employment in it.
Thomas Jefferson
Letter to Peter Carr, June 22, 1792

25.9   Battledore and shuttlecock's a wery good game, vhen you an't the shuttlecock and two lawyers the battledores, in which case it gets too excitin' to be pleasant.
Charles Dickens
Pickwick Papers, 1836–1837

25.10   I would rather have clients than be somebody's lawyer.
Louis D. Brandeis
Ernest Poole, Interview, *American Magazine,* vol. 71, no. 492, 1911

25.11   . . . ideal client—"the very wealthy man in very great trouble."
John C. Sterling, American publisher
John C. Payne, "Lawyers and the Laws of Economics," 46 *American Bar Association Journal* 365 (April 1960)

25.12   Most of the clients that I represent in a criminal case I detest. . . . As a matter of fact, . . . the more I become involved emotionally in my client's cause, the less I am able to [do] for him.
Joseph A. Ball, American lawyer; president, American College of Trial Lawyers
Speech, American Bar Association, reported in the *Los Angeles Herald-Examiner,* August 23, 1970

25.13   You can't earn a living defending innocent people.
Maurice Nadjari
New York Post, May 8, 1975

25.14   If there is any truth to the old proverb that "one who is his own lawyer, has a fool for a client," the Court . . . now bestows a *constitutional* right on one to make a fool of himself.
Harry Blackmun
Faretta v. California (1975)

25.15   There is never a deed so foul that something couldn't be said for the guy; that's why there are lawyers.
Melvin Belli
Los Angeles Times, December 18, 1981

26. COMMON LAW

26.1   The unwritten law—the "common law."
Latin legal phrase
W. Gurney Benham, *Putnam's Complete Book of Quotations, Proverbs and Household Words,* 1927

26.2   Things which restrict the common law are to be interpreted rigidly.
Latin legal phrase
W. Gurney Benham, *Putnam's Complete Book of Quotations, Proverbs and Household Words,* 1927

26.3   We ourselves of the present age, chose our common law, and consented to the most ancient Acts of Parliament, for we lived in our ancestors 1,000 years ago, and those ancestors are still living in us.

Sir Robert Atkyns, English jurist
Trial of Sir Edward Hales (1686), 11 How. St. Tr. n. p. 1204

26.4   Its [The common law's] origin . . . is as undiscoverable as the Head of the Nile.

Sir Matthew Hale
History of the Common Law, 1713

26.5   The common law is nothing else but statutes worn out by time. . . .

Sir John Eardley Wilmot, English jurist; chief justice
Collins v. Blantern (1767), 2 Wils, K.B., 341, 348

26.6   The first requirement of a sound body of law is, that it should correspond with the actual feelings and demands of the community, whether right or wrong.

Oliver Wendell Holmes
The Common Law, 1881

26.7   The common law is not a brooding omnipresence in the sky but the articulate voice of some sovereign or quasi-sovereign that can be identified. . . .

Oliver Wendell Holmes
Southern Pacific Co. v. Jensen, 244 U.S. 205, 221 (1917)

26.8   [Common law] stands as a monument slowly raised, like a coral reef, from the minute accretions of past individuals, of whom each built upon the relics which his predecessors left, and in his turn left a foundation upon which his successors might work.

Learned Hand
"Review of Judge Cardozo's *The Nature of the Judicial Process,*" 35 *Harvard Law Review,* 481 (1922)

26.9   We always exempt ourselves from the common laws. When I was a boy and the dentist pulled out a second tooth, I thought to myself that I would grow a third if I needed it. Experience discouraged this prophecy.

Oliver Wendell Holmes, *1841–1936*
Think, October 1959

26.10   . . . Churchill never minded contemplating the mystery of death. Once a friend inquired: "What makes you think you will reach the bar of Heaven?" He interjected with solemn assurance: "Surely the Almighty must observe the principles of English common law and consider a man innocent until proven guilty."

Sir Winston S. Churchill, *1874–1965*
New York Times, February 1, 1965

27. COMPETITION

27.1   One bush, they say, can never hide two thieves.
Aristophanes
The Wasps, 422 B.C.

27.2   Not hate, but glory, made these chiefs contend. . . .
Alexander Pope
Verse translation of Homer's *"Iliad"*
1715–1720

27.3   Free competition is worth more to society than it costs.
Oliver Wendell Holmes
Vegelahn v. Guntner, 167 Mass. 92, 44 N.E. 1077, 1080 (1896)

27.4   . . . competition has many times caused distress and failure; for competition does not think or feel; still, thus far, we have found nothing to take the place of competition excepting monopoly, which is but a modern form of slavery. Unrestricted business tends toward monopoly. It gives an advantage to the strong, the clever, the selfish and unscrupulous. It is the rule of the jungle. The problem in business, and in life, has always been to preserve freedom without monopoly. . . . We have solved it as we do most questions by taking both courses at the same time.
Clarence Darrow, *1857–1938*
Arthur and Lila Weinberg, *Verdicts Out of Court,* 1963

27.5   For excesses of competition lead to monopoly. . . .
John Gardner
Excellence: Can We Be Equal and Excellent Too?, 1961

28. CONFESSION

28.1   Silence [in court] may be equivalent to confession.
Talmud, *Yevamot*

28.2   Confession of our faults is the next thing to innocency.
Publilius Syrus, Latin writer
Sententiae, c.43 B.C.

28.3   The confession of evil works is the first beginning of good works.
St. Augustine, *354–430*
Franklin Pierce Adams, *F.P.A. Book of Quotations,* 1952

28.4   Confess and be hanged.
Christopher Marlowe
The Jew of Malta, 1589

28.5   Hamlet: Confess yourself to heaven: Repent what's past; avoid what is to come.
Shakespeare
Hamlet, III, 4, 1600–1601

28.6   He's half absolv'd who has confessed.
Matthew Prior
Alma, 1715–1717

28.7   There is no refuge from confession but suicide; and suicide is confession.
Daniel Webster
Argument on the murder of Captain White, April 6, 1830

28.8   A confession is wholly and incontestably voluntary only if a guilty person gives himself up to the law and becomes his own accuser.
Robert H. Jackson
Ashcraft v. Tennessee, 322 U.S. 143, 161 (1944)

29. CONSCIENCE

29.1   It is always Term-Time in the Court of Conscience.
Proverb
Thomas Fuller, *Gnomologia,* 1732

29.2   No guilty man is ever acquitted at the bar of his own conscience.
Juvenal
Satires, c.120

29.3   Conscience and reputation are two things. Conscience is due to yourself, reputation to your neighbor.
St. Augustine, *354–430*

29.4   My conscience hath a thousand several tongues,
And every tongue brings in a several tale,
And every tale condemns me for a villain.
Shakespeare
Richard III, V, 3, 1592–1593

29.5   Why should not Conscience have vacation
As well as other Courts o' the nation?
Samuel Butler
Hudibras, 1663–1678

29.6   Two things fill my mind with ever-increasing wonder and awe . . . the starry heavens above me and the moral law within me.
Immanuel Kant
Critique of Pure Reason, 1787

29.7   Labor to keep alive in your breast that little spark of celestial fire, called Conscience.
George Washington, *1732–1799*
Moral Maxims: Virtue and Vice,
Conscience

29.8   A man's vanity tells him what is honour,
a man's conscience what is justice.
Walter Savage Landor, English writer
Imaginary Conversations, 1824

29.9   The sting of conscience, like the gnawing of a dog at a bone, is mere foolishness.
Nietzsche, *1844–1900*
Human All-too-Human

29.10   The roots of valid law . . . are, and can only be, within the individual conscience.
Harold J. Laski
The State in Theory and Practice,
1935

30. CONSEQUENCES

30.1   When anything is forbidden, everything which leads to the same result is also forbidden.
> Latin legal expression
> W. Gurney Benham, *Putnam's Complete Book of Quotations, Proverbs and Household Words,* 1927

30.2   It is the common fate of the indolent to see their rights become a prey to the active. The condition upon which God hath given liberty to man is eternal vigilance; which condition if he break, servitude is at once the consequence of his crime and the punishment of his guilt.
> John Philpot Curran, Irish jurist
> Speech upon the Right of Election, 1790

30.3   If a man will make a purchase of a chance he must abide by the consequences.
> Sir Richard Richards, English jurist
> *Hitchcock v. Giddings* (1817), 4 Price, 135

30.4   The degree of civilization which a people has reached, no doubt, is marked by their anxiety to do as they would be done by.
> Oliver Wendell Holmes
> *The Common Law,* 1881

30.5   Logical consequences are the scarecrows of fools and the beacons of wise men.
> Thomas H. Huxley
> *Animal Automatism,* 1884

30.6   Consequences cannot alter statutes, but may help to fix their meaning.
> Benjamin N. Cardozo
> *In re Rouss,* 116 N.E. 782, 785 (1917)

31. CONSTITUTION

31.1   What are twenty acts of Parliament amongst friends?
John Selden, *1584–1654*
Table-Talk, c.1689

31.2   It [the Constitution] is a good canvas, on which some strokes only want retouching.
Thomas Jefferson
Letter to James Madison, July 31, 1788

31.3   Constitutions should consist only of general provisions; the reason is that they must necessarily be permanent, and that they cannot calculate for the possible change of things.
Alexander Hamilton
Speech in the Senate, 1788

31.4   . . . no society can make a perpetual constitution, or even a perpetual law. The earth belongs always to the living generation. . . . Every constitution then, and every law, naturally expires at the end of 19 years.
Thomas Jefferson
Letter to James Madison, September 6, 1789

31.5   Our Constitution is in actual operation; everything appears to promise that it will last; but in this world nothing is certain but death and taxes.
Benjamin Franklin
Letter to Jean Baptiste Le Roy, November 13, 1789

31.6   We, the people of the United States, in Order to form a more perfect Union, establish Justice, insure domestic Tranquility, provide for the common Defense, promote the general Welfare, and secure the Blessings of Liberty to ourselves and our Posterity, do ordain and establish this Constitution for the United States of America.
Framers of the Constitution
Preamble to the Constitution of the United States, 1789

31.7   The American constitutions were to liberty, what a grammar is to language: they define its parts of speech, and practically construct them into syntax.
Thomas Paine
The Rights of Man, 1791

31.8   We must never forget that it is a constitution we are expounding.
John Marshall
McCulloch v. Maryland, 17 U.S. (4 Wheat.) 316, 415 (1819)

31.9   A Constitution should be short and
obscure.
> Napoleon Bonaparte, *1769–1821*
> Franklin Pierce Adams, *F.P.A. Book
> of Quotations,* 1952

31.10   Laws and institutions must go
hand in hand with the progress of
the human mind . . . We might as
well require a man to wear the coat
that fitted him as a boy, as civilized
society to remain ever under the regime of their ancestors.
> Thomas Jefferson, *1743–1826,*
> referring to constitutions
> Franklin Pierce Adams, *F.P.A. Book
> of Quotations,* 1952

31.11   "Here we stan' on the Constitution,
by thunder!
It's a fact o' wich ther's bushils o'
proofs;
Fer how could we trample on't so, I
wonder,
Ef't worn't thet it's ollers under our
hoofs?"
Sez John C. Calhoun, sez he.
> James Russell Lowell
> *The Biglow Papers,* 1848

31.12   But there is a higher law than the
Constitution. . . .
> William H. Seward
> Speech, U.S. Senate, March 11, 1850

31.13   The Constitution of the United
States was made not merely for the
generation that then existed, but for
posterity—unlimited,   undefined,
endless, perpetual posterity.
> Henry Clay
> Speech, U.S. Senate, 1850

31.14   "We, the people of the United
States." Which "We, the people"?
The women were not included.
> Lucy Stone, American suffragist
> Speech, reported in the *New York
> Tribune,* April 1853

31.15   A majority held in restraint by
constitutional checks and limitations, and always changing easily
with deliberate changes of popular
opinions and sentiments, is the only
true sovereign of a free people.
> Abraham Lincoln
> First inaugural address, March 4,
> 1861

31.16   If by the mere force of numbers a
majority should deprive a minority
of any clearly written constitutional
right, it might, in a moral point of
view, justify revolution.
> Abraham Lincoln
> First inaugural address, March 4,
> 1861

31.17   The Constitution of the United
States is a law for rulers and people,
equally in war and in peace, and cov-
ers with the shield of its protection
all classes of men, at all times, and
under all circumstances.
> David Davis, American jurist
> *Ex parte Milligan,* 71 U.S. (4 Wall.) 2,
> 120–21 (1866)

31.18   I am sworn to uphold the Constitution as Andy Johnson understands
it and interprets it.
> Andrew Johnson, *c.1865–1869,* in
> vetoing the act of Congress that
> created the National Bank
> Thad Stem, Jr. and Alan Butler, *Sam
> Ervin's Best Short Stories,* 1973

31.19   What's the Constitution between
friends?
> Timothy J. Campbell, American
> politician; Tammany Hall (New York
> City) congressman
> Communication to President Grover
> Cleveland, c.1885

31.20   Our Constitution is color-blind.
John M. Harlan
Plessy v. Ferguson, 163 U.S. 537, 559,
41 L.Ed. 256, 263, 16 S. Ct. 1138
(1896)

31.21   Constitutions are intended to preserve practical and substantial rights,
not to maintain theories.
Oliver Wendell Holmes
Davis v. Mills, 194 U.S. 451, 457
(1904)

31.22   . . . the accident of our finding certain opinions natural and familar, or
novel, and even shocking, ought not
to conclude our judgment upon the
question whether statutes embodying
them conflict with the Constitution
of the United States.
Oliver Wendell Holmes
Lochner v. New York, 198 U.S. 45, 76
(1905)

31.23   We are under a Constitution, but
the Constitution is what judges say it
is.
Charles Evans Hughes
Speech, Elmira, New York, May 3,
1907

31.24   Constitutional rights like others
are matters of degree.
Oliver Wendell Holmes
Martin v. District of Columbia, 205
U.S. 135, 139 (1907)

31.25   . . . the Constitution of the United
States is not a mere lawyers' docu-
ment: it is a vehicle of life, and its
spirit is always the spirit of the age.
Woodrow Wilson
*Constitutional Government in the
United States,* 1908

31.26   Whenever the Constitution comes
between men and the virtue of the

white women of South Carolina, I
say—to Hell with the Constitution!
Cole L. Blease, American politician;
governor, South Carolina
Public statement, 1911

31.27   Constitutional law like other mortal contrivances has to take some
chances.
Oliver Wendell Holmes
Blinn v. Nelson, 222 U.S. 1, 7 (1911)

31.28   There is truth in the reply of a
great lawyer when asked how the
lawyers who formed the United
States Constitution had such a mastery of legal principles: "Why, they
had so few books."
Charles Warren
"The Colonial Lawyer's Education,"
A History of the American Bar, 1911

31.29   But the provisions of the Constitution are not mathematical formulas
having their essence in their form;
they are organic living institutions
transplanted from English soil. Their
significance is vital, not formal. . . .
Oliver Wendell Holmes
Gompers v. United States, 233 U.S.
604, 610 (1914)

31.30   The Fourteenth Amendment . . .
was adopted with a view to the protection of the colored race, but has
been found to be equally important
in its application to the rights of
all. . . .
Oliver Wendell Holmes
United States v. Mosley, 238 U.S. 383,
388 (1915)

31.31   Our constitution . . . is an experi-
ment as all life is an experiment.
Oliver Wendell Holmes
Abrams v. United States, 250 U.S.
616, 630, 63 L.Ed. 1175, 1180, 40 S.
Ct. 17 (1919)

31.32 Without general elections, without freedom of the press, freedom of speech, freedom of assembly, without the free battle of opinions, life in every public institution withers away, becomes a caricature of itself, and bureaucracy rises as the only deciding factor.
Rosa Luxemburg, *1870–1919*
Paul Froelich, *Die Russische Revolution,* 1940

31.33 Constitutional rights should not be frittered away by arguments so technical and unsubstantial. "The Constitution deals with substance, not shadows."
Louis D. Brandeis
Milwaukee Social Democratic Publishing Co. v. Burleson, 255 U.S. 407, 431 (1921)

31.34 The great generalities of the Constitution have a content and a significance that vary from age to age.
Benjamin N. Cardozo
The Nature of the Judicial Process, 1921

31.35 If the thing has been practiced for two hundred years by common consent, it will need a strong case for the Fourteenth Amendment to affect it. . . .
Oliver Wendell Holmes
Jackson v. Rosenbaum Co., 260 U.S. 22, 31 (1922)

31.36 The interpretation of constitutional principles must not be too literal. We must remember that the machinery of government would not work if it were not allowed a little play in its joints.
Oliver Wendell Holmes
Springer v. Philippine Islands, 277 U.S. 189, 209–210 (1928)

31.37 The United States Constitution has proven itself the most marvelously elastic compilation of rules of government ever written.
Franklin D. Roosevelt
Radio speech, March 2, 1930

31.38 . . . the theory that the Constitution is a written document is a legal fiction. The idea that it can be understood by a study of its language and the history of its past development is equally mythical. It is what the Government and the people who count in public affairs recognize and respect as such, what they think it is.
Charles A. and Mary Beard
The American Leviathan, 1931

31.39 If the provisions of the Constitution be not upheld when they pinch as well as when they comfort, they may as well be abandoned.
George Sutherland, American jurist
Home Building & Loan Assn. v. Blaisdell, 290 U.S. 398, 483 (1934)

31.40 I hope that your committee will not permit doubt as to constitutionality, however reasonable, to block the suggested legislation [the Guffey Coal Control Bill].
Franklin D. Roosevelt
Letter to Representative Samuel B. Hill, July 1935

31.41 Do the people of this land . . . desire to preserve those [liberties] so carefully protected by the First Amendment. . . . If so, let them withstand all *beginnings* of encroachment. For the saddest epitaph which can be carved in memory of a vanished liberty is that it was lost because its possessors failed to stretch forth a saving hand while yet there was time.

George Sutherland, American jurist
Associated Press v. National Labor Relations Board, 301 U.S. 103, 141 (1937)

31.42   If the Constitution is to be construed to mean what the majority at any given period in history wish the Constitution to mean, why a written Constitution?

Frank J. Hogan
Presidential address, American Bar Association, San Francisco, July 10, 1939

31.43   . . . the ultimate touchstone of constitutionality is the Constitution itself and not what we have said about it.

Felix Frankfurter
Graves v. New York ex rel. O'Keefe, 306 U.S. 466; 83 L.Ed. 927; 59 Sup. Ct. 595 (1939)

31.44   While the Declaration was directed against an excess of authority, the Constitution was directed against anarchy.

Robert H. Jackson
The Struggle for Judicial Supremacy, 1941

31.45   Is that which was deemed to be of so fundamental a nature as to be written into the Constitution to endure for all times to be the sport of shifting winds of doctrine?

Felix Frankfurter
West Virginia State Board of Education v. Barnette, 319 U.S. 624, 642 (1943)

31.46   The Constitution does not provide for first and second class citizens.

Wendell L. Willkie
An American Program, 1944

31.47   The Constitution was built for rough as well as smooth roads. In time of war the nation simply changes gears and takes the harder going under the same power.

Harold H. Burton, American jurist
Duncan v. Kahanamoku, 327 U.S. 304, 342 (1946)

31.48   Our protection against all kinds of fanatics and extremists, none of whom can be trusted with unlimited power over others, lies not in their forbearance but in the limitations of our Constitution.

Robert H. Jackson
American Communications Association v. Douds, 339 U.S. 382, 439 (1950)

31.49   . . . the validity of a doctrine does not depend on whose ox it gores.

Robert H. Jackson
Wells v. Simonds Abrasive Co., 345 U.S. 514, 525 (1953)

31.50   The Constitution favors no racial group, no political or social group.

William O. Douglas
Uphaus v. Wyman, 364 U.S. 388, 406 (1960)

31.51   We believe . . . that when the men who met in 1787 to make a Constitution made the best political document ever made, they did it very largely because they were great compromisers.

Learned Hand
Irving Dilliard, *The Spirit of Liberty,* 1960

31.52   The layman's Constitutional view is that what he likes is Constitutional and that which he doesn't like is unconstitutional. That about measures up the Constitutional acumen of the average person.

Hugo L. Black
New York Times, February 26, 1971

32. CONTRACTS

32.1 *Caveat emptor.* [Let a purchaser beware.]
Latin legal maxim

32.2 He who derives the advantage ought to sustain the burthen.
Legal maxim

32.3 No cause of action arises from a bare promise.
Legal maxim

32.4 To break an oral agreement which is not legally binding is morally wrong.
Talmud, *Bava Metzi'a*

32.5 Necessitous men are not, truly speaking, free men, but, to answer a present exigency, will submit to any terms that the crafty may impose upon them.
Lord Thomas Henley, English jurist
Vernon v. Bethell (1762), 2 Eden. 110, 113

32.6 The movement of progressive societies has hitherto been a movement from status to contract.
Sir Henry James Sumner Maine, English jurist and legal historian
Ancient Law; Its Connection with the Early History of Society, and Its Relation to Modern Ideas, 1861

32.7 The law has outgrown its primitive stage of formalism when the precise word was the sovereign talisman, and every slip was fatal. It takes a broader view today. A promise may be lacking, and yet the whole writing may be "instinct with an obligation," imperfectly expressed. . . . If that is so, there is a contract.
Benjamin N. Cardozo
Wood v. Lucy, Lady Duff-Gordon, 1917

32.8 There is grim irony in speaking of the freedom of contract of those who, because of their economic necessities, give their service for less than is needful to keep body and soul together.
Harlan Fiske Stone
Morehead v. N. Y. ex rel. Tipaldo, 298 U.S. 587, 632 (1936)

32.9 A verbal contract isn't worth the paper it's written on.
Samuel Goldwyn
Laurence J. Peter, *Peter's Quotations,* 1977

33. CORRUPTION

33.1   There was never anything by the wit of man so well devised, or so sure established, which in continuance of time hath not been corrupted.
"Concerning the Service," Book of Common Prayer

33.2   King: In the corrupted currents of this world
Offence's gilded hand may shove by justice,
And oft 'tis seen the wicked prize itself
Buys out the law: but 'tis not so above;
There is no shuffling, there the action lies
In his true nature; and we ourselves compell'd
Even to the teeth and forehead of our faults,
To give in evidence.
Shakespeare
Hamlet, III, 3, 1600–1601

33.3   Asebia: We never valued right and wrong
But as they serve our cause.
Zelota: Our business was to please the throng,
And court their wild applause.
Asebia: For this we bribed the lawyer's tongue

And then destroyed the laws.
John Dryden
Albion and Albanius, 1685

33.4   Corruption's not of modern date;
It hath been tried in ev'ry state.
John Gay
Fables, 1738

33.5   Touch but a cobweb in Westminster Hall, and the old spider of the law is out upon you with all his vermin at his heels.
Henry Fox, 1705–1774
Marshall Brown, Wit and Humor of Bench and Bar, 1899

33.6   He that accuses all mankind of corruption ought to remember that he is sure to convict only one.
Edmund Burke
Letter to the sheriffs of Bristol, 1777

33.7   The time to guard against corruption and tyranny is before they shall have gotten hold of us. It is better to keep the wolf out of the fold than to trust to drawing his teeth and talons after he shall have entered.
Thomas Jefferson
Notes on the State of Virginia, c.1781–1783

33.8 He is a man of splendid abilities, but utterly corrupt.
He shines and stinks like a rotten mackerel by moonlight.
> John Randolph, *1773–1833,* in an attack on Edward Livingston
> Thad Stem, Jr. and Alan Butler, *Sam Ervin's Best Stories,* 1973

33.9 There is no odor so bad as that which arises from goodness tainted.
> Henry David Thoreau
> *Walden,* 1854

33.10 "Your laws are ineffective," Wen declared. "Why? Because no system of control will work as long as most of those administering the law against an evil have more than a finger dipped into it themselves."
> Han Suyin, Chinese physician and writer
> *Destination Chungking,* 1942

33.11 We are born in innocence. . . . Corruption comes later. The first fear is a corruption, the first reaching for a something that defies us. The first nuance of difference, the first need to feel better than the different one, more loved, stronger, richer, more blessed—these are corruptions.
> Laura Z. Hobson
> *Gentlemen's Agreement,* 1946

33.12 "Corruption continues with us beyond the grave," she said, "and then plays merry hell with all ideals. . . ."
> Daphne Du Maurier
> *Mary Anne,* 1954

33.13 . . . the accomplice to the crime of corruption is frequently our own indifference.
> Bess Myerson
> Claire Safran, "Impeachment?"
> *Redbook,* April 1974

34. COURTS

34.1 A court may not permit one litigant to sit and compel the other to stand, one to speak all his desires and the other to be brief.
> Talmud, *Shevu'ot*

34.2 For friend in court ay better is
Than peny in purs, certis.
> Jean de Meun, French poet, *c.1279–?*
> *Roman de la Rose*

34.3 Lo, in this pond be fishe and froggis bothe.
> Sir Thomas More
> *Fortune,* c.1500

34.4 The place of justice is a hallowed place.
> Francis Bacon
> "Of Judicature," *Essayes,* 1625

34.5 The law can take an open purse in court,

while it condemns a less delinquent for 't.
Samuel Butler, *1612–1680*
Miscellaneous Thoughts

34.6 The charge is prepared; the lawyers are met,
The judges all ranged (a terrible show!).
John Gay
The Beggar's Opera, 1728

34.7 Laws are a dead letter without courts to expound and define their true meaning and operation.
Alexander Hamilton
The Federalist, 1788

34.8 The business of the court is to try the case, and not the man; and a very bad man may have a very righteous cause.
Anonymous
Thompson v. Church (1791), 1 Root 312

34.9 The man that has no friend at court,
Must make the laws confine his sport;
But he that has, by dint of flaws,
May make his sport confine the laws.
Thomas Chatterton
The Revenge, 1795

34.10 Suitors, whose aching backs do break
With costs, and penalities, and pains,
We take—at least you'll own—we take
Judicial notice that it rains.
Showell Rogers
"Ballade of Judicial Notice," c.1845

34.11 Fresh from brawling courts
And dusty purlieus of the law.
Tennyson
In Memoriam, 1850

34.12 A revolt of the judiciary is more dangerous to a government than any other, even a military revolt. Now and then it uses the military to suppress disorder, but it defends itself every day by means of the courts.
Alexis de Tocqueville, *1805–1859*
W. H. Auden and Louis Kronenberger, *The Viking Book of Aphorisms,* 1962

34.13 The prophecies of what the courts will do in fact, and nothing more pretentious, are what I mean by the law.
Oliver Wendell Holmes
"Path of the Law," 10 *Harvard Law Review* 457, 461 (1897)

34.14 I know of no duty of the Court which it is more important to observe, and no powers of the Court which it is more important to enforce, than its power of keeping public bodies within their rights. The moment public bodies exceed their rights they do so to the injury and oppression of private individuals. . . .
Nathaniel Lindley, English jurist
Robert v. Gwyrfai District Council (1899), L.R. 2 C.D. 614

34.15 The decisions of the courts on economic and social questions depend on their economic and social philosophy.
Theodore Roosevelt, *1858–1919*
Laurence J. Peter, *Peter's Quotations,* 1977

34.16 No court can make time stand still.
Felix Frankfurter
Scripps-Howard Radio v. Federal Communications Commission, 316 U.S. 4, 9 (1942)

34.17   A court which yields to the popular will thereby license itself to practice despotism, for there can be no assurance that it will not on another occasion indulge its own will.
Felix Frankfurter
American Federation of Labor v. American Sash & Door Co., 335 U.S. 538, 557 (1949)

34.18   Madrigal: Truth doesn't ring true in a court of law.
Enid Bagnold, English dramatist
The Chalk Garden, 1953

34.19   The penalty for laughing in a courtroom is six months; if it were not for this penalty the jury would never hear the evidence.
H. L. Mencken, *1880–1956*
Kenneth Redden, *Modern Legal Glossary*, 1983

34.20   Courtroom: A place where Jesus Christ and Judas Iscariot would be equals, with the betting odds in favor of Judas.
H. L. Mencken, *1880–1956*
Laurence J. Peter, *Peter's Quotations*, 1977

34.21   If respect for the courts and for their judicial process is gone or steadily weakened, no law can save us as a society. Lawyers, whatever their views on controversial decisions, must inspire respect for the judiciary.
William T. Gossett, American lawyer; president, American Bar Association
Speech, Canadian Bar Association, Ottawa, September 3, 1969

34.22   The courts are institutional cripples, stumbling along in the pattern of an outworn tradition, compiling a record of incredible inefficiency.
John V. Lindsay
Address, Association of the Bar of the City of New York, reported in the *New York Times*, February 21, 1970

34.23   The flagrant disregard in the courtroom of elementary standards of proper conduct should not and cannot be tolerated. We believe trial judges confronted with disruptive, contumacious, stubbornly defiant defendants must be given sufficient discretion to meet the circumstances in each case.
Hugo L. Black
New York Times, April 1, 1970

34.24   I have nothing but utter contempt for the courts of this land.
George C. Wallace
Plainview (Texas) *Daily Herald*, September 24, 1971

34.25   The court should be a place where anybody can come—whatever they have in their pocket—and be able to file a complaint in simple fashion and at least have somebody give consideration to it and give them an opportunity to be heard.
Thomas T. Curtin, American jurist; judge, U.S. District Court
New York Times, October 7, 1971

34.26   No one can ever be sure how courts will interpret any new law or amendment.
Susan C. Ross, American lawyer
The Rights of Women, 1973

34.27   The court will even make up or accept a spurious purpose for the law in order to justify differential treatment.
Susan C. Ross, American lawyer
The Rights of Women, 1973

34.28　　I do think people are putting too much reliance on courts. I also believe the courts are too prone to take on problems that they have no business getting into. To me, the idea of a court deciding whether or not girls should be permitted to play Little League baseball is ludicrous. Congress too contributes to this glut which I call legal pollution.

> Thomas Ehrlich, American educator; dean, Stanford University School of Law
> *U.S. News & World Report,* July 21, 1975

34.29　　The courts hold a unique position among our democratic institutions. In a sense, they represent one of our last bastions of participatory democracy, in which disputants go directly before a judge or jury to resolve an issue. In no other governmental context does an individual have the opportunity to take a problem to a decision-maker who represents the full force and power of that particular branch of government. This direct interchange between the individual and the state is at the heart of the democratic process. . . . We must protect this unique heritage and strive to preserve the values it represents.

> Rose E. Bird, American jurist; chief justice, Supreme Court of California
> *Los Angeles Times,* November 16, 1977

34.30　　We should get away from the idea that a court is the only place in which to settle disputes. People with claims are likely people with pains. They want relief and results and they don't care whether it's in a courtroom with lawyers and judges, or somewhere else.

> Warren E. Burger
> Address, American Bar Association, New Orleans, reported in the *Los Angeles Times,* August 27, 1978

34.31　　If our courts lose their authority and their rulings are no longer respected, there will be no one left to resolve the divisive issues that can rip the social fabric apart. . . . The courts are a safety valve without which no democratic society can survive.

> Rose E. Bird, American jurist; chief justice, Supreme Court of California
> *Los Angeles Times,* September 11, 1978

34.32　　The court is a political institution. All of us here were appointed by politicians and none of us can deny we were chosen in part for our political belief. To suggest that doesn't influence our thinking now that we are judges is just naive.

> William P. Clark, Jr., American jurist; justice, Supreme Court of California
> *Los Angeles Times,* November 23, 1978

34.33　　The young judge spends the first third of his life in fear that he might be reversed by the court of appeals, the middle third in the conviction that the court of appeals was always wrong and the last third not caring whether it was right or wrong.

> Patrick Devlin, English jurist
> *The Judge,* 1979

34.34　　There is a reciprocal relationship between the U.S. Supreme Court and the state courts. As the Supreme Court's own energy flags or it reaches the limits of appropriate

Federal judicial activity, it may nonetheless have marked the path that creative state jurists will want to follow. In the long view of history, most of the truly creative developments in the American law have come from the states.

> Laurence H. Tribe, American educator; professor, Harvard University
> *New York Times,* May 19, 1982

34.35 We must use our courage to ensure a judiciary not governed by the daily polls but by the rules of law, serving not the special interest of the few but the best interest of all, devoted not to self-preservation, but to the preservation of those great Constitutional principles which history has bequeathed to us.

> Rose E. Bird, American jurist; chief justice, Supreme Court of California
> *Los Angeles Times,* July 20, 1982

34.36 The courts are an easy scapegoat because at a time when everything has to be boiled down to easy slogans, we speak in subtleties.

> Rose E. Bird, American jurist; chief justice, Supreme Court of California
> *Newsweek,* August 9, 1982

34.37 [The court] is the lengthened shadow of many men.

> C. J. Field
> Observance of the 250th Anniversary of the Supreme Court

35.   CRIME

35.1 The number of the Malefactors, authorizes not the Crime.

> Proverb
> Thomas Fuller, *Gnomologia,* 1732

35.2 The greatest crimes are caused by surfeit, not by want. Men do not become tyrants in order that they may not suffer cold.

> Aristotle
> *Politics,* c.322 B.C.

35.3 Crime and intention of crime are equal in their nature.

> Cicero,   *106–43 B.C.*
> W. Gurney Benham, *Putnam's Complete Book of Quotations, Proverbs and Household Words,* 1927

35.4 The man upright in his life, and free from crime, does not need Moorish javelins or bow.

> Horace
> *Odes,* 23 B.C.

35.5 No crime is founded upon reason.

> Livy
> *History of Rome,* c.10 B.C.

35.6   Evil booty does not bring good luck.
Ovid,   *43 B.C.-?A.D. 7*
Amores

35.7   Crime must be safeguarded by crime.
Seneca
De Clementia, c.55

35.8   A happy issue makes some crimes honorable.
Seneca
Hippolytus, c.60

35.9   There is no crime without a precedent.
Seneca
Hippolytus, c.60

35.10   The safe way to crime is always through crime.
Seneca,   *4 B.C.?-A.D. 65*
Agamemnon

35.11   With a differing fate, men commit the same crimes: one man gets a cross as a reward of villainy, another a crown.
Juvenal
Satires, c.120

35.12   What man was ever content with one crime?
Juvenal
Satires, c.120

35.13   No crime is rooted out once and for all.
Tertullian
The Christian's Defense, c.215

35.14   If little faults, proceeding on distemper,
Shall not be wink'd at, how shall we stretch our eye

When capital crimes, chew'd, swallow'd, and digested,
Appear before us?
Shakespeare
Henry V, II, 2, 1598-1599

35.15   Tremble, thou wretch,
That hast within thee undivulged crimes.
Unwhipp'd of justice.
Shakespeare
King Lear, III, 2, 1605-1606

35.16   A deed without a name.
Shakespeare
Macbeth, IV, 1, 1605-1606

35.17   The source of every crime is some defect of the understanding, or some error in reasoning, or some sudden force of the passions.
Thomas Hobbes
Leviathan, 1651

35.18   If poverty is the mother of crime, then want of sense is its father.
Jean de La Bruyère
Caractères, 1688

35.19   For crime is all the shame of punishment.
Daniel Defoe
Hymn to the Pillory, 1703

35.20   All, all look up with reverential awe, at crimes that 'scape, or triumph o'er the law.
Alexander Pope
Epilogue, Satires, 1738

35.21   The history of the great events of this world is scarcely more than the history of crimes.
Voltaire
Essai sur les moeurs, 1740-1743

35.22   He that carries a small Crime easily, will carry it on when it comes to be an ox.
Benjamin Franklin
Poor Richard's Almanack, 1758

35.23   Crimes not against forms, but against those eternal laws of justice, which are our rule and birthright.
Edmund Burke
Impeachment of Warren Hastings,
February 15, 1788

35.24   For you'll ne'er mend your fortunes, nor help the just cause,
By breaking of windows, or breaking of laws.
Hannah More, English writer
Address to the Meeting in Spa Fields,
1817

35.25   Nor florid prose, nor honeyed lines of rhyme,
Can blazon evil deeds, or concentrate a crime.
Lord Byron
Childe Harold, 1812–1818

35.26   That ill-gotten gain never prospers is the trite consolation administered to the easy dupe, when he has been tricked out of his money or estate.
Charles Lamb,   *1775–1834*
Bergen Evans, *Dictionary of Quotations,* 1968

35.27   It is worse than a crime, it is a blunder.
Attributed to Talleyrand,   *1754–1838*
William S. Walsh, *International Encyclopedia of Prose and Poetical Quotations,* 1951

35.28   Petty laws breed great crimes.
Ouida (pseudonym of Marie Louise de la Ramée), English writer
"Pipistrello" (1880), *Wisdom, Wit and Pathos,* 1884

35.29   An English historian, contrasting the London of his day with the London of the time when its streets, supplied only with oil lamps, were scenes of nightly robberies, says that "the adventurers in gas lights did more for the prevention of crime than the government had done since the days of Alfred."
John M. Harlan
New Orleans Gas Light Co. v. Louisiana Light Mfg. Co., 115 U.S.
650, 658 (1885)

35.30   The real significance of crime is in its being a breach of faith with the community of mankind.
Joseph Conrad
Lord Jim, 1900

35.31   Crime is only the retail department of what, in wholesale, we call penal law.
George Bernard Shaw
Man and Superman, 1903

35.32   For de little stealin' dey gits you in jail soon or late. For de big stealin' dey makes you emperor and puts you in de Hall o' Fame when you croaks.
Eugene O'Neill
The Emperor Jones, 1920

35.33   The more featureless and commonplace a crime is, the more difficult it is to bring it home.
Sir Arthur Conan Doyle,   *1859–1930*
W. H. Auden and Louis Kronenberger, *The Viking Book of Aphorisms,* 1962

35.34   To say that crime brings its own punishment is by way of being a platitude, and yet in my opinion nothing can be truer.
Agatha Christie
The Tuesday Club Murders, 1933

35.35   It ain't no sin if you crack a few laws now and then, just so long as you don't break any.
Mae West
Every Day's a Holiday (film), 1937

35.36   [Coercion:] The unpardonable crime.
Dorothy Miller Richardson, English writer
Pilgrimage, 1938

35.37   To initiate a war of aggression . . . is not only an international crime; it is the supreme international crime differing only from other war crimes in that it contains within itself the accumulated evil of the whole.
Judgement, *Trial of the Major War Criminals Before the International Military Tribunal,* vol.2, Nürnberg, Germany, 1947

35.38   When a man wants to murder a tiger, he calls it sport: when the tiger wants to murder him, he calls it ferocity. The distinction between crime and justice is no greater.
George Bernard Shaw, *1856–1950*
W. H. Auden and Louis Kronenberger, *The Viking Book of Aphorisms,* 1962

35.39   The duty to disclose knowledge of crime rests upon all citizens.
Robert H. Jackson
Stein v. New York, 346 U.S. 156, 184 (1953)

35.40   I hate this "crime doesn't pay" stuff. Crime in the U.S. is perhaps one of the biggest businesses in the world today.
Paul Kirk
Wall Street Journal, February 26, 1960

35.41   If we were brought to trial for the crimes we have committed against ourselves, few would escape the gallows.
Paul Eldridge
Maxims for a Modern Man, 1965

35.42   [If crime is increasing nationally], it is due in large part to the fact that waiting in the wings are lawyers willing to go beyond their professional responsibility, professional rights and professional duty.
Julius J. Hoffman, American jurist
At the trial of the Chicago 7, reported in the *Los Angeles Times,* February 16, 1970

35.43   Premeditated crime: the longer the meditating, the dreaming, the more triumphant the execution!
Joyce Carol Oates, writer
Do with Me What You Will, 1970

35.44   When is conduct a crime, and when is a crime not a crime? When Somebody Up There—a monarch, a dictator, a Pope, a legislator—so decrees.
Jessica Mitford, writer
Kind and Unusual Punishment, 1971

35.45   . . . a crime is anything that a group in power chooses to prohibit.
Freda Adler, American educator
Sisters in Crime, 1975

36. CRIMINALS

36.1 Lawmakers ought not to be law-breakers.
English proverb
Geoffrey Chaucer, "The Man of
Law's Tale," *The Canterbury Tales,*
c.1386

36.2 All criminals turn preachers under the gallows.
Italian proverb
H. L. Mencken, *A New Dictionary of
Quotations,* 1946

36.3 The act is not criminal unless the mind is criminal.
Legal maxim

36.4 The wrathful man does not see the law.
Publilius Syrus, Latin writer, *1st
century B.C.*
W. Gurney Benham, *Putnam's
Complete Book of Quotations, Proverbs
and Household Words,* 1927

36.5 It is better that a criminal be not accused than that he be acquitted.
Livy
History of Rome, c.10 B.C.

36.6 Who breaks no law is subject to no kings.
George Chapman
Revenge of Bussy d'Ambois, 1613

36.7 A man is not born a knave; there must be time to make him so, nor is he presently discovered after he becomes one.
Sir John Holt, English jurist; chief
justice
Reg. v. Swendson (1702), 14 How. St.
Tr. 596

36.8 Let me remember, when I find myself inclined to pity a criminal, that there is likewise a pity due to the country.
Sir Matthew Hale
History of the Pleas of the Crown,
1736

36.9 People crushed by law have no hope but from power. If laws are their enemies, they will be enemies to laws; and those who have much to hope and nothing to lose will always be dangerous, more or less.
Edmund Burke
Letter to the Honorable C. J. Fox,
October 8, 1777

36.10 If there were no bad people there would be no good lawyers.
Charles Dickens
The Old Curiosity Shop, 1841

36.11 The law's made to take care o' raskills.
George Eliot
The Mill on the Floss, 1860

36.12   Laws and institutions require to be adapted, not to good men, but to bad.
John Stuart Mill
The Subjugation of Women, 1869

36.13   When a felon's not engaged in his employment,
Or maturing his felonious little plans,
His capacity for innocent enjoyment
Is just as great as any other man's.
W. S. Gilbert
The Pirates of Penzance, 1880

36.14   When the enterprising burglar's not a-burgling,
When the cutthroat isn't occupied in crime,
He loves to hear the little brook a-gurgling,
And to listen to the merry village chime.
W. S. Gilbert
The Pirates of Penzance, 1880

36.15   Whether you're an honest man or
Whether you're a thief,
Depends on whose solicitor has given me a brief.
W. S. Gilbert
Utopia Limited, 1893

36.16   Imagination is the first faculty wanting in those that do harm to their kind.
Margaret Oliphant, Scottish writer
and historian, *1828–1897*
"Innocent"

36.17   Given a child falling into a river, an old person in a burning building, and a woman fainting in the street, a band of convicts would risk their lives to give aid as quickly at least as a band of millionaires.
Clarence Darrow
Resist Not Evil, 1903

36.18   We have to choose, and for my part I think it a less evil that some criminals should escape than that the Government should play an ignoble part.
Oliver Wendell Holmes
Olmstead v. United States, 277 U.S. 438, 470 (1928)

36.19   It's not the people in prison who worry me. It's the people who aren't.
Arthur Gore, earl of Arran
New York Times, January 7, 1962

36.20   There are certain characters who, unable to read a writ from the court of conscience and reason, must be served with one from a court—even though it be inferior—whose language they understand.
A. B. Smith
W. H. Auden and Louis
Kronenberger, *The Viking Book of Aphorisms,* 1962

36.21   Americans are solicitous enough concerning the rights of the individual criminal; they need to cultivate regard for the rights of the community.
Anonymous judge
Richard O'Connor, *Courtroom Warrior,* 1963

36.22   Eichmann, much less intelligent and without any education to speak of, at least dimly realized that it was not an order but a law which had turned them all into criminals. The distinction between an order and the Führer's word was that the latter's validity was not limited in time and space, which is the outstanding characteristic of the former.
Hannah Arendt
Eichmann in Jerusalem, 1963

36.23   The trouble with Eichmann was precisely that so many were like him, and that the many were neither perverted nor sadistic, that they were, and still are, terribly and terrifyingly normal. From the viewpoint of our legal institutions and of our moral standards of judgment, this normality was much more terrifying than all the atrocities put together, for it implied—as had been said at Nuremberg over and over again by the defendants and their counsels—that this new type of criminal, who is in actual fact *hostis generis humani,* commits his crimes under circumstances that make it well-nigh impossible for him to know or to feel that he is doing wrong.

Hannah Arendt
Eichmann in Jerusalem, 1963

36.24   "How does a person become an outlaw, DuBois?" Elgar inquired mildly. . . .

"One is born to the calling," DuBois answered. "Many are called, but few choose. You see, society decides which of its segments are going to be outside its borders. Society says, 'These are the legitimate channels to my rewards. They are closed to you forever.' So then the outlawed segments must seek rewards through illegitimate channels."

Kristin Hunter, American writer
The Landlord, 1966

36.25   Maleness remains a recessive genetic trait like color-blindness and hemophilia, with which it is linked. The suspicion that maleness is abnormal and that the Y chromosome is an accidental mutation boding no good for the race is strongly supported by the recent discovery by geneticists that congenital killers and criminals are possessed of not one but *two* Y chromosomes, bearing a double dose, as it were, of genetically undesirable maleness.

Elizabeth Gould Davis, American
librarian
The First Sex, 1971

36.26   Radical and revolutionary ideologies are seeping into the prisons. Whereas formerly convicts tended to regard themselves as unfortunates whose accident of birth at the bottom of the heap was largely responsible for their plight, today many are questioning the validity of the heap.

Jessica Mitford, English-American
writer
Kind and Unusual Punishment, 1971

36.27   One of the nicest American scientists I know was heard to say, "Criminals in our penitentiary are fine experimental material—much cheaper than chimpanzees." I hope the chimpanzees don't come to hear of this.

Jessica Mitford, English-American
writer
Kind and Unusual Punishment, 1971

---

37.   CROSS-EXAMINATION

37.1   When you have no basis for argument, abuse the plaintiff.
> Cicero, *106–43 B.C.*
> Louis Levinson, *Bartlett's Unfamiliar Quotations,* 1971

37.2   Then, if at any time you find you have the worst end of the staff, leave off your cause and fall upon the person of your adversary; put it boldly and enough of't, and somewhat must stick; no matter how true or false, it begets a prejudice to a person, and many times forejudges the cause.
> Christopher North (pseudonym of John Wilson), *1785–1854*
> *The Cheats*

37.3   And yet as he sat down he knew that she had been guilty! . . . That those witnesses had spoken truth he also knew, and yet he had been able to hold them up to the execration of all around them as though they had committed the worst of crimes from the foulest of motives! And more than this, stranger than this, worse than this,—when the legal world knew—as the legal world soon did know—that all this had been so, the legal world found no fault with Mr. Furnival, conceiving that he had done his duty by his client in a manner becoming an English barrister and an English gentleman.
> Anthony Trollope
> *Orley Farm,* 1862

37.4   Be mild with the mild, shrewd with the crafty, confiding to the honest, rough to the ruffian, and a thunderbolt to the liar. But in all this, never be unmindful of your own dignity.
> David Paul Brown
> Marshall Brown, *Wit and Humor of Bench and Bar,* 1899

37.5   More cross-examinations are suicidal than homicidal.
> Emory R. Buckner
> Francis Lewis Wellman, *Art of Cross-Examination,* 1936

37.6   Never, never, never, on cross-examination ask a witness a question you don't already know the answer to was a tenet I absorbed with my baby-food. Do it, and you'll often get an answer you don't want, an answer that might wreck your case.
> Harper Lee
> *To Kill a Mockingbird,* 1960

37.7   Challenging an expert and questioning his expertise is the lifeblood of our legal system—whether it is a psychiatrist discussing mental disturbances, a physicist testifying on the environmental impact of a nuclear power plant, or a General Motors executive insisting on the impossiblity of meeting Federal anti-pollution standards by 1975. It is the only way a judge or jury can decide whom to trust.

David L. Bazelon, American jurist;
chief judge, U.S. Court of Appeals
Dallas Times Herald, May 13, 1973

---

38. CUSTOM

38.1 Custom makes law.
English proverb
John Wycliffe, *Seven Werkys of Merely Bodyly,* 1382

38.2 Custom is held as Law.
Latin legal phrase
W. Gurney Benham, *Putnam's Complete Book of Quotations, Proverbs and Household Words,* 1927

38.3 Custom has the force of law.
Proverb
Rosalind Fergusson, *The Facts On File Dictionary of Proverbs,* 1983

38.4 Every land has its own law.
Proverb
Rosalind Fergusson, *The Facts On File Dictionary of Proverbs,* 1983

38.5 With customs we live well, but laws undo us.
Proverb
Rosalind Fergusson, *The Facts On File Dictionary of Proverbs,* 1983

38.6 The law follows custom.
Plautus
Trinummus, c.190 B.C.

38.7 Modesty forbids that to be done which the law does not forbid.
Seneca
Hippolytus, c.60

38.8 As laws are necessary that good manners may be preserved, so good manners are necessary that laws may be maintained.
Machiavelli
Discourses on Livy, 1513

38.9 Custom, that is before all law;
Nature, that is above all art.
Samuel Daniel, English poet
A Defence of Rhyme, 1603

38.10 We must not make a scarecrow of the law,
Setting it up to fear the birds of prey,
And let it keep one shape, till custom make it
Their perch and not their terror.
Shakespeare
Measure for Measure, II, 1, 1604–1605

38.11 Custom, that unwritten law,
By which the people keep even kings
in awe.
Sir William Davenant, *1606–1668*
Circe

38.12 Let the law never be contradictory
to custom: for if the custom be good,
the law is worthless.
Voltaire
Philosophical Dictionary, 1764

38.13 Laws and customs may be creative
of vice; and should be therefore per-
petually under process of observation and correction: but laws and
customs cannot be creative of virtue. . . .
Harriet Martineau, American writer
and critic
"Marriage," *Society in America,* 1837

38.14 There are two kinds of restrictions
upon human liberty—the restraint of
law and that of custom. No written
law has ever been more binding than
unwritten custom supported by
popular opinion.
Carrie Chapman Catt
Speech, February 8, 1900

38.15 . . . when common understanding
and practice have established a way
it is a waste of time to wander in by-
paths of logic.
Oliver Wendell Holmes
Ruddy v. Rossi, 248 U.S. 104, 111
(1918)

38.16 . . . where is the society which does
not struggle along under a dead-
weight of tradition and law inherited
from its grandfathers?
Suzanne LaFollette, American
feminist and writer
"The Beginnings of Emancipation,"
Concerning Women, 1926

38.17 "Custom is before all law." As
soon as you begin to say "We have
always done things this way—perhaps *that* might be a better way,"
conscious law-making is beginning.
As soon as you begin to say "*We* do
things this way—*they* do things that
way—what is to be done about it?"
men are beginning to feel towards
justice, that resides between the endless jar of right and wrong.
Helen M. Cam, English historian
Lecture, Girton College, February 18,
1956

38.18 Custom has furnished the only ba-
sis which ethics have ever had.
Joseph Wood Krutch
The Modern Temper, 1956

38.19 Superfluity, excess of custom, and
superstition would climb like a chok-
ing vine on the Fence of the Law if
skepticism did not continually hack
them away to make freedom for pu-
rity.
Cynthia Ozick
"The Pagan Rabbi" (1966), *The
Pagan Rabbi and Other Stories,* 1971

D

39. DEBT

39.1 He who desireth to sleep soundly, let him buy the bed of a bankrupt.
English proverb
John Ray, *English Proverbs,* 1678

39.2 Thou canst not fly high with borrowed Wings.
Proverb
Thomas Fuller, *Gnomologia,* 1732

39.3 If one wants to know the real value of money he needs but to borrow some from his friends.
Confucius
Analects, c.500 B.C.

39.4 He that buildeth his house with other men's money,
Is as one gathering stones for his sepulchre.
Ben Sira
Old Testament, *Ecclesiasticus* 21:8, c.190 B.C.

39.5 A trifling debt makes a man your debtor, a large one makes him your enemy.
Seneca
Epistulae Morales ad Lucilium 63–65

39.6 Do not borrow, for you will incur the derision of the proverb, "I am unable to carry the goat, so put the ox upon me."
Plutarch
"On Borrowing," *Moralia,* 97

39.7 The man who is once involved in debt remains a debtor all his life, exchanging, like a horse that has once been bridled, one rider for another.
Plutarch
"On Borrowing," *Moralia,* 97

39.8 Neither a borrower nor a lender be: For loan oft loses both itself and friend,
And borrowing dulls the edge of husbandry.
Shakespeare
Hamlet, I, 3, 1600–1601

39.9 He that would have a short Lent, let him borrow money to be repaid at Easter.
Benjamin Franklin
Poor Richard's Almanack, 1738

39.10   Creditors have better memories than debtors.
Benjamin Franklin
Poor Richard's Almanack, 1758

39.11   Never spend your money before you have it.
Thomas Jefferson, *1743–1826*
Franklin Pierce Adams, *F.P.A. Book of Quotations,* 1952

39.12   Debt is the prolific mother of folly and of crime.
Benjamin Disraeli
Henrietta Temple, 1837

39.13   . . . it is the policy of the law that the debtor be just before he be generous.
Edward R. Finch, American jurist
Hearn 45 St. Corp. v. Jano, 283 N.Y. 139, 142 (1940)

40. DECISIONS

40.1   Out of thy own mouth I will judge thee.
New Testament, *Luke* 19:22

40.2   How a good meaning
May be corrupted by a misconstruction.
Thomas Middleton
The Old Law, 1656

40.3   As mathematical and absolute certainty is seldom to be attained in human affairs, reason and public utility require that judges and all mankind in forming their opinion of the truth of facts should be regulated by the superior number of probabilities on the one side or the other.
Sir William Murray, Lord Mansfield, English jurist; chief justice
1705–1793
Francis L. Wellman, *The Art of Cross-Examination,* 1936

40.4   Evil stands the case when it is to be said of a judicial decree as the saying goes in the play of the "Two Gentlemen of Verona" . . .
'I have no other but a woman's reason;
I think him so, because I think him so.'
Benjamin N. Cardozo
The Nature of the Judicial Process, 1921

40.5   Lines should not be drawn simply for the sake of drawing lines.
Felix Frankfurter
Pearce v. Commissioner of Internal Revenue, 314 U.S. 593, 62 S. Ct. 98, 86 L.Ed. 479 (1942)

40.6   To the somnambulist, sleep-walking may seem more pleasant and less hazardous then wakeful walking, but the latter is the wiser mode of locomotion

in the congested traffic of a modern
community. It is about time to aban-
don judicial somnambulism.
  Jerome Frank
  Law and the Modern Mind, 1963

41.   DEFENSE

41.1   My rule is this, in doubtful cases,
when men are upon their lives, I had
rather hear what is impertinent, than
not let them make a full defence.
  Sir William Scroggs, English jurist;
  lord chief justice
  Whitehead's Case, 1679

41.2   The laws of God and man both give
the party an opportunity to make his
defence, if he has any. I remember to
have heard it observed by a very
learned man upon such an occasion,
that even God himself did not pass
sentence upon *Adam* before he was
called upon to make his defence.
Adam (says God), where art thou?
Hast thou eaten of the tree, whereof I
commanded thee that thou shouldest
not eat? And the same question was
put to *Eve* also.
  William Fortescue, English jurist
  The King v. Chancellor, etc. of the
  University of Cambridge (1723), 1 Str.
  566

41.3   In the early days of English criminal jurisprudence, when even a trifling
larceny was punishable with death,

there was reason why the judicial
mind should exhaust its ingenuity in
aid of the defense, and seize upon every technicality to avert from the prisoner a punishment so disproportion-
ate to his crime. . . . The reason for
resorting to mere technicality to enable the criminal to evade the sanc-
tions of the law no longer exists, and
the practice to which that reason led
should therefore cease.
  Bennet Van Syckel, American jurist
  Patterson v. State, 48 N.J.L. 381, 383,
  4A. 449, 450 (1886)

41.4   The right to be heard would be, in
many cases, of little avail if it did not
comprehend the right to be heard by
counsel.
  George Sutherland, American jurist
  Powell v. Alabama, 287 U.S. 45, 53 S.
  Ct. 55, 77 L.Ed. 158 (1932)

41.5   The pair were playing a game that
defied   intervention;   they   were
matched like reel and rod and there
was no unwinding. They juggled in
jargon, dabbled in *double-entendres,*

wallowed in each other's witticisms, and all at the expense of the Defendant.
> Daphne Du Maurier
> *Mary Anne,* 1954

41.6 It is a lawyer's duty to represent a guilty man, but not to free him.
> Grant B. Cooper, American lawyer
> *Los Angeles Times,* April 13, 1969

41.7 The insanity defense is a key part of our criminal justice system which is founded on the belief that [people] normally choose whether or not to obey the law.
> Elyce Zenoff, American educator;
> professor, George Washington
> University
> *U.S. News & World Report,* July 5, 1982

41.8 I am a mercenary. A person who is accused of something comes into my office and he wants me to be his sword, he wants me to protect his rights. I must, if I accept his case, close my eyes to the needs of society and I do what I can to protect him within legal ethics, without any regard to society's needs or anyone else's needs. The fact is that society gains most of all by seeing to it that the rule of law applies to all. It is not tested with the law-abiding middle class, but with the people who need it most.
> Jay Goldberg, American lawyer
> *New York Times,* May 24, 1969

41.9 . . . he believed in the justice of his using any legal methods he could improvise to force the other side into compromise or into dismissals of charges, or to lead a jury into the verdict he wanted. Why not? He was a defense lawyer, not a judge or a juror or a policeman or a legislator or a theoretician or an anarchist or a murderer.
> Joyce Carol Oates
> *Do with Me What You Will,* 1970

41.10 I am not interested in my client's innocence or guilt; I am not interested in seeing that justice is done when I'm the defense attorney. I am interested in seeing them acquitted. It's not the defense attorney's job to do justice. His job is to defend vigorously his client. . . . It's not a happy experience to get people off who are guilty. I don't expect any prizes or plaudits for it. . . . What we do is a necessary evil—a very necessary evil.
> Alan M. Dershowitz
> *Los Angeles Herald-Examiner,* May 26, 1982

42. DELAYS

42.1 Delays in the law are hateful.
Latin legal phrase
W. Gurney Benham, *Putnam's Complete Book of Quotations, Proverbs and Household Words,* 1927

42.2 No delay [in law] is long concerning the death of a man.
Latin legal phrase
W. Gurney Benham, *Putnam's Complete Book of Quotations, Proverbs and Household Words,* 1927

42.3 For who would bear the whips and scorns of time,
The oppressor's wrong, the proud man's contumely,
The pangs of dispriz'd love, the law's delay,
The insolence of office, and the spurns,
That patient merit of the unworthy takes,
When he himself might his quietus make
With a bare bodkin
Shakespeare
Hamlet, III, 1, 1600–1601

42.4 It is not to be imagined that the King will be guilty of vexatious delays.
Sir Dudley Ryder, English jurist; lord chief justice
Rex v. Berkley and another (1754), Sayer's Rep. 124

42.5 Delay will frequently have . . . considerable influence upon the judgment which ought to be formed upon the evidence adduced.
Frederic Thesiger, 1st Lord Chelmsford, English jurist; lord chancellor
Cuno v. Cuno (1873), L.R. 2 Sc. & D. 302

42.6 In any event, mere speed is not a test of justice. Deliberate speed is. Deliberate speed takes time. But it is time well spent.
Felix Frankfurter
First Iowa Coop. v. Power Comm'n., 328 U.S. 152, 188 (1946)

42.7 The judgments below . . . are accordingly reversed and the cases are remanded to the District Courts to take such proceedings and enter such orders and decrees consistent with this opinion as are necessary and proper to admit to public schools on a racially nondiscriminatory basis with all deliberate speed the parties to these cases.
Earl Warren
Brown v. Board of Education of Topeka, 349 U.S. 294, 301 (1955)

43. DEMOCRACY

43.1   Democracy . . . a charming form of government, full of variety and disorder, and dispensing a sort of equality to equals and unequals alike.
Plato
The Republic, c.370 B.C.

43.2   If liberty and equality, as is thought by some, are chiefly to be found in democracy, they will be best attained when all persons alike share in the government to the utmost.
Aristotle
Politics, c.322 B.C.

43.3   Democracy arose from men thinking that if they are equal in any respect they are equal in all respects.
Aristotle
Politics, c.322 B.C.

43.4   Republics are brought to their ends by luxury, monarchies by poverty.
de Montesquieu
The Spirit of the Laws, 1748

43.5   The tyranny of a multitude is a multiplied tyranny.
Edmund Burke
Letter to Thomas Mercer, 1790

43.6   The republican is the only form of government which is not eternally at open or secret war with the rights of mankind.
Thomas Jefferson,   *1743–1826*
Franklin Pierce Adams, *F.P.A. Book of Quotations,* 1952

43.7   A minority is powerless while it conforms to the majority.
Henry David Thoreau
Civil Disobedience, 1849

43.8   Any man more right that his neighbors constitutes a majority of one already.
Henry David Thoreau
Civil Disobedience, 1849

43.9   There are nine hundred and ninety-nine patrons of virtue to one virtuous man.
Henry David Thoreau
Civil Disobedience, 1849

43.10   Among free men there can be no successful appeal from the ballot to the bullet.
Abraham Lincoln,   *1809–1865*
Franklin Pierce Adams, *F.P.A. Book of Quotations,* 1952

43.11   As I would not be a *slave,* so I would not be a *master.* This expresses my idea of democracy. What-

ever differs from this, to the extent of the difference, is no democracy.
Abraham Lincoln
"Fragment on Slavery," August 1, 1858

43.12 . . . ballots are the rightful and peaceful successors of bullets.
Abraham Lincoln
Message to Congress, July 4, 1861

43.13 The ship of Democracy, which has weathered many storms, may sink through the mutiny of those on board.
Grover Cleveland
Letter to Wilson S. Bissell, 1894

43.14 It was we, the people; not we, the white male citizens; nor yet we, the male citizens; but we the whole people who formed the Union . . . not to give the blessings of liberty, but to secure them . . . to the whole people—women as well as men.
Susan B. Anthony, *1820–1906*
A Woman's Right to Suffrage

43.15 The world must be made safe for democracy.
Woodrow Wilson
Address to Congress, April 2, 1917

43.16 All the ills of democracy can be cured by more democracy.
Alfred E. Smith
Speech, June 27, 1933

43.17 We must be the great arsenal of democracy.
Franklin Delano Roosevelt
Radio address, 1940

43.18 People who want to understand democracy should spend less time in the library with Aristotle and more time on the buses and in the subway.
Simeon Strunsky, American journalist and author
No Mean City, 1944

43.19 Our people do not want barren theories from their democracy, Maury Maverick has expressed very quaintly, but clearly, what they really want when he says: "We Americans want to talk, pray, think as we please-*and eat regular.*"
Robert H. Jackson, *1892–1954*
"Back to the American Way,"
Unpublished Speeches, vol. 5, no. 14, as quoted in Eugene C. Gerhart, *America's Advocate: Robert H. Jackson,* 1958

43.20 There is a basic inconsistency between popular government and judicial supremacy.
Robert H. Jackson, *1892–1954*
Thomas C. Cochran and Wayne Andrews, eds., *Concise Dictionary of American History,* 1962

43.21 Democracy is no harlot to be picked up in the street by a man with a tommy gun.
Sir Winston S. Churchill
F. B. Czarnomski, ed., *The Wisdom of Winston Churchill,* 1956

43.22 The conception of political equality from the Declaration of Independence to Lincoln's Gettysburg Address, to the Fifteenth, Seventeenth, and Nineteenth Amendments can mean only one thing—one person, one vote.
William O. Douglas
Gray v. Sanders, 372 U.S. 368, 381 (1963)

44. DISSENT

44.1   Dissent, not satisfied with toleration, is not conscience, but ambition.
Edmund Burke
Speech on the Acts of Uniformity,
House of Commons, February 1772

44.2   A little rebellion now and then is a good thing.
Thomas Jefferson
On the Shays' Rebellion, c.1790

44.3   But freedom to differ is not limited to things that do not matter much. That would be a mere shadow of freedom. The test of its substance is the right to differ as to things that touch the heart of existing order.
Robert H. Jackson
*West Virginia State Board of
Education v. Barnette,* 319 U.S. 624,
642 (1943)

44.4   The whole drift of our law is toward the absolute prohibition of all ideas that diverge in the slightest form from the accepted platitudes, and behind that drift of law there is a far more potent force of growing custom, and under that custom there is a natural philosophy which erects conformity into the noblest of virtues and the free

functioning of personality into a capital crime against society.
H. L. Mencken,   *1880–1956*
New York Times Magazine, August 9,
1964

44.5   The right to dissent is the only thing that makes life tolerable for a judge of an appellate court.
William O. Douglas
America Challenged, 1960

44.6   Dissent and dissenters have no monopoly on freedom. They must tolerate opposition. They must accept dissent from their dissent. And they must give it the respect and the latitude which they claim for themselves.
Abe Fortas
"The Limits of Civil Disobedience,"
New York Times Magazine, May 12,
1968

44.7   The long history of antiobscenity laws makes it very clear that such laws are most often invoked against political and life-style dissidents.
Gloria Steinem
"Gazette News: Obscene?" *Ms.,*
October 1973

44.8   The "flatfoot mentality" insists that any individual or organization that wants to change *anything* in our present system is somehow subversive of

"the American way," and should be under continuous surveillance—a task that appears to absorb most of our resources for fighting genuine crime.
Toni Carabillo, American writer
"The 'Flatfoot Mentality,' "
Hollywood NOW News, August 1975

44.9 One generation's dissents have often become the rule of law years later.
Irving Kaufman, American jurist
"Keeping Politics Out of the Court,"
New York Times, December 9, 1984

45. DOUBT

45.1 How long halt thee between two opinions?
Old Testament, *I Kings* 4:25

45.2 To know much is often the cause of doubting more.
Michel de Montaigne
Essais, 1588

45.3 What do I know? What does it matter?
Michel de Montaigne, *1533–1592*
Motto

45.4 If a man will begin with certainties, he shall end in doubts; but if he will be content to begin with doubts, he shall end in certainties.
Francis Bacon
The Advancement of Learning, 1605

45.5 . . . certaintie is the mother of quietness and repose, and uncertaintie the cause of variance and contentions.
Sir Edward Coke
The Institutes of the Lawes of England, vol. 1, 1628–1641

45.6 Doubt grows with knowledge.
Goethe
Sprüche in Prosa, 1819

45.7 I always thought it better to allow myself to doubt before I decided, than to expose myself to the misery after I had decided, of doubting whether I had decided rightly and justly.
John Scott, Lord Eldon, *1751–1838*
Horace Twiss, *Life of Lord Eldon*, 1844

45.8 I may be wrong, and often am, but I never doubt.
Sir George Jessel, English jurist, replying to question about whether he had any doubts in reference to the *Alabama* claims (1871–1872)
M. Frances McNamara, *Ragbag of Legal Quotations*, 1960

45.9 . . . all things are presumed to have been rightly done unless there is reasonable ground shown for doubting it.
Sir James Hannen, British jurist
Woodhouse v. Balfour (1887), L.R. 13 Pr. D. 4

45.10   But certainty is generally illusion, and repose is not the destiny of man.
Oliver Wendell Holmes
"The Path of the Law," 10 *Harvard Law Review* 457 (1897)

45.11   To have doubted one's own first principles is the mark of a civilized man.
Oliver Wendell Holmes
"Ideals and Doubts," 10 *Illinois Law Review* 3 (1915)

45.12   To rest upon a formula is a slumber that, prolonged, means death.
Oliver Wendell Holmes
"Ideals and Doubts," 10 *Illinois Law Review* 3 (1915)

45.13   An honest man can never surrender an honest doubt.
Walter Malone, *1866–1915*
Bergen Evans, *Dictionary of Quotations,* 1968

45.14   . . . in my first years upon the bench. . . . I sought for certainty. I was oppressed and disheartened when I found that the quest for it was futile. I was trying to reach land, the solid land of fixed and settled rules, the paradise of a justice that would declare itself by tokens plainer and more commanding than its pale and glimmering reflections in my own vacillating mind and conscience.
Benjamin N. Cardozo
The Nature of the Judicial Process, 1921

45.15   Just think of the tragedy of teaching children not to doubt.
Clarence Darrow, *1857–1938*
Franklin Pierce Adams, *F.P.A. Book of Quotations,* 1952

45.16   . . . the old rule of "Give the accused the benefit of the doubt."
Freeman W. Crofts, Irish mystery writer
Circumstantial Evidence, 1941

45.17   Increasingly constructive doubt is the sign of advancing civilization. We must put question marks alongside many of our inherited legal dogmas, since they are dangerously out of line with social facts.
Jerome Frank
Law and the Modern Mind, 1963

45.18   The rather random observations and any tentative conclusions reached in this paper rest on opinion; here, the opinion of one who claims no special competence to observe or judge. Hence the Apologia:
Sage: My son, a man who is absolutely certain of anything is a fool!
Son: Are you sure?
Sage: Positive!
Laurens Williams
Toward More Effective Coordination of the Work of Government Personnel and Professional Groups in Tax Legislation, American Law Institute, 1964

46. DRUNKENNESS

46.1   Let us eat and drink, for tomorrow we die.
New Testament, *I Corinthians,* 15:32

46.2   Let him who sins when drunk, be punished when sober.
Anonymous
Kendrick v. Hopkins (1580), Cary's
Rep. 133

46.3   Oons, Sir! do you say that I am drunk? I say, Sir, that I am as sober as a judge; . . .
Henry Fielding
Don Quixote in England, 1734

46.4   Men intoxicated are sometimes stunned into sobriety.
Sir James Mansfield, English jurist;
chief justice *1733–1821*
Rex v. Wilkes (1769), 4 Burr. Part IV.
2563

46.5   There is in all men a demand for the superlative, so much so that the poor devil who has no other way of reaching it attains it by getting drunk.
Oliver Wendell Holmes
"Natural Law," 82 *Harvard Law
Review* (1918)

46.6   The prohibition law, written for weaklings and derelicts, has divided the nation, like Gaul, into three parts—wets, drys and hypocrites.
Florence Sabin, American scientist
Speech, February 9, 1931

46.7   The horse and mule live thirty years
And nothing know of wines and beers;
The goat and sheep at twenty die,
And never taste of Scotch or Rye;
The cow drinks water by the ton
And at eighteen is mostly done;
Without the aid of rum and gin
The dog at fifteen cashes in;
The cat in milk and water soaks,
And then at twelve years old she croaks;
The modest, sober bone-dry hen
Lays eggs for nogs and dies at ten;
All animals are strictly dry;
They sinless live and swiftly die,
While sinful, gleeful rum-soaked men
Survive for three score years and ten.
And some of us—a mighty few—
Stay pickled 'till we're ninety-two.
Harlan Fiske Stone, *1872–1946*
Alpheus Thomas Mason, *Harlan Fisk
Stone, Pillar of the Law,* 1956

47. DUE PROCESS

47.1   No man should be condemned unheard.
Legal maxim

47.2   That no man of what estate or condition, shall be put out of land or ten-
ement, nor taken nor imprisoned, nor
disinherited, nor put to death, without
being brought in answer by due process of law.
Statute of Westminister, c.13th
century

47.3   Nor shall any person . . . be deprived of life, liberty, or property,
without due process of law.
Constitution of the United States,
Fifth Amendment, 1791

47.4   . . . nor shall any State deprive any
person of life, liberty, or property,
without due process of law. . . .
Constitution of the United States,
14th Amendment, 1868

47.5   Whatever disagreement there may
be as to the scope of the phrase "due
process of law" there can be no doubt
that it embraces the fundamental conception of a fair trial, with opportunity to be heard.
Oliver Wendell Holmes
Frank v. Mangum, 237 U.S. 309, 347
(1915)

47.6   Due process is a growth too sturdy
to succumb to the infection of the
least ingredient of error.
Benjamin Cardozo
Roberts v. New York, 295 U.S. 264,
278, 79 L.Ed. 1429, 1436, 55 S. Ct.
669 (1935)

47.7   Bad men, like good men, are entitled to be tried and sentenced in accordance with law, . . .
Hugo L. Black
Green v. United States, 365 U.S. 301,
309-310 (1961)

47.8   . . . freedom of personal choice in
matters of marriage and family life is
one of the liberties protected by the
Due Process Clause of the Fourteenth
Amendment. . . . That right necessarily includes the right of a woman to
decide whether or not to terminate her
pregnancy.
Harry Blackmun
Roe v. Wade, 410 U.S. 113, 93 S. Ct.
705, 35 L.Ed.2d 147 (1973)

47.9   The due process of law . . . rests
squarely on the liberal idea of conflict
and resolution.
June L. Tapp, American psychologist
Gordon Bermant, "The Notion of
Conspiracy Is Not Tasty to
Americans," *Psychology Today,* May
1975

47.10   The worse the society, the more
          law there will be. In Hell there will
          be nothing but law and due process
          will be meticulously observed.
          Grant Gilmore
          New York Times, February 23, 1977

E

48. EQUALITY

48.1   What is lawful to Jupiter is not lawful to the ox.
   Latin proverb
   W. Gurney Benham, *Putnam's Book of Quotations, Proverbs and Household Words,* 1927

48.2   The rich break the laws, and the poor are punished for it.
   Spanish proverb
   Charles Cahier, *Quelques Six Milles Proverbes,* 1856

48.3   Obey the law, whoever you be that made the law.
   Pittacus, Greek statesman and sage, c.650–570 B.C.
   Maxim

48.4   Would you say that all men are equal in excellence, or is one man better than another?
   Plato
   Republic, c.370 B.C.

48.5   The law for the rich and poor is not the same.
   Plautus
   Cistellaria, c.200 B.C.

48.6   The nets not stretched to catch the hawk,

Or kite, who do us wrong; but laid for those
Who do us none at all.
   Terence
   Phormio, 161 B.C.

48.7   The censor absolves the crow, and passes sentence on the dove.
   Juvenal
   Satires, c.120

48.8   For if all things were equally in all men, nothing would be prized.
   Thomas Hobbes
   Leviathan, 1651

48.9   It follows as a common law of nature that every man esteem and treat another as one who is naturally his equal, and who is a man as well as he.
   John Wise, *1652–1725*
   Vindication of the Government of New England Churches

48.10   It is not true that equality is a law of nature. Nature knows no equality. Its sovereign law is subordination and dependence.
   Marquis de Vauvenargues, French moralist
   Réflexions, 1746

48.11   Law has no power to equalize men in defiance of nature.
Marquis de Vauvenargues, French moralist, *1715–1747*
W. Gurney Benham, *Putnam's Complete Book of Quotations, Proverbs and Household Words,* 1927

48.12   All men have equal rights to liberty, to their property, and to the protection of the laws.
Voltaire
Essay on Manners, 1756

48.13   Laws are always useful to those who possess and vexatious to those who have nothing.
Jean Jacques Rousseau
Du Contrat Social, 1762

48.14   We hold these truths to be self-evident; that all men are created equal; that they are endowed by their Creator with certain unalienable rights; that among these are life, liberty, and the pursuit of happiness. . . .
Declaration of Independence, July 4, 1776

48.15   One law for the ox and the ass is oppression.
William Blake, *1757–1827*
W. H. Auden and Louis Kronenberger, *The Viking Book of Aphorisms,* 1962

48.16   Four score and seven years ago our fathers brought forth on this continent, a new nation, conceived in Liberty, and dedicated to the proposition that all men are created equal.
Abraham Lincoln
Gettysburg Address, November 19, 1863

48.17   Equality may be as much as anything equality of misery.
Rudolph von Jhering, German jurist, *1818–1892*
Law as a Means to an End

48.18   . . . there never will be complete equality until women themselves help to make laws and elect lawmakers.
Susan B. Anthony
"The Status of Women, Past, Present and Future," *The Arena,* May 1897

48.19   The law, in its majestic equality, forbids all men to sleep under bridges, to beg in the streets, and to steal bread—the rich as well as the poor.
Anatole France
Crainquebille, 1902

48.20   The Procrustean bed is not a symbol of equality.
Felix Frankfurter
New York v. United States, 331 U.S. 284, 353 (1947)

48.21   It was a wise man who said that there is no greater inequality than the equal treatment of unequals.
Felix Frankfurter
Dennis v. United States, 339 U.S. 162, 184 (1950)

48.22   If the affluent flagrantly disregard the law, the poor and the deprived will follow their leadership.
Robert M. Morgenthau
New York Times, June 26, 1969

48.23   The brutal fact is that convicted women . . . have not yet won the right to equal treatment in the criminal and juvenile justice system.
Susan C. Ross, American lawyer
The Rights of Women, 1973

48.24 The American Republic is now almost 200 years old, and in the eyes of the law women are still not equal with men. The special legislation which will remedy that situation is the Equal Rights Amendment. Its language is short and simple:

Equality of rights under the law shall not be abridged in the United States or by any state on account of sex.
Clare Boothe Luce
Bulletin of the Baldwin School,
Pennsylvania, September 1974

49. EQUITY

49.1 A legal fiction is always consistent with equity.
Legal maxim

49.2 Equity is that idea of justice, which contravenes the written law.
Aristotle
Rhetoric, c.322 B.C.

49.3 The umpire has regard to equity, the judge to law.
Aristotle
Rhetoric, c.322 B.C.

49.4 It is difficult, when you desire to assist everyone, to preserve equity, which appertains most especially to justice.
Cicero
De Officiis, c.45–44 B.C.

49.5 You wish nothing to be lawful to me, and all things to you.
Martial, Roman epigrammatist
Epigrams, 85

49.6 All the sentences of precedent judges that have ever been cannot altogether make a law contrary to natural equity.
Thomas Hobbes
Leviathan, 1651

49.7 Equity, in law, is the same that the spirit is in religion: What everyone pleases to make it.
John Selden, English legal antiquarian and politician,
1584–1654
"Equity," *Table-Talk,* 1689

49.8 Equity is a rougish thing. For Law we have to measure, know what to trust to; Equity is according to the conscience of him that is Chancellor, and as that is larger or narrower, so is Equity. 'Tis all one as if they should make the standard for the measure we call a "foot" a Chancellor's foot; what an uncertain measure would this be! One Chancellor has a long foot, another a short foot, a third an indifferent foot. 'Tis the same thing in the Chancellor's conscience.
John Selden, *1584–1654*
"Equity," Table-Talk, 1689

49.9   Equality is equity.
Richard Francis
Maxims of Equity, 1728

49.10   There is but one law for all, namely, that law which governs all law, the law of our Creator, the law of humanity, justice, equity—the law of nature and of nations.
Edmund Burke, on May 28, 1794
W. Gurney Benham, *Putnam's Complete Book of Quotations,* 1927

49.11   There are two, and only two, foundations of law . . . equity and utility.
Edmund Burke,   *1729-1797*
Tracts on the Popery Laws

49.12   Law and equity are two things which God has joined, but which man hath put asunder.
Charles Caleb Colton
Lacon, 1820

49.13   He who seeks equity must do equity.
Joseph Story
Equity Jurisprudence, 1896

49.14   Equity speaks softly and wins in the end.
Caroline Bird, American writer
Born Female, 1968

50.   ERROR(S)

50.1   The cautious seldom err.
Confucius
Analects, c.500 B.C.

50.2   I would rather err with Plato than perceive the truth with others.
Cicero,   *106–43 B.C.*
Tusculanae Disputationes

50.3   An error is not counted as a crime.
Seneca
Hercules Octaeus, c.60

50.4   The strength of our persuasions is no evidence at all of their own rectitude: crooked things may be as stiff and inflexible as straight: and men may be as positive and peremptory in error as in truth.
John Locke
An Essay Concerning Human Understanding, 1690

50.5   The progress of rivers to the ocean is not so rapid as that of man to error.
Voltaire
A Philosophical Dictionary: Rivers, 1764

50.6   I know but of one Being to whom error may not be imputed.
Edward Law, Lord Ellenborough, English jurist; chief justice
Rex v. Lambert and Perry (1810), 2 Camp. 402

50.7   Delay is preferable to error.
Thomas Jefferson
To George Washington, May 16,
1792

50.8   Mistakes are the inevitable lot of mankind.
Sir George Jessel, English jurist
Tomlin v. Underhay (1882), L.R. 22
C.D. (1883)

50.9   Lack of recent information . . . is responsible for more mistakes of judgment than erroneous reasoning.
Matthew Arnold, *1822–1888*
Louis D. Brandeis, "The Living
Law," *The Curse of Bigness,* 1935

50.10   If someone made a mistake he [Darrow] would drawl, "Hell, that's why they make erasers."
Clarence Darrow, *1857–1938*
Irving Stone, *Clarence Darrow for the Defense,* 1941

50.11   One utterance of [Oliver Cromwell] has always hung in my mind. It was just before the Battle of Dunbar; he beat the Scots in the end, as you know, after a very tough fight; but he wrote them before the battle, trying to get them to accept a reasonable composition. These were his words: "I beseech ye in the bowels of Christ, think that ye may be mistaken." I should like to have that written over the portals of every church, every school, and every court house, and, may I say, of every legislative body in the United States.
Learned Hand
Irving Dilliard, *The Spirit of Liberty,*
1960

51. ESTATES

51.1   When a festive occasion our spirit unbends
We should never forget the profession's best friends.
So we'll pass round the wine
And a light bumper fill
To the jolly testator who makes his own will.
Anonymous
Jacob M. Brande, *Lifetime Speaker's Encyclopedia,* 1962

51.2   Land was never lost for want of an heir.
English proverb
John Ray, *Compleat Collection of English Proverbs,* 1670

51.3   All things which are so written in a will as to be unintelligible are to be on that account regarded as though they were not written.

Latin legal phrase
W. Gurney Benham, *Putnam's Complete Book of Quotations, Proverbs and Household Words,* 1927

51.4   That which is ill-gotten a third heir hardly ever enjoys.

Latin phrase
Thomas Walsingham, *Historia Anglicana,* c.1422

51.5   No one can be heir during the life of his ancestor.

Legal maxim

51.6   The bestower of a gift has a right to regulate its disposal.

Legal maxim

51.7   Dowries and inheritances bring no luck.

Yiddish proverb
Joseph L. Baron, *A Treasury of Jewish Quotations,* 1956

51.8   Who comes for the inheritance is often made to pay for the funeral.

Yiddish proverb
Joseph L. Baron, *A Treasury of Jewish Quotations,* 1956

51.9   A lawyer's dream of heaven—every man reclaimed his property at the resurrection, and each tried to recover it from all his forefathers.

Samuel Butler, *1612–1680*
W. H. Auden and Louis Kronenberger, *The Viking Book of Aphorisms,* 1962

51.10   There is no instance where men are so easily imposed upon, as at the time of their dying under the pretence of charity.

William Cowper, English jurist; lord chancellor
Attorney-General v. Barnes et uxor (1707), Gilbert Eq. Ca. 5

51.11   . . . man with all his wisdom, *toils for heirs he knows not who.*

Andrew Kirkpatrick, American jurist
William Nevision et al. v. James Taylor, 8 N.J.L. 43, 46 (1824)

51.12   There is an objection to the taxation of the inheritance of personal property of a very serious kind. It is that it is one law for the rich and another for the poor.

J. E. T. Rogers, English economist
The Economic Interpretation of History, 1888

52. ETHICS

52.1   "Virtue down the middle," said the Devil as he sat down between two lawyers.
Danish proverb
H. L. Mencken, *A New Dictionary of Quotations,* 1946

52.2   The law often permits what honor forbids.
Bernard Joseph Saurin, French tragic writer
Spartacus, 1760

52.3   Just to the windward of the law.
Charles Churchill, English dramatist
The Ghost, 1762–1763

52.4   . . . the man whose probity consists in merely obeying the laws, cannot be truly virtuous or estimable; for he will find many opportunities of doing contemptible and even dishonest acts, which the laws cannot punish.
Stephanie Félicité Genlis, French harpist and author
"Laws," *Tales of the Castle,* c.1793

52.5   We do not believe the less in astronomy and vegetation because we are writhing and roaring in our beds with rheumatism.
Walt Whitman
The Sovereignty of Ethics, 1878

52.6   I will not counsel or maintain any suit or proceeding which shall appear to me to be unjust, nor any defense except such as I believe to be honestly debatable under the law of the land.
Oath for Candidates for Admission to the Bar, American Bar Association, c.1925

52.7   There are . . . many forms of professional misconduct that do not amount to crimes.
Benjamin N. Cardozo
People ex rel. Karlin v. Culkin, 248 N.Y. 465, 470 (1928)

52.8   As to ethics, the parties seem to me as much on a parity as the pot and the kettle.
Robert H. Jackson
Mercoid Corporation v. Mid-Continent Co. 320 U.S. 661, 679 (1944)

52.9   We [lawyers] must alter our prime axiom—that we are combat mercenaries available indifferently for any cause or purpose a client is ready to finance. . . . We should all be what I would term "ministers of justice." As such, we would have to reconsider and revise a system of loyalty to clients that results too often in coverups, frauds, and injury to innocent people. A favorite quotation in the legal profession . . . is Lord Brougham's declaration that an advocate "knows but one person in all the world, and that person is his client. . . ." For him Lord Brougham said, the advocate would stand against the world . . . Lord Brougham was wrong; we should be less willing to fight the world and . . .

more concerned to save our own souls. As ministers of justice, we should find ourselves more positively concerned than we now are with the pursuit of truth.
> Marvin E. Frankel, American jurist;
> judge, U.S. District Court
> *Washington Post,* May 7, 1978

53. EVIDENCE

53.1　　Judge a man not by the words of his mother, but from the comments of his neighbors.
> Jewish folk saying
> Leo Rosten, *Treasury of Jewish Quotations,* 1972

53.2　　The drunkard smells of whiskey—but so does the bartender.
> Jewish folk saying
> Joseph L. Baron, *A Treasury of Jewish Quotations,* 1956

53.3　　To assume is to fool one's self.
> Jewish folk saying
> Joseph L. Baron, *A Treasury of Jewish Quotations,* 1956

53.4　　Where there is room for question, something is wrong.
> Jewish folk saying
> Joseph L. Baron, *A Treasury of Jewish Quotations,* 1956

53.5　　You don't have to see the lion if you see his hair.
> Jewish folk saying
> Joseph L. Baron, *A Treasury of Jewish Quotations,* 1956

53.6　　And I would sooner trust the smallest slip of paper for truth, than the strongest and most retentive memory, ever bestowed on mortal man.
> Joseph Henry Lumpkin, American jurist
> *Miller and others v. Cotton and others,* 5 Ga. 341, 349 (1848)

53.7　　If a man go into the London Docks sober without means of getting drunk, and comes out of one of the cellars very drunk wherein are a million gallons of wine, I think that would be reasonable evidence that he had stolen some of the wine in that cellar, though

you could not prove that any wine was stolen, or any wine was missed.
Sir William Henry Maule, English jurist
Reg. v. Burton (1854), Dearsly's C. C. 284

53.8 Some circumstantial evidence is very strong, as when you find a trout in the milk.
Henry David Thoreau, *1817–1862*
W. H. Auden and Louis Kronenberger, *The Viking Book of Aphorisms,* 1962

53.9 Human nature constitutes a part of the evidence in every case.
Elisha R. Potter, American jurist
Green v. Harris, HRI 5, 17 (1875)

53.10 But evidence drawn empirically from facts, though it may justify the action of the practical man, is not scientifically conclusive.
Beatrice Potter Webb, English sociologist and social reformer
"The Economics of Factory Legislation," *Socialism and National Minimum,* 1909

53.11 My friend—I had to save him. The evidence of a woman devoted to him would not have been enough—you hinted as much yourself. But I know something of the psychology of crowds. Let my evidence be wrung from me, as an admission, damning me in the eyes of the law, and a reaction in favor of the prisoner would immediately set in.
Agatha Christie
Witness for the Prosecution, 1924

53.12 It is for ordinary minds, and not for psychoanalysts, that our rules of evidence are framed.
Benjamin N. Cardozo
Shepard v. United States, 290 U.S. 96, 104 (1933)

53.13 Chemists employed by the police can do remarkable things with blood. They can find it in shreds of cloth, in the interstices of floor boards, on the iron of a heel, and can measure it and swear to it and weave it into a rope to hang a man.
Margery Allingham, English writer
The Tiger in the Smoke, 1952

53.14 . . . the allowance of the privilege to withhold evidence that is demonstrably relevant in a criminal trial would cut deeply into the guarantee of due process of law and gravely impair the basic function of the courts.
Warren E. Burger
United States v. Nixon, 418 U.S. 683, 94 S. Ct. 3090, 41 L.Ed.2d 1039 (1974)

54. EVIL

54.1 That which is evil is soon learn't.
English proverb
John Ray, *English Proverbs,* 1670

54.2 Virtue and vice divide the world; but vice has got the greater share.
German proverb
Thomas Fuller, *Gnomologia,* 1732

54.3 Better suffer a great evil than do a little one.
Proverb
H. G. Bohn, *Handbook of Proverbs,* 1855

54.4 Why does the way of the wicked prosper?
Old Testament, *Jeremiah* 12:1

54.5 For the good that I would I do not: but the evil which I would not, that I do.
Now if I do that I would not, it is no more I that do it, but sin that dwelleth in me.
I find then a law, that, when I would do good, evil is present with me.
New Testament, *Romans* 7:19–21

54.6 Abstain from all appearances of evil.
New Testament, *I Thessalonians* 5:22

54.7 Evil deeds never prosper.
Homer
Odyssey, c.8th century B.C.

54.8 It is not noble to return evil for evil; at no time ought we do an injury to our neighbors.
Plato
Crito, c.350 B.C.

54.9 To a good man nothing that happens is evil.
Plato, *427–347 B.C.*
Apology

54.10 One evil flows from another.
Terence
Eunuchus, c.160 B.C.

54.11 He who is bent on doing evil can never want occasion.
Publilius Syrus, Latin writer
Sententiae, c.43 B.C.

54.12 An evil life is a kind of death.
Ovid
Epistulae ex Ponto, c.5

54.13 The evil best known is the most tolerable.
Livy
History of Rome, c.10

54.14 It is not goodness to be better than the worst.
Seneca
Epistulae Morales ad Lucilium, c.63–65

54.15 Although it be with truth thou speakest evil, this also is a crime.
St. John Chrysostom
Homilies, c.388

54.16 Justice has but one form, evil has many.
Moses Ben Jacob Meir Ibn Ezra,
Spanish-Hebrew poet and
philosopher, *c.1070–1130*
Shirat Yisrael, 1924

54.17 Of two evils we should always choose the less.
Thomas Kempis
Imitation of Christ, c.1420

54.18 There are three all-powerful evils: lust, anger and greed.
Tulsī Dās, Hindu poet
Rāmāyan, 1574

54.19 All evils become equal when they are extreme.
Pierre Corneille, French dramatist
Horace, 1639

54.20 There are men of whom we can never believe evil without having seen it. Yet there are few in whom we should be surprised to see it.
La Rochefoucauld
Maximes, 1665

54.21 Where two evils [are] present, a wise administration, if there be room for an option, will choose the least.
Sir Michael Foster, English jurist
Case of Pressing Mariners (1743), 18
How. St. Tr. 1330

54.22 No evil without its advantages.
William Hone
Every-Day Book, 1827

54.23 I think the old, sound, and honest maxim that "*you shall not do evil that good may come,*" is applicable in law as well as in morals.
Sir Alexander James Edmund
Cockburn, British jurist; lord chief
justice
Reg. v. Hicklin and another (1868), 11
Cox, C.C. 27; S.C. 3 L.R.Q.B. 372

54.24 There is in many, if not in all men, a constant inward struggle between the principles of good and evil; and because a man has grossly fallen, and at the time of his fall added the guilt of hypocrisy to another sort of immorality, it is not necessary, therefore, to believe that his whole life has been false, or that all the good which he ever professed was insincere or unreal.
Roundell Palmer, 1st earl of Selborne,
British jurist; lord chancellor
Symington v. Symington (1875), L.R. 2
Sc. & D. 428

54.25 It is a sin to believe evil of others, but it is seldom a mistake.
H.. L. Mencken,
A Book of Burlesques, 1916

54.26 Evil becomes an operative motive far more easily than good. . . .
Simone Weil, French philosopher
L' Enracinement, 1949

54.27 They did not know . . . that the same force that had made him tolerant, was now the force that made him ruthless—that the justice which would forgive miles of innocent errors of knowledge, would not forgive a single step taken in conscious evil.
Ayn Rand
Atlas Shrugged, 1957

54.28   It is by the promise of an occult sense of power that evil often attracts the weak.
Eric Hoffer, American philosopher
W. H. Auden and Louis Kronenberger, *The Viking Book of Aphorisms,* 1962

54.29   Here's a rule I recommend. Never practice two vices at once.
Tallulah Bankhead,   *1903–1968*

54.30   When choosing between two evils, I always like to try the one I've never tried before.
Mae West,   *1892–1980*

F

55. FACTS

55.1 We should not investigate facts by the light of arguments, but arguments by the light of facts.
Myson, of Chen, one of the Seven Sages, *c.600 B.C.*
Burton Stevenson, *Home Book of Proverbs, Maxims and Familiar Phrases,* 1948

55.2 When speculation has done its worst, two and two still make four.
Samuel Johnson
The Idler, c.1758

55.3 Facts are apt to alarm us more than the most dangerous principles.
Junius, unidentified English letter writer
A letter to the *Public Advertiser,* 1769

55.4 There is nothing more horrible than the murder of a beautiful theory by a brutal gang of facts.
La Rochefoucauld, *1747–1827*

55.5 Facts are stubborn things.
Ebenezer Elliott, *1781–1849*
Field Husbandry

55.6 The state of a man's mind is as much fact as the state of his digestion.
Charles Bowen, English jurist
Edgington v. Fitzmaurice (1884), 29 L.R., Ch. Div. 459, 483

55.7 Truly it has been said, that to a clear eye the smallest fact is a window through which the Infinite may be seen.
Thomas H. Huxley
"The Study of Zoology", *Discourses, Biological and Geological,* 1896

55.8 Fact and fancy look alike across the years that link the past with the present.
Helen Keller
The Story of My Life, 1903

55.9 The ultimate umpire of all things in life is—Fact.
Agnes C. Laut, Canadian journalist
The Conquest of the Great Northwest, 1908

55.10 This is not a matter for polite presumptions; we must look facts in the face.
Oliver Wendell Holmes
Frank v. Mangum, 237 U.S. 309, 347 (1915)

55.11 No law, apart from a Lawgiver, is a proper object of reverence. It is merely a brute fact.
William Temple, English clergyman; archbishop of Canterbury
Nature, Man, and God, 1934

55.12 ... take as your motto this thought from Huxley: "God give me strength to face a fact though it slay me."
Bernard Baruch
A Philosophy for Our Time, 1954

55.13 ". . . facts are like cows. If you look them in the face hard enough they generally run away."
Dorothy L. Sayers
Clouds of Witness, 1956

55.14 While it is not always profitable to analogize "fact" to "fiction," La Fontaine's fable of the crow, the cheese, and the fox demonstrates that there is a substantial difference between holding a piece of cheese in the beak and putting it in the stomach.
Felix Frankfurter
Alleghany Corp. v. Breswick & Co., 353 U.S. 151, 170 (1957)

55.15 We want the facts to fit the preconceptions. When they don't, it is easier to ignore the facts than to change the preconceptions.
Jessamyn West, American writer
The Quaker Reader, 1962

55.16 Facts do not cease to exist because they are ignored.
Aldous Huxley, *1894–1963*
A Note on Dogma

55.17 The ends of criminal justice would be defeated if judgements were to be founded on a partial or speculative presentation of the facts. The very integrity of the judicial system and public confidence in the system depend on full disclosure of all the facts, within the framework of the rules of evidence.
Warren E. Burger
United States v. Nixon, 418 U.S. 683, 94 S. Ct. 3090, 41 L.Ed.2d 1039 (1974)

56. FALSEHOOD

56.1 No law for lying.
Proverb
Rosalind Fergusson, *The Facts On File Dictionary of Proverbs,* 1983

56.2 A hair perhaps divides the false and true.
Omar Khayyám, *1048?–1122*
The Rubáyiát

56.3 This is a false, perjured, and for-
sworn man.
> Inscription on a paper put over the
> head of a man set up in the pillory in
> the market place, Canterbury,
> England, 1524

56.4 As false as dicers' oaths.
> Shakespeare
> *Hamlet,* III, 4, 1600–1601

56.5 Sin has many tools, but a lie is the
handle which fits them all.
> Oliver Wendell Holmes
> *The Autocrat of the Breakfast Table,*
> 1858

56.6 There are three kinds of lies: lies,
damned lies, and statistics.
> Benjamin Disraeli
> Franklin Pierce Adams, *F.P.A. Book
> of Quotations,* 1952

56.7 When Falsehood saw he had no
legs, he made himself wings.
> Simchah Ben Zion, Hebrew translator
> *Luah Ahiasaf,* 1897

56.8 To have no occasion for lying does
not yet mean to be honest.
> Arthur Schnitzler
> *Buch der Sprüche und Bedenken,* 1927

56.9 I know the face of Falsehood and her
tongue
Honeyed with unction, plausible with
guile. . . .
> Edna St. Vincent Millay
> "Fatal Interview," *Fatal Interview,*
> 1931

57. FEES

57.1 A lawyer and a wagon-wheel must
be well greased.
> German proverb
> H. L. Mencken, *A New Dictionary of
> Quotations,* 1946

57.2 Doctors purge the body, preachers
the conscience, lawyers the purse.
> German proverb
> Charles Cahier, *Quelques Six Mille
> Proverbes,* 1856

57.3 A lawyer's opinion is worth nothing
unless paid for.
> Proverb
> Rosalind Fergusson, *The Facts On
> File Dictionary of Proverbs,* 1983

57.4 Lawyers' houses are built on the
heads of fools.
> Proverb
> Thomas Fuller, *Gnomologia,* 1732

57.5 Law's costly: tak' a pint and 'gree.
Scottish proverb
W. Gurney Benham, *Putnam's
Complete Book of Quotations, Proverbs
and Household Words,* 1927

57.6 O! then, I see, Queen Mab hath been
with you. . . .
And in this state she gallops night by
night
Through lovers' brains, and then they
dream of love;
O'er courtiers' knees, that dream on
curt'sies straight,
O'er lawyers' fingers, who straight
dream on fees. . . .
Shakespeare
Romeo and Juliet, I, 4, 1594–1595

57.7 No fee, no law.
Gabriel Harvey, English writer
Works, 1597

57.8 Agree, for the law is costly.
William Camden, English antiquarian
and historian
Remains, 1605

57.9 'Tis like the breath of an unfee'd lawyer;
you gave me nothing for 't.
Shakespeare
King Lear, I, 4, 1605–1606

57.10 A man may as well as open an oyster without a knife, as a lawyer's
mouth without a fee.
Barten Holyday, English writer
Technogamia, 1618

57.11 Litigious terms, fat contentions
and flowing fees.
John Milton
Tractate on Education, 1644

57.12 If you simply buy a house,
He will take note of every interview,
And charge you for receiving your
instructions,

Charge you likewise for drawing up
the same—
Eight folio pages with a world of
margin;
Charge you likewise for copying the
same,
Charge you likewise for reading you
the same,
And reading of it to the other party;
Charge you likewise for reading long
reply
From Finden, lawyer, with a draft
agreement;
Charge you likewise perusing said
draft;
Charge you likewise transmitting
draft agreement.
James Hurnard
"The Setting Sun," 1871

57.13 First, I charge a retainer; then I
charge a reminder; next I charge a
refresher; and then I charge a fin-
isher.
Judah P. Benjamin, *1811–1884*
P. J. Clark, *Great Sayings by Great
Lawyers,* 1926

57.14 Go to the court o' last resort
For the sake o' your poor family!
The Lord sustain! My client's gane,
He's ruined—but I've got my fee!
George Outram
Legal and Other Lyrics, 1888

57.15 The old judge had a picture,
prominently displayed, of an English
barrister flourishing an oyster on a
fork as two countrymen, holding the
shells, looked on agape. Underneath
was the couplet:
A pearly shell for you and me;
The oyster is the lawyer's fee.
Harvey O'Connor
*Mellon's Millions, The Biography of a
Fortune,* 1933

57.16   I dislike sending in professional charges to friendly people, but we have a saying here that offices like individuals have to live.
Reginald L. Hine, American jurist
Confessions of an Un-Common Attorney, 1945

57.17   When there's a rift in the lute, the business of a lawyer is to widen the rift and gather the loot.
Arthur Garfield Hays, American lawyer, *1881–1954*
Leonard Lewis Levinson, *Bartlett's Unfamiliar Quotations,* 1971

57.18   I get paid for seeing that my clients have every break the law allows. I have knowingly defended a number of guilty men. But the guilty never escape unscathed. My fees are sufficient punishment for anyone.
F. Lee Bailey
Los Angeles Times, January 9, 1972

57.19   I don't charge by the hour or by the day. I'm not a mechanic. I'm an artist. If you are going to use the time to be a bookkeeper, you can't be a trial lawyer.
Percy Foreman
Dallas Times Herald, May 12, 1972

57.20   . . . lawyers do not unfairly charge their clients. Rather, they simply do not dispense legal services efficiently.
James D. Fellers, American lawyer; president, American Bar Association
Los Angeles Times, May 30, 1975

57.21   For many middle-income people, using a lawyer is like going to a dentist. They only go when they have to, because the costs of legal services prevent their using lawyers for preventive services.
Philip J. Murphy, American lawyer
New York Times, January 18, 1976

57.22   The cost of rendering legal services today has become so high that in modest matters lawyers cannot afford to undertake the work and prospective clients cannot afford to retain lawyers.
Justin A. Stanley, American lawyer; president, American Bar Association
New York Times, May 2, 1976

57.23   The legal profession has indicated in its operative canons of ethics that the principal responsibility for the representation of people unable to afford legal fees ought to be placed on the profession itself. . . . The bar has a fundamental responsibility to undertake that which its own set of ethics imposes. And we do think it somewhat troublesome that a bar whose members' total gross income now substantially exceeds $20 billion a year needs to lobby for a wholly Federally funded program in order to exercise its own responsibility.
Michael J. Horowitz, American lawyer
New York Times, June 28, 1981

57.24   The [legal] fees are outrageous. With the cost of litigation these days, I think clients would often be better off if they just met in the halls and threw dice. Certainly it would be cheaper.
Walter McLaughlin, American jurist; chief justice, Supreme Court of Massachusetts
Time, July 27, 1981

58. FRAUD

58.1   He is not deemed to give consent who is under a mistake.
Latin legal phrase
W. Gurney Benham, *Putnam's Complete Book of Quotations, Proverbs and Household Words,* 1927

58.2   No one can bring an action upon his own fraud.
Latin legal phrase
W. Gurney Benham, *Putnam's Complete Book of Quotations, Proverbs and Household Words,* 1927

58.3   Frauds are not frauds, unless you make a practice of deceit.
Plautus,   *254?–184 B.C.*
Captivi

58.4   Fraud and deceit abound in these days more than in former times.
Sir Edward Coke
Twyne's Case, 1602

58.5   Fraud may consist as well in the suppression of what is true as in the representation of what is false.
Justice Heath, English jurist
Tapp v. Lee (1803), 3 Bos. & Pull, 371

58.6   The strongest mind cannot always contend with deceit and falsehood.
Sir William Draper Best, Lord Wynford, British jurist; chief justice
Blackford v. Christian (1829), 1 Knapp, 77

58.7   Fraud includes the pretense of knowledge when knowledge there is none.
Benjamin Cardozo
Ultramares Corporation v. Touche, 255 N.Y. 170, 179 (1931)

58.8   Laws are made to protect the trusting as well as the suspicious.
Hugo L. Black
Federal Trade Commission v. Standard Education Society, 302 U.S. 112, 116 (1937)

58.9   . . . nobody wants a prosaic explanation of fraud and greed.
Margery Allingham, English writer
The Villa Marie Celeste, 1960

59. FREEDOM

59.1   Slavery and freedom, when excessive, are evils; but when moderate are altogether good.
Plato, *427–347 B.C.*
Epistle 8

59.2   Law alone can give us freedom.
Goethe, *1749–1832*
W. Gurney Benham, *Putnam's Complete Book of Quotations, Proverbs and Household Words,* 1927

59.3   The law will never make men free; it is men who have got to make the law free.
Henry David Thoreau
Slavery in Massachusetts, 1854

59.4   In giving freedom to the slave we assure freedom to the free—honorable alike in what we give and what we preserve.
Abraham Lincoln
Annual Message to Congress, 1862

59.5   . . . true emancipation begins neither at the polls nor in courts. It begins in women's soul.
Emma Goldman
"The Tragedy of Women's Emancipation," *Anarchism and Other Essays,* 1911

59.6   . . . sunlight is the best of disinfectants. . . .
Louis D. Brandeis, *1856–1941*
New York Times, February 15, 1984

59.7   The mark of a truly civilized man is confidence in the strength and security derived from the inquiring mind.
Felix Frankfurter
Dennis v. United States, 341 U.S. 494, 556 (1951)

59.8   . . . if there is one invention that has influenced freedom . . . it is the clock, the chiming hour and the pocket watch. With that and a myriad of inventions . . . freedom has been reduced not by the tyrant's decree but by the mere nature of things. Traffic lights curtailing liberty mark a technical progress that can be traced back through the centuries. Each freedom gained in theory is balanced by one lost in fact.
C. Northcote Parkinson
New York Law Journal, December 19, 1963

59.9   The function of freedom is to free somebody else.
Toni Morrison, *1931–*

G

60. GOD'S LAW

60.1   . . . he that keepeth the law, happy is he.

Old Testament, *Proverbs* 29:18

60.2   But his delight is in the law of the Lord; and in his law will he exercise himself day and night.

Old Testament, *Psalms* 1:2

60.3   But the fruit of the Spirit is love, joy, peace, longsuffering, gentleness, goodness, faith.

Meekness, temperance: against such there is no law.

New Testament, *Galatians* 5:22–23

60.4   If ye then, being evil, know how to give good gifts unto your children, how much more shall your Father which is in heaven give good things to them that ask him?

Therefore all things whatsoever ye would that men should do to you, do ye even so to them: for this is the law and the prophets.

New Testament, *Matthew* 7:11–12

60.5   Jesus said unto him, Thou shalt love the Lord thy God with all thy heart, and with all thy soul, and with all thy mind.

This is the first and great commandment.

And the second is like unto it, Thou shalt love thy neighbor as thyself.

On these two commandments hang all the law and the prophets.

New Testament, *Matthew* 22:37–40

60.6   For when the Gentiles, which have not the law, do by nature the things contained in the law, these, having not the law, are a law unto themselves.

New Testament, *Romans* 2:14

60.7   Render therefore to all their dues: tribute to whom tribute is due; custom to whom custom; fear to whom fear, honour to whom honour.

Owe no man any thing, but to love one another: for he that loveth another hath fulfilled the law.

New Testament *Romans* 13:7–8

60.8   Just as it is forbidden to permit that which is prohibited, so it is forbidden to prohibit that which should be permitted.

Talmud, *Terumot*

119

60.9   Charity itself fulfills the law.
        Shakespeare
        Love's Labour's Lost, I, 3, 1594–1595

60.10   Who sees not, that whosoever min-
        isters to the poor, ministers to God?
        as it appears in that solemn sentence
        of the last day, Inasmuch as you did
        feed, clothe, lodge the poor, you did
        it unto me.
        Sir Henry Hobart, English jurist;
        chief justice
        Pits v. James (1614), Lord Hobart's
        Rep. 125

60.11   The wildest scorner of his Maker's
        laws
        Finds in a sober moment time to
        pause.
        William Cowper,   *1731–1800*
        Tirocinium

60.12   Be just—not like man's law, which
        seizes on one isolated fact, but like
        God's judging angel, whose clear,
        sad eye saw all the countless canker-
        ing days of this man's life. . . .
        Rebecca Harding Davis, American
        social critic and writer
        "Life in the Iron Mills," *Atlantic
        Monthly,* April 1861

60.13   But men never violate the laws of
        God without suffering the conse-
        quences, sooner or later.
        Lydia M. Child, American
        abolitionist and editor
        "Toussaint L'Ouverture," *The
        Freedman's Book,* 1865

60.14   A difficult form of virtue is to try
        in your own life to obey what you
        believe to be God's will.
        John Duke Coleridge, English jurist;
        lord chief justice
        Reg. v. Ramsey (1883), 1 Cababé and
        Ellis's Q.B.D. Rep. 145

60.15   Once early in the morning . . .
        when the master was asleep, the
        books in the library began to quarrel
        with each other as to which was the
        king of the library. The dictionary
        contended quite angrily that he was
        the master of the library because
        without words there would be no
        communication at all. The book of
        science argued stridently that he was
        the master of the library for without
        science there would have been no
        printing press or any of the other
        wonders of the world. The book of
        poetry claimed that he was . . . the
        master of the library, because he
        gave surcease and calm to his master
        when he was troubled. The books of
        philosophy, the economic books, all
        put in their claims, and the clamor
        was great and the noise at its height
        when a small low voice was heard
        from an old brown book lying in the
        center of the table and the voice said,
        "The Lord is my shepherd, I shall
        not want." And all of the noise and
        the clamor in the library ceased, and
        there was a hush in the library, for all
        of the books knew who the real mas-
        ter of the library was.
        Louis Nizer
        "Ministers of Justice," *Tennessee Law
        Review,* Fall 1963

61. GOVERNMENT

61.1   The makers of laws are the majority who are weak; they make laws and distribute praises and censures with a view to themselves and to their own interests; and they terrify the stronger sort of men, and those who are able to get the better of them, in order that they may not get the better of them.
Plato
Gorgias, c.360 B.C.

61.2   A good government produces citizens distinguished for courage, love of justice, and every other good quality; a bad government makes them cowardly, rapacious, and the slaves of every foul desire.
Dionysius of Halicarnassus
Antiquities of Rome, c.20 B.C.

61.3   . . . governments rather depend upon men than men upon governments.
William Penn
Preface to Pennsylvania's Frame of Government, 1682–1684

61.4   . . . an Act of Parliament can do no wrong, though it may do several things that look pretty odd; . . .
Sir John Holt, English jurist; chief justice
City of London v. Wood (1701), 12 Mod. 669, 687

61.5   If men be good, government cannot be bad.
William Penn,   *1644–1718*
Fruits of Solitude

61.6   Governments derive their just powers from the consent of the governed.
Declaration of Independence, 1776

61.7   Laws always lose in energy what the government gains in extent.
Immanuel Kant
Perpetual Peace, 1795

61.8   And having looked to Government for bread, on the first scarcity they will turn and bite the hand that fed them.
Edmund Burke,   *1729–1797*
Thoughts and Details on Scarcity

61.9   Though in a state of society some must have greater luxuries and comforts than others, yet all should have the necessaries of life; and if the poor cannot exist, in vain may the rich look for happiness or prosperity. The legislature is never so well employed as when they look to the interests of those who are at a distance from them in the ranks of society. It is their duty to do so; religion calls for it; humanity calls for it; and if there are hearts who are not awake to either of those

feelings, their own interests would dictate it.
Sir Lloyd Kenyon, English jurist; lord
chief justice
Rex v. Rusby (1800), Peake's N.P.
Cases 192

61.10   The will of the people is the only legitimate foundation of any government, and to protect its free expression should be our first object.
Thomas Jefferson
First inaugural address, March 4,
1801

61.11   The will of the people is the only legitimate foundation of any government, and to protect its free expression should be our first object.
Thomas Jefferson
Letter to Benjamin Waring, 1801

61.12   A single good government is a blessing to the whole earth.
Thomas Jefferson
Letter to George Flower, 1817

61.13   Self-government is the natural government of man.
Henry Clay
Speech, 1818

61.14   That one hundred and fifty lawyers should do business together ought not to be expected.
Thomas Jefferson, *1743–1826,*
referring to the Congress of the
United States
Autobiography, 1853

61.15   The spirit of resistance to government is so valuable on certain occasions that I wish it to be always kept alive.
Thomas Jefferson, *1743–1826*
To Abigail Adams

61.16   The whole of government consists in the art of being honest.
Thomas Jefferson, *1743–1826*
Letter to John Adams

61.17   Were we directed from Washington when to sow, and when to reap, we should soon want bread.
Thomas Jefferson, *1743–1826*
Autobiography, 1853

61.18   Government is a trust, and the officers of the government are trustees; and both the trust and the trustees are created for the benefit of the people.
Henry Clay
Speech, 1829

61.19   Any people anywhere being inclined and having the power have the right to rise up and shake off the existing government, and form a new one that suits them better. This is a most valuable, a most sacred right— a right which we hope and believe is to liberate the world.
Abraham Lincoln
Speech, Congress, January 12, 1848

61.20   Why does [the government] always crucify Christ, and excommunicate Copernicus and Luther, and pronounce Washington and Franklin rebels?
Henry David Thoreau
Civil Disobedience, 1849

61.21   The people's government, made for the people, made by the people, and answerable to the people.
Daniel Webster, *1782–1852*
Franklin Pierce Adams, *FPA Book of
Quotations,* 1952

61.22　　. . . no man is good enough to govern another man without that other's consent.
Abraham Lincoln
Speech, Peoria, Illinois, October 16, 1854

61.23　　"A house divided against itself cannot stand."* I believe this government cannot endure permanently half-slave and half-free.
Abraham Lincoln
Speech, Republican State Convention, Springfield, Illinois, June 16, 1858

61.24　　The decisions of the House of Lords are binding on me and upon all the Courts except itself.
Sir John Romilly, English jurist
Attorney-General v. The Dean and Canons of Windsor (1858), 24 Beav. 715

61.25　　The only government that I recognize . . . is that power that establishes justice in the land, never that which establishes injustice.
Henry David Thoreau
John Brown's Body, 1859

61.26　　While the people retain their virtue and vigilance, no administration, by any extreme of wickedness or folly, can very seriously injure the government in the short space of four years.
Abraham Lincoln
First Inaugural Address, March 4, 1861

61.27　　. . . that this nation, under God, shall have a new birth of freedom, and that government of the people, by the people, for the people, shall not perish from the earth.
Abraham Lincoln
Gettysburg Address, November 19, 1863

*New Testament, *Mark* 3:25

61.28　　You can fool some of the people all of the time, and all of the people some of the time, but you cannot fool all of the people all of the time.
Abraham Lincoln, *1809-1865*

61.29　　The divine right of kings may have been a plea for feeble tyrants, but the divine right of government is the keystone of human progress, and without it government sinks into police and a nation into a mob.
Benjamin Disraeli
Preface, *Lothair,* 1870

61.30　　The government is us; we are the government, you and I.
Theodore Roosevelt
Speech, 1902

61.31　　Men must turn square corners when they deal with the Government.
Oliver Wendell Holmes
Rock Island C. R.R. v. United States, 254 U.S. 141, 143 (1920)

61.32　　At the foundation of our civil liberty lies the principle which denies to government officials an exceptional position before the law and which subjects them to the same rules of conduct that are commands to the citizen.
Louis D. Brandeis
Burdeau v. McDowell, 256 U.S. 465, 477 (1921)

61.33　　Experience should teach us to be most on our guard to protect liberty when the Government's purposes are beneficent.
Louis D. Brandeis
Olmstead v. United States, 277 U.S. 438, 478 (1928)

61.34   If the law is upheld only by government officials, then all law is at an end.
Herbert Hoover
Message to Congress, 1929

61.35   I have given you my Law, and you set up commissions.
T. S. Eliot
The Rock, 1934

61.36   That government which thinks in terms of humanity will continue.
Franklin Delano Roosevelt
Campaign speech, 1936

61.37   This government is ours whether it be local, county, State, or Federal. It doesn't belong to anybody but the people of America. Don't treat it as an impersonal thing; don't treat it as something to sneer at; treat it as something that belongs to you.
Harry L. Hopkins
Speech, 1939

61.38   I can retain neither respect nor affection for a Government which has been moving from wrong to wrong in order to defend its immorality.
Mohandas Gandhi,   *1869–1948*
Franklin Pierce Adams, *F.P.A. Book of Quotations,* 1952

61.39   . . . all power tends to develop into a government in itself. Power that controls the economy should be in the hands of elected representatives of the people, not in the hands of an industrial oligarchy. Industrial power should be decentralized. It should be scattered into many hands so that the fortunes of the people will not be dependent on the whim or caprice, the political prejudices, the

emotional stability of a few self-appointed men.
William O. Douglas
United States v. Steel Co., 334 U.S. 495, 536 (1948)

61.40   You had the famous American maxim, "Governments derive their just powers from the consent of the governed," and we both noticed that the world was divided into peoples that owned the governments and governments that owned the peoples.
Winston Churchill
Speech, 1949

61.41   Government is like fire. If it is kept within bounds and under the control of the people, it contributes to the welfare of all. But if it gets out of place, if it gets too big and out of control, it destroys the happiness and even the lives of the people.
Harold E. Stassen,   *1907–*
Franklin Pierce Adams, *F.P.A. Book of Quotations,* 1952

61.42   Thought control is a copyright of totalitarianism, and we have no claim to it. It is not the function of our Government to keep the citizen from falling into error; it is the function of the citizen to keep the Government from falling into error.
Robert H. Jackson
American Communications Assn. v. Douds, 339 U.S. 382, 442–43 (1950)

61.43   Government can easily exist without law, but law cannot exist without government.
Bertrand Russell
"Ideas That Have Helped Mankind,"
Unpopular Essays, 1951

61.44   The task of law is to maintain an ever-readjusted balance between the needful restraint on the powers of

government and the needful exercise of the powers of government.
Leon Jaworski
Address, American Bar Association, New York, reported in the *Boston Globe,* July 5, 1971

61.45   Under current law, it is a crime for a private citizen to lie to a government official, but not for the government to lie to the people.
Donald M. Fraser
Laurence J. Peter, *Peter's Quotations,* 1977

62.   GUILT

62.1   Nothing is more wretched than the mind of a man conscious of guilt.
Plautus,   *c.254–184 B.C.*
Mostellaria

62.2   Queen: So full of artless jealousy is guilt,
It spills itself in fearing to be spilt.
Shakespeare
Hamlet, IV, 5, 1600–1601

62.3   The pot calls the kettle black.
Cervantes
Don Quixote, 1605

62.4   Sire, we have little defense against the opinion of a monarch, and even the most innocent man who ever lived will begin to be guilty if the king thinks him so.
Pierre Corneille, French poet and dramatist
Horace, 1640

62.5   Guilt has very quick ears to accusation.
Henry Fielding
Amelia, 1752

62.6   Give him rope enough and he will hang himself.
Charlotte Brontë
Shirley, 1849

62.7   *. . . if we see cruelty or wrong that we have the power to stop, and do nothing, we make ourselves sharers in the guilt.*
Anna Sewell, British writer
Black Beauty, 1877

62.8   . . . the twofold aim [of criminal justice] is that guilt shall not escape or innocence suffer.
Berger v. United States, 295 U.S. 78 (1935)

62.9   Now, if any fundamental assumption underlies our system, it is that guilt is personal not inheritable.
Robert H. Jackson
Korematsu v. United States, 323 U.S. 214 (1944)

H

63. HUMAN NATURE

63.1   No man is so exquisitely honest or upright in living but that ten times in his life he might not lawfully be hanged.
Michel de Montaigne
Essais, 1588

63.2   Those who fear men like laws.
Marquis de Vauvenargues, French moralist
Réflexions, 1746

63.3   For behaviour, men learn it, as they take diseases, one of another.
Francis Bacon
The Advancement of Learning, 1605

63.4   Nature never deceives us; it is always we who deceive ourselves.
Jean-Jacques Rousseau
Emile, 1762

63.5   Every law which the state enacts indicates a fact in human nature.
Ralph Waldo Emerson
"History," *Essays*, 1899

63.6   Man may be a little lower than the angels, but he has not yet shaken off the brute. . . . His path is strewn with carnage, murder lurks always not far beneath, to break out from time to time, peace resolution to the contrary notwithstanding.
Learned Hand
"Democracy! Its Presumptions and Realities" 1 *Federal Bar Association Journal* 2 (1932)

63.7   I wish I loved my fellow men more than I do, but to love one's neighbor as oneself, taken literally, would mean to realize all his impulses as one's own, which no one can, and which I humbly think would not be desirable if one could.
Oliver Wendell Holmes,   *1841–1935*
Harry C. Shriver, ed., *Justice Oliver Wendell Holmes: His Book Notices and Uncollected Letters and Papers,* 1936

63.8   Possibly gaiety is the miasmic mist of misery.
Oliver Wendell Holmes,   *1841–1935*
Mark De Wolfe Howe, *Holmes-Pollock Letters,* 1946

63.9   Neither Law nor Human Nature is an exact science.
George W. Keeton, ed., *Harris's Hints on Advocacy,* 1943

63.10 . . . [government employees] are subject to that very human weakness, especially displayed in Washington, which leads men to "crook the pregnant hinges of the knee where thrift may follow fawning."
Robert H. Jackson
Frazier v. United States, 335 U.S. 497, 515 (1948)

63.11 Law is born from despair of human nature.
José Ortega y Gasset, *1883–1955*
W. H. Auden and Louis Kronenberger, *The Viking Book of Aphorisms,* 1962

63.12 But Corwin's Law was established in advice he gave a budding speaker: "Never make people laugh. If you would succeed in life, you must be solemn, solemn as an ass. All the great monuments are built over solemn asses."
Thomas Corwin, American politician
Clayton Fritchey, "A Politician Must Watch His Wit," *New York Times Magazine,* July 3, 1960

I

64. IGNORANCE

64.1 Ignorance of the law does not prevent the losing lawyer from collecting his bill.
Anonymous
Laurence J. Peter, *Peter's Quotations,*
1977

64.2 Ignorance of the law excuses no man; not that all men know the law, but because 'tis an excuse every man will plead, and no man can tell how to refute him.
John Selden *1584–1654*
"Law," *Table-Talk,* 1689

64.3 Ignorance is preferable to error; and he is less remote from the truth who believes nothing, than he who believes what is wrong.
Thomas Jefferson
Notes on the State of Virginia,
c.1781–1783

64.4 Ignorance of the law is not excuse in any country. If it were, the laws would lose their effect, because it can always be pretended.
Thomas Jefferson
To M. Limozin, December 22, 1787

64.5 If a nation expects to be ignorant and free, in a state of civilization, it expects what never was and never will be.
Thomas Jefferson
Letter to Charles Yancy, January 6,
1816

64.6 Lawyers are the only persons in whom ignorance of the law is not punished.
Ascribed to Jeremy Bentham,
1748–1832
Wolfe D. Goodman, "Sole Practice, Partnership or Merger," 9 *Canadian Bar Journal* 3 (June 1966)

64.7 To be conscious that you are ignorant is a great step to knowledge.
Benjamin Disraeli
Sybil, 1845

64.8 And there comes a point where this Court should not be ignorant as judges of what we know as men.
Felix Frankfurter
Watts v. Indiana, 338 U.S. 49, 52
(1949)

65. IMPRISONMENT

65.1 Golden fetters.
Diogenes, *c.4th century B.C.*
William S. Walsh, *International Encyclopedia of Prose and Poetical Quotations,* 1968

65.2 No freeman shall be taken or imprisoned or disseised or exiled or in any way destroyed, nor will we go upon him nor will we send upon him, except by the lawful judgment of his peers or by the law of the land.
Magna Carta 1215

65.3 A foole I doe him firmly hold,
That loves his fetters, though they were of gold.
Edmund Spenser
Fairie Queene, 1589

65.4 Experience hath shewn, that between the prisons and the graves of princes, the distance is very small.
Sir Michael Foster, English jurist
Foster's Crown Case. (1762),
Discourse I. c. 1, s. 3

65.5 Durance vile.
W. Kendrick, British dramatist
Falstaff's Wedding, 1776

65.6 A learned county court judge told me that at first he used to make orders of committal for a short time and he found that the people went to prison. He then lengthened the period, and he found that fewer people went to prison; and he found that the longer the period for which he committed people to prison for not paying, the shorter was the total amount of imprisonment suffered by debtors, because when they were committed for the whole six weeks they moved heaven and earth among their friends to get the funds and pay; whereas if the term was a short one, they underwent the punishment.
Lord William Bramwell, English jurist
Stonor v. Fowle (1887), L.R. 13 Ap.
Ca. 28

65.7 I know not whether Laws be right,
Or whether Laws be wrong;
All that we know who lie in gaol
Is that the wall is strong;
And that each day is like a year,
A year whose days are long.
Oscar Wilde
The Ballad of Reading Gaol, 1898

65.8 You have put me in here [jail] a cub, but I will come out roaring like a lion, and I will make all hell howl!
Carry Nation
Carleton Beals, *Cyclone Carry,* c.1901

65.9   Whilst we have prisons, it matters little which of us occupy the cells.
George Bernard Shaw,   *1856–1950*
W. H. Auden and Louis Kronenberger, *The Viking Book of Aphorisms,* 1962

65.10   No doubt like schools, old-age homes, mental hospitals, and other closed institutions that house the powerless, prisons afford a very special opportunity to employees at all levels for various kinds of graft and thievery.
Jessica Mitford, English-American writer
Kind and Unusual Punishment, 1971

65.11   . . . if you think only terrible people go to prison, that solves that problem.
Alta, American poet
Untitled Poem, 1972

65.12   Jails and prisons are designed to break human beings, to convert the population into specimens in a zoo— obedient to our keepers, but dangerous to each other.
Angela Davis
Angela Davis: An Autobiography, 1974

65.13   More than half of the jail population have never been convicted of anything, yet they languish in those cells.
Angela Davis
Angela Davis: An Autobiography, 1974

66.   INJUSTICE

66.1   Woe to him who builds his house by . . . injustice, who uses his neighbor's services without wages.
Old Testament, *Jeremiah* 22:13

66.2   If it were not for injustice, men would not know justice.
Heraclitus,   *c.540–c.480 B.C.*
Marjorie P. Katz and Jean S. Arbeiter, *Pegs to Hang Ideas On,* 1973

66.3   Is not injustice the greatest of all threats of the state?
Plato
The Republic, c.370 B.C.

66.4   To do evil to men differs in no respect from injustice.
Plato
Crito, c.350 B.C.

66.5   Extreme law is often extreme injustice.
Terence
The Self-Tormentor, 163 B.C.

66.6   How lightly do we sanction a law unjust to ourselves.
Horace
Satires, 35 B.C.

66.7   A good man should and must
Sit rather down with loss,
Than rise unjust.
Ben Jonson
Sejanus, 1603

66.8   When one has been threatened with a great injustice, one accepts a smaller as a favour.
Jane Welsh Carlyle, Scottish woman of letters and diarist
Journal entry, November 21, 1855, *Letters and Memorials,* 1883 ff.

66.9   Nothing can be permanently useful which is unjust.
Leone Levi, English jurist and statistician
International Law, 1888

66.10   A fruitful parent of injustice is the tyranny of concepts.
Benjamin N. Cardozo,   *1870–1938*
"The Paradoxes of Legal Science,"
Selected Writings of Benjamin Nathan Cardozo, edited by Margaret E. Hall, 1947

66.11   . . . justice can never be done in the midst of injustice.
Simone de Beauvoir
The Second Sex, 1953

67. INNOCENCE

67.1   He who is free from fever does not fear to eat watermelons.
Chinese proverb
William Scarborough, *Chinese Proverbs,* 1875

67.2   God will not cast away an innocent man.
Old Testament, *Job* 8:20

67.3   When innocence is frightened
The judge is condemned.
Publilius Syrus, Latin writer
Sententiae, c.43 B.C.

67.4   The next best to guiltless hands is ignorance of guilt itself.
Seneca,   *4 B.C.–A.D. 65*
Hercules Furens

67.5   I should, indeed, prefer twenty guilty men to escape death through mercy, than one innocent to be condemned unjustly.
Sir John Fortescue, English jurist; chief justice
De Laudibus Legum Angliae, c.1470

67.6   Innocence has more power than all the deceits of an evil man.
Giambattista Battista Giraldi (aka Cinthio)
Selene, c.1549

67.7   Innocence is not nearly so well shielded as crime.
La Rochefoucauld
Maximes, 1665

67.8   It is better to risk saving a guilty man than to condemn an innocent one.
Voltaire
Zadig, 1747

67.9   It is better than ten guilty persons escape than one innocent suffer.
Sir William Blackstone
Commentaries on the Laws of England,
1765-1769

67.10   In England a man is presoomed to be innicent till he's proved guilty an' they take it f'r granted he's guilty. In this counthry a man is presoomed to be guilty ontil he's proved guilty an' afther that he's presoomed to be innicent.
Finley Peter Dunne, *1867-1936*
Edward J. Bander, ed., *Mr. Dooley on the Choice of Law,* 1963

67.11   Our national nostrum, "Not Proven" . . . a verdict which has been construed by the profane to mean "Not Guilty, but don't do it again."
William Roughead
The Art of Murder, 1943

J

68. JUDGES

68.1   The judge is nothing but the law speaking.
Aphorism
Benjamin Whichcote, *Moral and Religious Aphorisms,* 1753

68.2   It is the duty of a judge to administer the law, not to make it.
Latin legal phrase
W. Gurney Benham, *Putnam's Complete Book of Quotations, Proverbs and Household Words,* 1927

68.3   It is the duty of a judge to judge according to what things are alleged and what things are proved.
Latin legal phrase
W. Gurney Benham, *Putnam's Complete Book of Quotations, Proverbs and Household Words,* 1927

68.4   The best law leaves the least discretion to the judge.
Latin proverb
H. L. Mencken, *A New Dictionary of Quotations,* 1946

68.5   A good judge conceives quickly, judges slowly.
Proverb
Rosalind Fergusson, *The Facts On File Dictionary of Proverbs,* 1983

68.6   A judge knows nothing unless it has been explained to him three times.
Proverb
Rosalind Fergusson, *The Facts On File Dictionary of Proverbs,* 1983

68.7   A judge and a stomach do their asking in silence.
Russian proverb
H. L. Mencken, *A New Dictionary of Quotations,* 1946

68.8   Tell God the truth but give the judge money.
Russian proverb
H. L. Mencken, *A New Dictionary of Quotations,* 1946

68.9   A judge who accepts bribes brings terror into the world.
Talmud, *Bava Batra*

68.10   Woe to the generation that judges its judges.
Talmud, *Bava Batra*

68.11   A habitual borrower is unfit to be a judge.
Talmud, *Ketubot*

68.12   A judge is disqualified for a case involving one he loves or hates.
Talmud, *Ketubot*

68.13   As Rabbi Samuel was boarding a ferry, a man rushed up to help him; the rabbi asked why he was so attentive, and the man said, "Because I have a lawsuit that will come up in your court." To which Rabbi Samuel replied, "Then I am forbidden to be your judge."
Talmud, *Ketubot*

68.14   When a court has pronounced a sentence of death, its members [judges] should taste nothing for the rest of that day.
Talmud, *Sanhedrin*

68.15   When a judge sits in judgment over a fellow man, he should feel as if a sword is pointed at his own heart.
Talmud, *Sanhedrin*

68.16   Disaster comes because of the kind of judges we have.
Talmud, *Shabbat*

68.17   I cannot try the case of one of my students, because I love him as myself, and no one can see a fault in himself.
Talmud, *Shabbat*

68.18   Four things belong to a judge: to hear courteously, to answer wisely, to consider soberly, and to decide impartially.
Socrates, *470–399 B.C.*
Franklin Pierce Adams, *F.P.A. Book of Quotations*, 1952

68.19   A judge should not be a youth, but old.
Plato
The Republic, c.370 B.C.

68.20   The Judge should not be young; he should have learned to know evil, not from his own soul, but from late and long observance of the nature of evil in others: knowledge should be his guide, not personal experience.
Plato
The Republic, c.370 B.C.

68.21   Ye judges who give judgments by law, ought to be obedient to the laws.
Cicero, *106–43 B.C.*
W. Gurney Benham, *Putnam's Complete Book of Quotations, Proverbs and Household Words*, 1927

68.22   He makes speed to repentance who judges hastily.
Publilius Syrus, Latin writer, *1st century B.C.*
In Judicando

68.23   First he [Radamanthus, the judge of Hell] punished before he heard, and when he had heard his denial, he compelled the party accused by torture to confess.
Virgil
Aeneid, c.19 B.C.

68.24   A good and faithful judge prefers what is right to what is expedient.
Horace
Carmina, c.13 B.C.

68.25   It is the duty of a judge to enquire not only into the matter but into the circumstances of the matter.
Ovid
Tristia, c.9–17

68.26   A judge is unjust who hears but one side of a case, even though he decide it justly.
Seneca, *4 B.C.–A.D. 65*
Medea

68.27   No one is ever innocent when his opponent is the judge.
Lucan, Roman poet, *39–65*
Pharsalia

68.28   A judge must bear in mind that when he tries a case he is himself on trial.
Philo
Special Laws, 1st century

68.29   Judges are best in the beginning; they deteriorate as time passes.
Tacitus
Annals, c.110

68.30   There must always be a goodly number of judges, for few will always do the will of the few.
Machiavelli
Discorsi, 1531

68.31   Portia: To offend, and judge, are distinct offices,
And of opposed natures.
Shakespeare
The Merchant of Venice, II, 9,
1596–1597

68.32   Shylock: A Daniel come to judgment!
Yea, a Daniel!
O, wise young judge, how I do honor thee!
Shakespeare
The Merchant of Venice, IV, 1,
1596–1597

68.33   Jacques: And then the justice
In fair round belly with good capon lined.
Shakespeare
As You Like It, II, 7, 1599–1600

68.34   Angelo: Thieves for their robbery have authority.
When judges steal themselves.
Shakespeare
Measure for Measure, II, 2, 1604–1605

68.35   Look with thine ears: see how yond justice rails upon yond simple thief. Hark, in thine ear: change places; and, handy-dandy, which is the justice, which is the thief.
Shakespeare
King Lear, IV, 3, 1605–1606

68.36   . . . a corrupt judge offendeth not so highly as a facile.
Francis Bacon
The Advancement of Learning, 1605

68.37   He who has the judge for his father goes into court with an easy mind.
Cervantes
Don Quixote, 1615

68.38   When a judge departs from the letter of the law he becomes a lawbreaker.
Francis Bacon
De Argumentis Scientiarum, 1623

68.39   Judges must beware of hard constructions and strained influences; for there is no worse torture than the torture of laws: specially in the case of laws penal, they ought to have care, that that which was meant for terror be not turned into rigor.
Francis Bacon
"Of Judicature," *Essayes,* 1625

68.40   You should be a light to jurors to open their eyes, but not a guide to lead them by their noses.
Lord Bacon's advice to Justice Hutton
Marshall Brown, *Wit and Humor of Bench and Bar,* 1899

68.41   When he [a judge] put on his robes, he put off his relation to any; and . . . becomes without pedigree.
Thomas Fuller
Holy State, 1642

68.42   When by a pardon'd murd'rer blood is spilt,
The judge that pardon'd hath the greatest guilt.
Sir John Denham, English poet,
1615–1669
On Justice

68.43   The most just man in the world may still not act as judge in his own case.
Pascal
Pensées, 1670

68.44   A popular judge is a deformed thing, and plaudits are fitter for players than for magistrates.
George Savile, 1st marquess of
Halifax, English politician,
1633–1695
W. H. Auden and Louis
Kronenberger, *The Viking Book of
Aphorisms,* 1962

68.45   The duty of a judge is to render justice; his art is to delay it.
Jean de La Bruyère, *1645–1696*

68.46   Tis but half a judge's task to know.
Alexander Pope
Essay on Criticism, 1711

68.47   God forbid that Judges upon their oath should make resolutions to enlarge jurisdiction.
William Cowper, English jurist; lord
chancellor
Reeves v. Buttler (1715), Gilbert, Eq.
Ca. 196

68.48   Judges . . . are picked out from the most dexterous lawyers, who are grown old or lazy, and having been biased all their lives against truth and equity, are under such a fatal necessity of favoring fraud, perjury, and oppression, that I have known several of them refuse a large bribe from the side where justice lay, rather than injure the faculty by doing any thing unbecoming their nature or their office.
Jonathan Swift
Gulliver's Travels, 1726

68.49   Laws should be made by legislators, not by judges.
Cesare Beccaria
Trattato dei delitti e delle pene, 1764

68.50   Set the sternest of judges to plead in his own case and then see how he expounds the law!
P. A. C. de Beaumarchais
Marriage of Figaro, 1784

68.51   Next to permanency in office, nothing can contribute more to the independence of the judges than a fixed provision for their support.
Alexander Hamilton
The Federalist, 1788

68.52   To vindicate the policy of the law is no necessary part of the office of a judge.
Gustavus Scott, American jurist
Evans v. Evans, 1790

68.53   The cold neutrality of an impartial judge.
Edmund Burke, *1729–1797*
Works

68.54   Knowing that religion does not furnish grosser bigots than law, I expect little from old judges.
Thomas Jefferson
Letter to Thomas Cooper, 1810

68.55 It is the judges . . . that make the common law. . . . When your dog does anything you want to break him of, you wait till he does it, and then beat him for it. This is the way you make laws for your dog: and this is the way the judges make law for you and me.
Jeremy Bentham
Truth v. Ashhurst (1823), 5 Works
233, 235

68.56 That part of the law of every country which was made by judges has been far better made than the part which consists of statutes enacted by the legislature.
John Austin
Austin's Jurisprudence, 1832

68.57 The acme of judicial distinction means the ability to look a lawyer straight in the eyes for two hours and not to hear a damned word he says.
John Marshall, *1755–1835*
Albert J. Beveridge, *The Life of John Marshall,* 1919

68.58 It is the duty of a Judge to make it disagreeable to counsel to talk nonsense.
John Singleton Copley, the younger,
1st Baron Lyndhurst, English jurist;
lord chancellor
John Campbell, *Lives of Lord Chancellors,* 1849

68.59 Judges, like *Caesar's* wife, should be above suspicion.
Charles Bowen, English jurist
Leeson v. General Council of Medical Education and Registration (1889),
L.R. 43 C.D. 385

68.60 Credulity is not esteemed a paramount virtue of the judicial mind.
Joseph Waldo Huston, American lawyer
Rankin v. Jauman, 4 Idaho, 394, 401 (1895)

68.61 There is a story of a Vermont justice of the peace before whom a suit was brought by one farmer against another for breaking a churn. The justice took time to consider, and then said that he had looked through the statutes and could find nothing about churns, and gave judgment for the defendant. The same state of mind is shown in all our common digests and textbooks.
Oliver Wendell Holmes
"The Path of the Law" (address), 1897

68.62 "If I had me job to pick out," said Mr. Dooley, "I'd be a judge. I've looked over all th' others an that's the on'y wan that suits. I have th' judicyal timperamint. I hate wurruk."
Finley Peter Dunne
Observations by Mr. Dooley: The Law's Delays, 1906

68.63 Judges are apt to be naif, simpleminded men, and they need something of Mephistopheles. We too need education in the obvious—to learn to transcend our own convictions and to leave room for much that we hold dear to be done away with short of revolution by the orderly change of law.
Oliver Wendell Holmes
"Law and the Court," 1913, *Collected Legal Papers,* 1920

68.64 But even judges sometimes progress.
Emma Goldman
"The Social Aspects of Birth Control," *Mother Earth,* April 1916

68.65 There are no more reactionary people in the world than judges.
Lenin
Political Parties and the Proletariat, 1917

68.66 . . . a judge of the United States is expected to be a man of ordinary firmness of character.
Oliver Wendell Holmes
Toledo Newspaper Co. v. United States, 247 U.S. 402, 424 (1918)

68.67 The great tides and currents which engulf the rest of men do not turn aside in their course, and pass the judges by.
Benjamin N. Cardozo
The Nature of the Judicial Process, 1921

68.68 Judges commonly are elderly men, and are more likely to hate at sight any analysis to which they are not accustomed, and which disturbs repose of mind, than to fall in love with novelties.
Oliver Wendell Holmes
Law in Science—Science in Law, 1921

68.69 We rate the judge who is only a lawyer higher than the judge who is only a philosopher.
Cuthbert W. Pound, American jurist
"Defective Law—Its Cause and Remedy," *New York State Bar Bulletin,* 1929

68.70 I venture to believe that it is important to a judge called upon to pass on a question of Constitutional law, to have at least a bowing acquaintance with Acton and Maitland, with Thucydides, Gibbon and Carlyle, with Homer, Dante, Shakespeare and Milton, with Machiavelli, Montaigne and Rabelais, with Plato, Bacon, Hume and Kant. . . . Men do not gather figs of thistles, nor supple institutions from judges whose outlook is limited by parish or class.
Learned Hand
"Sources of Tolerance," 79 *University of Pennsylvania Law Review* 1, 12 (1930)

68.71 I could carve out of a banana a judge with more backbone than that.
Oliver Wendell Holmes, *1841–1935*
New York Times, February 23, 1984

68.72 . . . one's final judge and only rival is oneself.
Oliver Wendell Holmes, *1841–1935*
Catherine Drinker Bowen, *Yankee from Olympus,* 1944

68.73 No judge writes on a wholly clean slate.
Felix Frankfurter
The Commerce Clause, 1937

68.74 A judge rarely performs his functions adequately unless the case before him is adequately presented.
Louis D. Brandeis, *1856–1941*
B. Donovan James, *Strangers on a Bridge,* 1964

68.75 The position of a judge has been likened to that of an oyster anchored in one place, unable to take the initiative, unable to go out after things, restricted to working on and digesting that which the fortuitous eddies and currents of litigation may bring his way.
Louis D. Brandeis, *1856–1941*
Felix Frankfurter, *Mr. Justice Brandeis,* 1932

68.76 I do not know whether it is the view of the Court that a judge must be thick-skinned or just thickheaded, but nothing in my experience or observation confirms the idea that he is insensitive to publicity. Who does not prefer good to ill report of his work? And if fame—a good public name—is, as Milton said, the "last infirmity of noble mind," it is frequently the first infirmity of a mediocre one.
Robert H. Jackson
Craig v. Harney, 331 U.S. 367, 396 (1947)

68.77   It has not been unknown that judges persist in error to avoid giving the appearance of weakness and vacillation.

Felix Frankfurter
Craig v. Harney, 331 U.S. 367, 392 (1947)

68.78   When my father became a Judge I said to him, "Be kind to the *young lawyers.*" When I became a Judge, he said to me, "Be kind to the *old lawyers.*"

Claude McColloch, American jurist
Notes of a District Judge, 1948

68.79   After all is said and done, we cannot deny the fact that a judge is almost of necessity surrounded by people who keep telling him what a wonderful fellow he is. And if he once begins to believe it, he is a lost soul.

Harold R. Medina, American jurist
"Some Reflections on the Judicial Function: A Personal Viewpoint," 38 *American Bar Association Journal* 107, 108 (1952)

68.80   What becomes decisive to a Justice's functioning on the Court . . . is his general attitude toward law, the habits of mind that he has formed or is capable of unforming, his capacity for detachment, his temperament or training for putting his passion behind his judgment instead of in front of it. The attitudes and qualities which I am groping to characterize are ingredients of what compendiously might be called dominating humility.

Felix Frankfurter
Forward, *Columbia Law Review,* April 1955

68.81   One of Judge Jerome Frank's [1889–1957] law clerks objected to the length of one of his opinions. He spent all of a week and finally cut it down from 65 pages to one-half page. He left both on Judge Frank's desk without comment. The following morning Judge Frank rushed into his clerk's office and shouted: "Bully for you," displaying the clerk's work, "we'll add it to the end."

Anonymous
Kenneth Redden, *Modern Legal Glossary,* 1983

68.82   A society whose judges have taught it to expect complaisance will exact complaisance; and complaisance under the pretense of interpretation is rottenness. If judges are to kill this thing they love, let them do it, not like cowards with a kiss, but like brave men with a sword.

Learned Hand
Irving Dilliard, *The Spirit of Liberty,* 1960

68.83   . . . a Judge who is both stupid and industrious is without question an unqualified disaster.

Dana Porter, Canadian jurist; chief justice, Province of Ontario
"What Once the Fleeting Hour Has Brought," 33 *New York State Bar Journal* 4 (August 1961)

68.84   I'm important in the County
I'm a Justice of the Peace
And I disbelieve Defendants
When they contradict the P'lice.

John A. Nordberg
"Farewell to Illinois J.P.'s–A Lesson from History," 44 *Chicago Bar Record* 10 (September 1963)

68.85   You see a court of appeals judge has a sort of intermediate status. It is the duty of a judge of a district court to be quick, courteous and wrong, but it must not be supposed from

that that the court of appeals must be slow, crapulous and right, for that would be to usurp the functions of the supreme court.
Editorial comment
Yearbook of the Canadian Bar Association, 1963

68.86 I found the compliments very disturbing; when a judge compliments you, it usually means you have lost.
James B. Donovan
Strangers on a Bridge, 1964

68.87 The judge who does not agonize before passing a sentence is a criminal.
John Ciardi
Saturday Review, February 13, 1965

68.88 It is upon their seats that judges shine most.
Sir Gerald Dodson, recorder, Old Bailey Criminal Court, *1884–1966*
New York Times, November 5, 1966

68.89 Our chief justices have probably had more profound and lasting influence on their times and on the direction of the nation than most presidents have had.
Richard M. Nixon
Television broadcast, May 21, 1969

68.90 When we put our judges in an ivory tower, you put justice in an ivory tower.
Bernard G. Segal, American lawyer; president, American Bar Association
Speech, American Bar Association, August 15, 1969

68.91 Like generals who have [had] no wars for a generation are out of practice, we judges have perhaps been sluggish in responding to the new ways of trying legal and factual issues. But in time we do respond . . . It would be foolhardy not to be con-

cerned about the turmoil and strife and violence we witness, much of it mindless and devoid of constructive ends. But concern must not give way to panic.
Warren E. Burger
Speech, American Law Institute, Washington, D.C., as reported in the *Washington Observer,* May 25, 1970

68.92 What a judge does with his time while he is not on the bench is of great interest to the public. It is absolutely necessary that the clear light of day should illuminate any off-the-bench activity by a judge—and particularly any money he makes off of it.
Roger J. Traynor, American jurist; chief justice, California Supreme Court
New York Times, August 9, 1970

68.93 It's easier to be cynical than to be correct. I know that from the judging business. It's easier to write a stinging dissent than a persuasive majority opinion.
Harry A. Blackmun
San Francisco Examiner, July 12, 1971

68.94 A great intellectual doesn't make a great trial judge. A man who's been a trial lawyer is a better judge of human nature than Professor X at Harvard, who's probably never been in the well of a courtroom. . . . The important question is whether a judge is honest and does he have the courage of his convictions to do what is right at the moment.
John J. Sirica
New York Times Magazine, November 4, 1973

68.95 Old magistrate to young lawyer: "Young man, quit jumping up and

saying 'I object. You are not proceeding according to law.' I'll have
you understand I am running this
court, and the law hasn't got a damn
thing to do with it!"
    Sam Ervin
    Thad Stem, Jr. and Alan Butler, *Sam
    Ervin's Best Stories,* 1973

68.96   There is always a tendency to judi-
cialize everything that goes wrong in
our criminal justice system. The
judge has one pill in his little black
bag: it is called judicialization. The
trouble with that is that solutions are
stuck into these problems, but no
one ever examines why the problems
arose in the first place.
    Donald Cressey, American educator;
    professor, University of California,
    Santa Barbara
    Center Magazine,
    November–December, 1975

68.97   If the judiciary is to be the primary agency for social reform,
shouldn't we be more concerned
about the quality of the people we
choose for judges? For the most part,
judges are narrow-minded lawyers
with little background for making social judgments.
    Philip B. Kurland, American
    educator; professor, University of
    Chicago Law School
    U.S. News & World Report, January
    19, 1976

68.98   Positivism holds that there is never
a single correct answer to novel, hard
questions of law. I disagree. An able
judge may properly think he can find
the right answer by considering written law—the Constitution, statutes
and previous court decisions—plus
all other considerations assumed in a

society that has respect for other
people's rights.
    Ronald Dworkin, professor, Oxford
    University
    Time, September 5, 1977

68.99   Judges are the weakest link in our
system of justice, and they are also
the most protected.
    Alan Dershowitz
    Newsweek, February 20, 1978

68.100   The more the courts are asked to
handle political issues, the more
their fragility is exposed. To some
extent, the questioning of the courts
is simply part of the increased attention that has been paid to all our
institutions over the past several
years. What concerns me is that the
focus of this questioning of the
courts seems to be not on matters of
substance but rather on points of
prejudice and personal pique. A
judge's integrity, fairness, temperament, and knowledge of the law are
all pertinent areas for public inquiry. However, what is happening
instead is that judges are being perceived as easy targets and are being
portrayed in a manner calculated to
create prejudice in the public mind.
    Rose E. Bird, American jurist; chief
    justice, California State Supreme
    Court
    San Francisco Examiner & Chronicle,
    October 22, 1978

68.101   The most important [judicial
qualities are]: quality and competence and temperament and character and diligence.
    Potter Stewart
    Washington Post, June 20, 1981

68.102   We must never forget that the
only real source of power that we as

judges can tap is the respect of the people.

Thurgood Marshall
Chicago Tribune, August 15, 1981

68.103   . . . has the judiciary's perception of right and wrong gone so far out of the mainstream of that society that people are concerned and alarmed? If they are, they should be

able to express it through the ballot box. They [justices] cannot become some kind of priesthood beyond the reach of people in a democratic society.

Gideon Kanner, American educator; professor, Loyola University
Christian Science Monitor, October 13, 1982

69. JUDGMENT

69.1   If a wicked man and a pious man are before you in court, do not say: I will turn judgment against the wicked.

Anonymous
Joseph L. Baron, *A Treasury of Jewish Quotations,* 1956

69.2   Only judge when you have heard all.

Greek proverb
Robert and Mary Collison, *The Dictionary of Foreign Quotations,* 1980

69.3   Before you start up a ladder, count the rungs.

Jewish folk saying
Joseph L. Baron, *A Treasury of Jewish Quotations,* 1956

69.4   Don't try to fill a sack that's full of holes.

Jewish folk saying
Joseph L. Baron, *A Treasury of Jewish Quotations,* 1956

69.5   Usage is the best interpreter of things.

Legal maxim

69.6   Give every man the benefit of the doubt.

Sayings of the Fathers
Joseph L. Baron, *A Treasury of Jewish Quotations,* 1956

69.7   Just as you listen to the poor man, listen to the rich man, for it is written, "Ye shall not favor persons in judgment."

Rabbi Nathan
Midrash, *Aboth de Rabbi Nathan*

69.8   He who passes judgment on fools is himself judged a fool.

Midrash

69.9   Judgment delayed is judgment voided.

Talmud, *Sanhedrin*

69.10   Judge every man charitably.
Joshua, the Son of Perachyah
Aboth: *Sayings of the Fathers,* c.200

69.11   O mortal men, be wary how ye judge.
Dante
Paradiso, 1320

69.12   A man had need of tough ears to hear himself judged.
Michel de Montaigne
Essais, 1588

69.13   The law is not exact upon the subject, but leaves it open to a good man's judgment.
Hugo Grotius,   *1583–1645*
W. Gurney Benham, *Putnam's Complete Book of Quotations, Proverbs and Household Words,* 1927

69.14   The greatest of all gifts is the power to estimate things at their true worth.
La Rochefoucauld
Maximes, 1665

69.15   Sir, as a man advances in life, he gets what is better than admiration—judgment, to estimate things at their true value.
Samuel Johnson
James Boswell, *The Life of Samuel Johnson,* 1791

69.16   Nothing is so easy as to be wise after the event.
Chief Justice Jervis
c.1859

69.17   A tendency toward enthusiasm and a chivalrous instinct have more than once been weighed as evidence of a lack of judgment.
Lloyd Paul Stryker
For the Defense, 1947

69.18   The state trial judges are being asked to make moral judgments. On abortion. On the question of when death occurs. These shouldn't be a judge's decisions. These should be scientific or theological decisions.
Jack P. Etheridge, American jurist; judge, Senior Circuit Court, Georgia
Christian Science Monitor, November 27, 1978

70.   JURIES

70.1   Let the judge answer on the question of law; the jury on the question of fact.
Latin legal phrase
W. Gurney Benham, *Putnam's Complete Book of Quotations, Proverbs and Household Words,* 1927

70.2   A fox should not be of the jury at a goose's trial.
Proverb
Thomas Fuller, *Gnomologia,* 1732

70.3   Keep your fellows' counsels and your own.
> Shakespeare
> Oath administered to a Grand Jury,
> *Much Ado About Nothing,* III, 3,
> 1598–1599

70.4   The jury, passing on the prisoner's life,
May in the sworn twelve have a thief or two
Guiltier than him they try.
> Shakespeare
> *Measure for Measure,* II, 1, 1604–1605

70.5   Wilt make haste to give up thy verdict because thou wilt not lose thy dinner.
> Thomas Middleton
> *A Trick to Catch the Old One,*
> c.1604–1611

70.6   As the law does think fit
No butchers shall on juries sit.
> Charles Churchill
> *The Ghost,* 1762–1763

70.7   Twelve good honest men shall decide in our cause,
And be judges of fact though not judges of law.
> William Pulteney, earl of Bath,
> *1684–1764*
> "The Honest Jury" (song)

70.8   Every new tribunal, erected for the decision of facts, without the intervention of a jury . . . is a step towards establishing aristocracy, the most oppressive of absolute governments.
> Sir William Blackstone
> *Commentaries on the Laws of England,*
> 1765–1769

70.9   There is no distinction between a good jury and a common jury.
> Charles Butler, English jurist
> *King v. Perry* (1793), 5 T.R. 460

70.10   In truth, it is better to toss up cross and pile [heads or tails] in a cause than to refer it to a judge whose mind is warped by any motive whatever, in that particular case. But the common sense of twelve honest men gives still a better chance of just decision than the hazard of cross and pile.
> Thomas Jefferson, *1743–1826*
> Saul K. Padover, *The Complete Jefferson,* 1943

70.11   In my mind, he was guilty of no error, he was chargeable with no exaggeration, he was betrayed by his fancy into no metaphor, who once said that all we see about us, kings, lords, and Commons, the whole machinery of the State, all the apparatus of the system, and its varied workings, end in simply bringing twelve good men into a box.
> Henry Peter Brougham, English
> jurist; lord chancellor
> "Present State of the Law" (speech),
> February 7, 1828

70.12   Juries, above all civil juries, help every citizen to share something of the deliberations that go on in the judge's mind; and it is these very deliberations which best prepare the people to be free.
> Alexis de Tocqueville
> *Democracy in America,* 1835–1840

70.13   I confess that in my experience I have not found juries specially inspired for the discovery of the truth . . . they will introduce into their verdict a certain amount—a very large amount, so far as I have observed— of popular prejudice, and thus keep the administration of the law in accord with the wishes and feelings of the community.
> Oliver Wendell Holmes
> Address, January 17, 1899

70.14   Th' lawyers make th' law, th' judges make th' errors, but th' editors make th' juries.
Finley Peter Dunne
American Magazine, October 1906

70.15   The jury has the power to bring in a verdict in the teeth of both law and facts.
Oliver Wendell Holmes
Horning v. District of Columbia, 249 U.S. 596, 39 S. Ct. 386, 63 L.Ed. 794 (1920)

70.16   Trial by jury is a rough scales at best; the beam ought not to tip for motes and straws.
Learned Hand
United States v. Brown, 79F (2d) 321, 326 (1935)

70.17   And how, milord, can we expect these twelve poor mutts on the jury—
The Judge: What is a mutt?
Sir Ethelred: Milord, a mutt—
The Judge: Sir Ethelred, no doubt you know best the lines of advocacy most likely to advance the interests of your clients; but is it quite wise to describe the jury as 'mutts', which, though I am not familiar with it, I judge instinctively to be a term of depreciation?
Sir Ethelred: Milord, 'mutt' is a relative term. The Prime Minister, if he were requested to transpose a musical composition in A flat major into the key of E minor would readily confess himself a mutt in relation to that particular task.
The Judge: Very well, Sir Ethelred. Proceed.
Sir Ethelred (turning to the jury): How, I say, can you poor mutts be expected to get a grip of this colossal conundrum *without the assistance of any documents at all?*
A. P. Herbert
Uncommon Law, 1936

70.18   But juries are not bound by what seems inescapable logic to judges.
Robert H. Jackson
Morissette v. United States, 342 U.S. 246, 276 (1952)

70.19   Jury service honorably performed is as important in the defense of our country, its Constitution and laws, and the ideals and standards for which they stand, as the service that is rendered by the soldier on the field of battle in time of war.
George H. Boldt, American jurist
United States v. Beck (1959)

70.20   A jury verdict is a quotient of the prejudices of twelve people.
Kenneth P. Grubb, American jurist
"False Fears," *Insurance Counsel Journal,* October 1959

70.21   Gentlemen, a court is no better than each man of you sitting before me on this jury. A court is only as sound as its jury, and a jury is only as sound as the men who make it up.
Harper Lee
To Kill a Mockingbird, 1960

70.22   A jury consists of 12 persons chosen to decide who has the better lawyer.
Robert Frost, *1874-1963*
Kenneth Redden, *Modern Legal Glossary,* 1983

70.23   The classic adversary system in the United States not only encourages, it demands that each lawyer attempt to empanel the jury most likely to understand his argument, or least likely to understand that of his opponent. You don't approach a case with the

philosophy of applying abstract justice. You go in to win.
Percy Foreman
New York Times, February 3, 1969

70.24   The day of manipulating a jury is absolutely gone, if there ever was such a day. Cases are won through preparation, dragging the facts into the courtroom. The lawyer excavates

the facts, and the more he digs, the more certain is he to win; and then he can pound upon the facts and an emotional appeal—that's the way of persuasion. But to play clever with a jury when you don't have the facts leaves them cold. They resent it.
Louis Nizer
San Francisco Examiner, May 29, 1974

71. JUSTICE

71.1   Justice delayed is worse than injustice.
Jewish folk saying
Joseph L. Baron, *A Treasury of Jewish Quotations,* 1956

71.2   A just balance preserves justice.
Latin proverb
W. Gurney Benham, *Putnam's Complete Book of Quotations, Proverbs and Household Words,* 1927

71.3   There is no wrong without a remedy.
Legal maxim

71.4   Be just before you are generous.
Proverb
Bergen Evans, *Dictionary of Quotations,* 1968

71.5   Much law, but little justice.
Proverb
Rosalind Fergusson, *The Facts On File Dictionary of Proverbs,* 1983

71.6   Justice pleaseth few in their own house.
Proverb
George Herbert, *Outlandish Proverbs,* 1639

71.7   Justice, justice shall you pursue.
Old Testament, *Deuteronomy* 16:20

71.8   Eye for eye, tooth for tooth, hand for hand, foot for foot.
Old Testament, *Exodus* 21:24

71.9   Just balances, just weights . . . shall ye have: . . .
Old Testament, *Leviticus* 19:36

71.10   Abraham said to God: "If you want the world to exist, you cannot insist upon complete justice; if it is complete justice you want, the world cannot endure."
Midrash, *Genesis Rabba*

71.11 Justice is but the interest of the stronger.
Plato
Republic, c.370 B.C.

71.12 It were to be wished that those who are at the head of the commonwealth were like the laws, which are moved to punish, not by anger, but by justice.
Cicero
De Officiis, 45–44 B.C.

71.13 The foundations of justice are that no one shall be harmed, and next that the common weal be served.
Cicero, *106–43 B.C.*
William S. Walsh, *International Encyclopedia of Prose and Poetical Quotations,* 1968

71.14 The people become more subservient to justice . . . when they see the author of a law obeying it himself.
Claudian (Claudius Claudianus)
Panegyricus de Quarto Consulatu Honorii Augusti, 398

71.15 If you see wicked men perverting justice, do not say: "Since they are many, I must follow after them."
Rashi (Rabbi Solomon Ben Isaac), *1040–1105*
Commentaries on the Pentateuch

71.16 To no one will we sell, to no one will we refuse or delay, right or justice.
Magna Carta, 1215

71.17 Kings gain greater riches through justice than do tyrants by rapacity.
St. Thomas Aquinas
On Princely Government, 1266

71.18 Let justice be done though the world perish.
Ferdinand I, emperor of the Holy Roman Empire, *1558–1564*
Motto

71.19 Law hath certain lawful fictions upon which it groundeth the truth of justice.
Michel de Montaigne
Essais, 1588

71.20 I beseech your Majesty, let me have Justice, and I will then trust the law.
Elizabeth Hoby Russell, English diarist and courtier
Spoken to King James I, 1603

71.21 Duke: . . . our decrees,
Dead to infliction, to themselves are dead;
And liberty plucks Justice by the nose.
Shakespeare
Measure for Measure, I, 3, 1604–1605

71.22 Lear: Plate sin with gold,
And the strong lance of justice hurtless breaks;
Arm it in rags, a pigmy's straw doth pierce it.
Shakespeare
King Lear, IV, 6, 1605–1606

71.23 The usurer hangs the cozener.*
Shakespeare
King Lear, IV, 6, 1605–1606

71.24 Justice may wink a while, but see at last.
Thomas Middleton
The Mayor of Quinborough, 1606

71.25 The weakest arm is strong enough that strikes,
With the sword of justice.
John Webster
The Duchess of Malfi, c.1614

71.26 Fresh justice is the sweetest.
Francis Bacon, on taking his seat as lord keeper
Speech, May 7, 1617

*i.e., the big cheat hangs the little cheat

71.27   . . . it is the worst oppression, that is done by colour of justice.
Sir Edward Coke
The Institutes of the Lawes of England,
vol. 2, 1628–1641

71.28   Where the fault springs, there let justice fall.
Robert Herrick
Hesperides, 1648

71.29   Justice is blind, he knows nobody.
John Dryden,
The Wild Gallant, 1663

71.30   Justice, while she winks at crimes,
Stumbles on innocence sometimes.
Samuel Butler
Hudibras, 1663–1678

71.31   The love of justice is simply, in the majority of men, the fear of suffering injustice.
La Rochefoucauld
Maximes, 1665

71.32   Justice is what is established; and thus all our established laws will be regarded as just, without being examined, since they are established.
Pascal
Pensées, 1670

71.33   Justice is lame as well as blind, amongst us.
Thomas Otway
Venice Preserved, 1682

71.34   A prince's favours but on few can fall,
But justice is a virtue shar'd by all.
John Dryden,   *1631–1700*
Britannia Rediviva

71.35   "There, take," says Justice, "take you each a shell.
We thrive at Westminster on fools like you.

'Twas a fat oyster—Live in peace—Adieu!"
Nicolas Boileau-Despréaux,
1636–1711
W. Gurney Benham, *Putnam's Complete Dictionary of Quotations, Proverbs and Household Words,* 1927

71.36   Hard is the task of justice, where distress
Excites our mercy, yet demands redress.
Colley Cibber
The Heroik Daughter, 1718

71.37   Poetic Justice, with her lifted scale,
Where in nice balance truth with gold she weighs,
And solid pudding against empty praise.
Alexander Pope
The Dunciad, 1728–1743

71.38   A good person once said that where mystery begins religion ends. Cannot I say, as truly at least, of human laws, that where mystery begins, justice ends?
Edmund Burke
A Vindication of Natural Society, 1761

71.39   Amongst the sons of men how few are known
Who dare be just to merit not their own?
Charles Churchill
Epistle to W. Hogarth, July 1763

71.40   Justice, that in the rigid paths of law, would still some drops from Pity's fountain draw.
John Langhorne, American poet
The Country Justice, c.1766

71.41 Let justice be done though the heavens fall.
Sir James Mansfield, English jurist; chief justice
Rex v. Wilkes (1769), 4 Burr. Part IV., p. 2549

71.42 It looks to me to be narrow and pedantic to apply the ordinary ideas of criminal justice to this great public contest. I do not know the method of drawing up an indictment against a whole people.
Edmund Burke
Speech on moving his resolutions for conciliation with the Colonies, March 22, 1775

71.43 I tremble for my country when I reflect that God is just; that his justice cannot sleep forever; that considering numbers, nature, and natural means only, a revolution of the wheel of fortune, an exchange of situation, is among possible events; that it may become probable by supernatural interference! The Almighty has no attribute which can take side with us in such a contest.
Thomas Jefferson
Notes on Virginia, 1786

71.44 There is one universal law that has been formed or at least adopted . . . by the majority of mankind. That law is justice. Justice forms the cornerstone of each nation's law.
Alexis de Tocqueville
Democracy in America, 1835

71.45 Justice is truth in action.
Benjamin Disraeli
Speech, House of Commons, February 11, 1851

71.46 The law does not generate justice. The law is nothing but a declaration and application of what is already just.
Pierre Joseph Proudhon
De la justice dans la révolution, 1858

71.47 It costs us nothing to be just.
Henry David Thoreau
John Brown's Body, 1859

71.48 Justice is like the Kingdom of God—it is not without us as a fact, it is within us as a great yearning.
George Eliot
Romola, 1862–1863

71.49 Justice travels with a leaden heel, but strikes with an iron hand.
Jeremiah S. Black, American jurist
Warning after the decision in the Hayes-Tilden presidential election count of 1876

71.50 Whoever fights, whoever falls, Justice conquers evermore.
Ralph Waldo Emerson, *1803–1882*
Voluntaries

71.51 We love justice greatly, and just men but little.
Joseph Roux
Meditations of a Parish Priest, 1886

71.52 But the sunshine aye shall light the sky,
As round and round we run;
And the truth shall ever come uppermost,
And justice shall be done.
Charles Mackay, Scottish writer, *1814–1889*
Eternal Justice

71.53 Of relative justice law may know something; of expediency it knows much; with absolute justice it does not concern itself.
Oliver Wendell Holmes, American physician and author
The Works of Oliver Wendell Holmes, 1891

71.54   The hope of all who suffer,
The dread of all who wrong.
John Greenleaf Whittier, *1807–1892*
Mantle of St. John De Matha

71.55   Injustice is relatively easy to bear;
what stings is justice.
H. L. Mencken
Prejudices: Third series, 1922

71.56   Justice is not to be taken by storm.
She is to be wooed by slow advances.
Benjamin N. Cardozo
The Growth of the Law, 1924

71.57   There is a justice, but we do not
always see it. Discreet, smiling, it is
there, at one side, a little behind injustice, which makes a big noise.
Jules Renard
Journal, 1925–1927

71.58   No system of justice can rise
above the ethics of those who administer it.
Report of the National (Wickersham)
Commission on Law Observance and
Law Enforcement, 1929

71.59   There is no such thing as justice—
in or out of court.
Clarence Darrow
New York Times, April 19, 1936

71.60   Justice is not a cloistered virtue:
she must be allowed to suffer the
scrutiny and respectful, even though
outspoken, comments of ordinary
men.
James Richard Atkin, 1st Baron of
Aberdovey
Ambard v. Attorney General for
Trinidad (1936), A.C. 322, 335

71.61   Justice, though due to the accused,
is due to the accuser also.
Benjamin N. Cardozo, *1870–1938*
Kenneth Redden, *Modern Legal*
Glossary, 1983

71.62   Why should there be not a patient
confidence in the ultimate justice of
the people?
Inscription over the main door of the
Manhattan Criminal Court Building,
1939

71.63   Justice is not a prize tendered to
the good-natured, nor is it to be
withheld from the ill-bred.
Charles L. Aarons
Hach v. Lewinsky et al., (1945)

71.64   Justice, I think, is the tolerable accommodation of the conflicting interests of society, and I don't believe
there is any royal road to attain such
accommodations concretely.
Learned Hand
Life, November 4, 1946

71.65   If we are to keep our democracy,
there must be one commandment:
Thou shalt not ration justice.
Learned Hand
Address, Legal Aid Society of New
York, February 16, 1951

71.66   Justice is too good for some people
and not good enough for the rest.
Norman Douglas, *1868–1952*
Laurence J. Peter, *Peter's Quotations,*
1977

71.67   Justice has been described as a
lady who has been subject to so
many miscarriages as to cast serious
reflections upon her virtue.
William L. Prosser, American
educator; dean, University of
California Law School
The Judicial Humorist, 1952

71.68   Fairness is what justice really is.
Potter Stewart
Time, October 20, 1958

71.69   The justice of the law is, therefore, a "statistical" justice, an average justice, a kind of rationed goods preserving all from want but sufficient for no one.
Moshe Silberg
"Law and Morals in Jewish Jurisprudence," 75 *Harvard Law Review* 306, 316 (1961)

71.70   "Look here," Furii said. "I never promised you a rose garden. I never promised you perfect justice. . . ."
Hannah Green, American writer
I Never Promised You a Rose Garden, 1964

71.71   They call it the Halls of Justice because the only place you get justice is in the halls.
Lenny Bruce, *1926–1966*
Kenneth Redden, *Modern Legal Glossary,* 1983

71.72   Justice delayed is not only justice denied—it is also justice circumvented, justice mocked and the system of justice undermined.
Richard M. Nixon
New York Times, March 12, 1971

71.73   The innately logical mind of woman, her unique sense of balance, orderliness, and reason, rebels at the terrible realization that justice has been an empty word, that she has been forced for nearly two millennia to worship false gods and to prostrate herself at their empty shrines.
Elizabeth Gould Davis, American librarian and writer
The First Sex, 1971

71.74   Ideas, ideals and great conceptions are vital to a system of justice, but it must have more than that—there must be delivery and execution. Concepts of justice must have hands and feet or they remain sterile abstractions. The hands and feet we need are efficient means and methods to carry out justice in every case in the shortest possible time and at the lowest possible cost. This is the challenge to every lawyer and judge in America.
Warren E. Burger
Address, American Bar Association, San Francisco, reported in *Vital Speeches,* October 1, 1972

71.75   The law is not the private property of lawyers, nor is justice the exclusive province of judges and juries. In the final analysis, true justice is not a matter of courts and law books, but of a commitment in each of us to liberty and mutual respect.
Jimmy Carter
Dallas Times-Herald, April 26, 1978

71.76   Justice is: JUST US.
Richard Pryor
In performance

L

72. LAW

72.1   Even as there are laws of poetry, so there is poetry in law.
Anonymous
Joseph L. Baron, *A Treasury of Jewish Quotations*, 1956

72.2   The glorious uncertainty of the law.
English phrase

72.3   Worse people worse laws.
English proverb
George England and A. W. Pollard, *Towneley Plays*, 1897

72.4   Good laws come from lewd lives.
French or English proverb
James Howell, *Proverbs*, 1659

72.5   The law has a wax nose.
French proverb
H. L. Mencken, *A New Dictionary of Quotations*, 1946

72.6   When a law is made the way to avoid it is found out.
Italian proverb
W. Gurney Benham, *Putnam's Book of Quotations, Proverbs and Household Words*, 1927

72.7   Without law, civilization dies.
Jewish folk saying
Leo Rosten's Treasury of Jewish Quotations, 1972

72.8   The disposition of law is more decisive and powerful than that of men.
Latin legal phrase
W. Gurney Benham, *Putnam's Complete Book of Quotations, Proverbs and Household Words*, 1927

72.9   The law aims at perfection.
Latin legal phrase
W. Gurney Benham, *Putnam's Complete Book of Quotations, Proverbs and Household Words*, 1927

72.10   The law effects injustice to no one; and does injury to no one.
Latin legal phrase
W. Gurney Benham, *Putnam's Book of Quotations, Proverbs and Household Words*, 1927

72.11   Laws are made by the conqueror, and accepted by the conquered.
Latin proverb
H. L. Mencken, *A New Dictionary of Quotations*, 1946

72.12   Like King, like law; like law, like people.
Portuguese proverb
W. Gurney Benham, *Putnam's Complete Book of Quotations, Proverbs and Household Words*, 1927

72.13   Be you never so high, the law is above you.
Proverb
Thomas Fuller, *Gnomologia*, 1732

72.14   Every law has a loophole.
Proverb
Rosalind Fergusson, *The Facts On File Dictionary of Proverbs*, 1983

72.15   Ill Kings make many good laws.
Proverb
Thomas Fuller, *Gnomologia*, 1732

72.16   Law governs man and reason the law.
Proverb
Thomas Fuller, *Gnomologia*, 1732

72.17   Laws catch flies but let hornets go free.
Proverb
Rosalind Fergusson, *The Facts On File Dictionary of Proverbs*, 1983

72.18   Many lords, many laws.
Proverb
Rosalind Fergusson, *The Facts On File Dictionary of Proverbs*, 1983

72.19   New lords, new laws.
Proverb
Rosalind Fergusson, *The Facts On File Dictionary of Proverbs*, 1983

72.20   New laws, new frauds.
Proverb
W. Gurney Benham, *Putnam's Complete Book of Quotations, Proverbs and Household Words*, 1927

72.21   The law is not the same at morning and at night.
Proverb
Rosalind Fergusson, *The Facts On File Dictionary of Proverbs*, 1983

72.22   The more laws, the more offenders.
Proverb
Rosalind Fergusson, *The Facts On File Dictionary of Proverbs*, 1983

72.23   Wrong laws make short governance.
Proverb
Rosalind Fergusson, *The Facts On File Dictionary of Proverbs*, 1983

72.24   A penny-weight of love is worth a pound of law.
Scottish proverb
James Kelly, *Complete Collection of Scottish Proverbs*, 1721

72.25   Show me the man, and I shall show you the law.
Scottish proverb
W. Gurney Benham, *Putnam's Book of Quotations, Proverbs and Household Words*, 1927

72.26   Ye shall have one manner of law, as well for the stranger, as for one of your own country. . . .
Old Testament, *Leviticus* 24:22

72.27   . . . the law is light. . . .
Old Testament, *Proverbs* 6:23

72.28   All things are lawful for me, but all things are not expedient: all things are lawful for me, but all things edify not.
New Testament, 1 *Corinthians* 10:23

72.29   . . . the letter killeth, but the spirit giveth life.
New Testament, 2 *Corinthians* 3:6

72.30 Is it not lawful for me to do what I will with mine own? Is thine eye evil, because I am good?
New Testament, *Matthew* 20:15

72.31 . . . where no law is, there is no transgression.
New Testament, *Romans* 4:15

72.32 But now we are delivered from the law, that being dead wherein we were held; that we should serve in newness of spirit, and not in the oldness of the letter.
New Testament, *Romans* 7:6

72.33 . . . the law is good, if a man use it lawfully.
New Testament, 1 *Timothy* 1:8

72.34 The law of the state is one law.
Talmud, *Gittin*

72.35 Taking the law into one's own hands.
Aesop, *c.620–560 B.C.*
Fables

72.36 The more mandates and laws are enacted, the more there will be thieves and robbers.
Lao-tze, *604?–?531 B.C.*
The Tao-te-ching

72.37 The people should fight for the law as for their city wall.
Heraclitus, *6th–5th century B.C.*
W. H. Auden and Louis Kronenberger, *The Viking Book of Aphorisms,* 1962

72.38 Law, lord of all, mortals and immortals, carries everything with a high hand.
Pindar
Fragments, c.480 B.C.

72.39 Law can never issue an injunction binding on all which really embodies what is best for each; it cannot prescribe with perfect accuracy what is good and right for each member of the community at any one time. The differences of human personality, the variety of men's activities and the inevitable unsettlement attending all human experience make it impossible for any act whatsoever to issue unqualified rules holding good on all questions at all times.
Plato, *427?–347 B.C.*
Politicus

72.40 Law, being a tyrant, compels many things to be done contrary to nature.
Plato
Protagoras, c.389 B.C.

72.41 Every law is the invention and gift of the gods.
Demosthenes, *385?–322 B.C.*
W. Gurney Benham, *Putnam's Complete Book of Quotations, Proverbs and Household Words,* 1927

72.42 Even when laws have been written down, they ought not always to remain unaltered.
Aristotle
Politics, c.322 B.C.

72.43 Good law means good order.
Aristotle
Politics, c.322 B.C.

72.44 Law is a pledge that citizens of a state will do justice to one another.
Aristotle
Politics, c.322 B.C.

72.45 The best laws should be constructed as to leave as little as possible to the decision of the judge.
Aristotle
Rhetoric, c.322 B.C.

72.46   The law is reason free from passion.
Aristotle,   *384–322 B.C.*
Laurence J. Peter, *Peter's Quotations*, 1977

72.47   Accept the law which you yourself make.
Cato
"Prologus," *Distichia,* c.175 B.C.

72.48   A people can be strong where the laws are strong.
Publilius Syrus, Latin writer,   *1st century B.C.*
W. Gurney Benham, *Putnam's Complete Book of Quotations, Proverbs and Household Words,* 1927

72.49   The universal law is that which ordains that we are to be born and to die.
Publilius Syrus, Latin writer,   *1st century B.C.*
W. Gurney Benham, *Putnam's Complete Book of Quotations, Proverbs and Household Words,* 1927

72.50   Law is the highest reason, implanted in Nature, which commands what ought to be done and forbids the opposite.
Cicero
De Legibus, 52 B.C.

72.51   The magistrate is a speaking law, but the law is a silent magistrate.
Cicero
De Legibus, 52 B.C.

72.52   The laws put the safety of all above the safety of one.
Cicero
De Finibus, c.50 B.C.

72.53   These laws being removed, the right appear wrong.
Cicero,   *106–43 B.C.*
W. Gurney Benham, *Putnam's Complete Book of Quotations, Proverbs and Household Words,* 1927

72.54   How rashly we sanction a law unfair to ourselves.
Horace
Satires, 35 B.C.

72.55   He gives laws to the peoples, and makes for himself a way to the heavens.
Virgil
Georgics, 30 B.C.

72.56   Time is the best interpreter of every doubtful law.
Dionysius of Halicarnassus
Antiquities of Rome, c.20 B.C.

72.57   No law perfectly suits the convenience of every member of the community; the only consideration is, whether upon the whole it be profitable to the greater part.
Livy
History of Rome, c.10 B.C.

72.58   Laws were made that the stronger might not in all things have his way.
Ovid
Fasti, c.8

72.59   The purpose of law is to prevent the strong always having their way.
Ovid
Fasti, c.8

72.60   Law has bread and butter in it.
Petronius
Satyricon, c.60

72.61   It is right that a law should be short in order that it may be the more easily grasped by the unlearned.
Seneca
Epistulae Morales ad Lucilium, 63–65

72.62   Some [laws] are good, some are middling, the most are bad.
Martial
Epigrams, 85

72.63   The prince is not above the laws, but the laws above the prince.
Pliny the Younger
Panegyricus Traianus, 100

72.64   As physicians are the preservers of the sick, so are the laws of the injured.
Epictetus
Encheiridion, c.110

72.65   Good men need no laws, and bad men are not made better by them.
Ascribed to Demonax of Cyprus,
Cynic philosopher,   *70–170*
H. L. Mencken, *A New Dictionary of Quotations*, 1946

72.66   Laws are spiders' webs, which stand firm when any light and yielding object falls upon them, while a larger thing breaks through them and escapes.
Solon
Diogenes Laërtius, *Lives of Eminent Philosophers*, 3rd Century

72.67   Good laws are produced by bad manners.
Macrobius, Latin writer and philosopher, fl. *c.400*
Saturnalia

72.68   The precepts of the law are these: to live honorably, to injure no other man, to render every man his due.
Justinian I
Institutes, c.533

72.69   The law is lordly.
William Langland
The Vision of William Concerning Piers the Plowman, c.1362–c.1390

72.70   Forthy [therefore] men seyn [say] ech contree hath his laws.
Chaucer
Troilus and Criseyde, c.1385

72.71   Do law away, what is a King?
Where is the right of any thing?
John Gower
Confessio Amantis, c.1390

72.72   And nowadays the law is ended as a man is friended.
Henry D. Brinklow
Henry Brinklow's Complaynt of Roderyck Mors, c.1542

72.73   It would be better to have no laws at all than it is to have so many as we have.
Michel de Montaigne
Essais, 1588

72.74   There is no one law governing all things.
Giordano Bruno
De Monade, numero, et figura, 1591

72.75   I have, perhaps, some shallow spirit of judgment;
But in these nice sharp quillets of the law,
Good faith, I am no wiser than a daw.
Shakespeare
1 *Henry VI*, II, 4, 1591–1592

72.76   Law, Logic and Switzers may be hired to fight for anybody.
Thomas Nashe
Christ's Tears, 1593

72.77   When law can do no right,
Let it be lawful that law bar no wrong.
Shakespeare
King John, III, 1, 1596–1597

72.78   Portia: The brain may devise laws for the blood;
but a hot temper leaps o'er a cold decree!
Shakespeare
The Merchant of Venice, I, 2, 1596–1597

72.79 There is no worse torture than the torture of laws.
Francis Bacon
"Of Judicature," *Essayes,* 1597

72.80 . . . old father antic the law?
Shakespeare
1 *Henry IV,* I, 2, 1597–1598

72.81 First Clown: Argal, he that is not guilty of his own death shortens not his own life.
Second Clown: But is this law?
First Clown: Ay, marry is't; crowner's quest law.
Shakespeare
Hamlet, V, 1, 1600–1601

72.82 Still you keep o' th' windy side of the law.
Shakespeare
Twelfth Night, III, 4, 1601–1602

72.83 The law hath not been dead, though it hath slept.
Shakespeare
Measure for Measure, II, 2, 1604–1605

72.84 Duke: The bloody book of law
You shall yourself read in the bitter letter
After your own sense.
Shakespeare
Othello, I, 3, 1604–1605

72.85 Some say men on the back of law
May ride and rule it like a patient ass,
And with a golden bridle in the mouth
Direct it into anything they please.
Nathaniel Field
A Woman Is a Weathercock, c.1610

72.86 The law is blind, and speaks in general terms.
Thomas May, English author
The Heir, c.1620

72.87 One of the Seven [wise men of Greece] was wont to say; That laws were like cobwebs, where the small flies were caught, and the great brake through.
Francis Bacon
Apophthagmes, 1625

72.88 The law obliges us to do what is proper, not simply what is just.
Hugo Grotius
De Jure Belli ac Pacis, 1625

72.89 Law is the safest helmet.
Sir Edward Coke
Inscription, on rings that he gave to friends, c.1630

72.90 The good needs fear no law,
It is his safety and the bad man's awe.
Phillip Massinger, *1583–1640*
The Old Law

72.91 Law is King.
Samuel Rutherford, Scottish clergyman
Lex Rex, 1644

72.92 Law is a pickpurse.
James Howell, Welsh writer
Familiar Letters, 1645–1655

72.93 Unnecessary laws are not good laws, but traps for money.
Thomas Hobbes
Leviathan, 1651

72.94 Ill Manners occasion Good laws, as the Handsome Children of Ugly Parents.
Thomas Fuller
The History of the University of Cambridge, 1655

72.95 Possession is nine points of the law.
Thomas Fuller, *1608–1661*
Holy War

72.96 So many Laws argue so many sins.
John Milton
Paradise Lost, 1667

72.97 Old laws have not been suffered to
be pointed,
To leave the sense at large the more
disjointed,
And furnish lawyers, with the greater
ease,
To turn and wind them any way they
please.
Samuel Butler, *1617–1680*
Miscellaneous Thoughts

72.98 No written laws can be so plain, so
pure,
But wit may gloss and malice may
obscure.
John Dryden
The Hind and the Panther, 1687

72.99 For in all the states of created beings, capable of laws, where there is
no law there is no freedom.
John Locke
Two Treatises on Civil Government,
1690

72.100 Shall free-born men, in humble
awe,
Submit to servile shame;
Who from consent and custom
draw
The same right to be ruled by law,
Which kings pretend to reign?
John Dryden, *1631–1700*
On the Young Statesman

72.101 All voice of nations and the course
of things
Allow that laws superior are to
kings.
Daniel Defoe
The True-Born Englishman, 1701

72.102 Laws are the sovereigns of sovereigns.
Louis XIV, *1638–1715*

72.103 The law of England is the greatest grievance of the nation, very ex-
pensive and dilatory.
Gilbert Burnet, Scottish bishop
History of My Own Times, 1723–1724

72.104 Where carcasses are, eagles will
gather,
And where good laws are, much
people flock thither.
Benjamin Franklin
Poor Richard's Almanack, 1734

72.105 Law [is] licensed breaking of the
peace.
Matthew Green, English poet
The Spleen, 1737

72.106 Laws too gentle are seldom
obeyed; too severe, seldom ex-
ecuted.
Benjamin Franklin
Poor Richard's Almanack, 1756

72.107 The law is a sort of hocus-pocus
science, that smiles in yer face while
it picks yer pocket.
Charles Macklin, English actor and
dramatist
Love à la Mode, 1759

72.108 Good laws lead to the making of
better ones; bad ones bring in
worse.
Jean-Jacques Rousseau
Du contrat social, 1762

72.109 Laws grind the poor, and rich
men rule the law.
Oliver Goldsmith
The Traveller, 1764

72.110 How small, of all that human hearts
endure,
That part which laws or kings can
cause or cure.
Oliver Goldsmith
The Traveller, 1764

72.111 Let all the laws be clear, uniform and precise; to interpret laws is almost always to corrupt them.
Voltaire
Philosophical Dictionary, 1764

72.112 What is the law, if those who make it
Become the forwardest to break it?
James Beattie
The Wolf and the Shepherds, 1776

72.113 The laws of a nation form the most instructive portion of its history. . . .
Edward Gibbon
The Decline and Fall of the Roman Empire, 1776

72.114 Bad laws are the worst sort of tyranny.
Edmund Burke
Speech at Bristol, 1780

72.115 Law is law—law is law; and as in such, and so forth, and hereby, and aforesaid, provided always, nevertheless, and notwithstanding. Law is like a country dance: people are led up and down it till they are tired. Law is like a book of surgery: there are a great many desperate cases in it. It is also like physic: they that take least of it are best off. Law is like a homely gentlewoman: very well to follow. Law is also like a scolding wife: very bad when it follows us. Law is like a new fashion: people are bewitched to get into it; it is also like bad weather: most people are glad when they get out of it.
George Stevenson, *?-1784*
Marshall Brown, *Wit and Humor of Bench and Bar,* 1899

72.116 The sober second thought of people shall be the law.
Fisher Ames, American politician
Congressional Speech, 1788

72.117 And sovereign Law, that State's collected will,
O'er thrones and globes elate,
Sits Empress, crowning good, repressing ill.
Sir William Jones, English Orientalist and jurist, *1746-1794*
Ode in Imitation of Alcaeus

72.118 Laws, like houses, lean on one another.
Edmund Burke, *1729-1797*
Tracts on the Popery Laws

72.119 . . . three things are always favoured in law—life, liberty and dower.
Dumsday v. Hughes (1803), 3 Bos. and Pull. 456

72.120 . . . but we find the law, as well as many other pursuits, requires much perseverance and patience to obtain the object; it is well for us that we do not always foresee the degree that it is necessary. . . .
Susannah Farnum Copley, American-English letter writer
Letter to her daughter, March 15, 1805

72.121 "That sounds like nonsense, my dear."
"Maybe so, my dear; but it may be very good law for all that."
Sir Walter Scott
Guy Mannering, 1815

72.122 The laws are with us and God is on our side.
Robert Southey
"Popular Disaffection," *Essays,* c.1820

72.123 Laws were made to be broken.
Christopher North (pseudonym of
John Wilson)
Noctes Ambrosianae, 1830

72.124 Law alone can give us freedom.
Goethe, *1749–1832*
W. Gurney Benham, *Putnam's Book
of Quotations, Proverbs and Household
Words,* 1927

72.125 Sancho: Me care for te laws when
te laws care for me.
Joanna Baillie, Scottish poet and
dramatist
The Alienated Manor, 1836

72.126 Law is whatever is boldly as-
serted and plausibly maintained.
Aaron Burr, *1756–1836*
Burton Stevenson, *Home Book of
Proverbs, Maxims and Familiar
Phrases,* 1948

72.127 Let reverence for the laws be
breathed by every American mother
to the lisping babe that prattles on
her lap; let it be taught in schools,
in seminaries, and in colleges; let it
be written in primers, spelling-
books, and in almanacs; let it be
preached from the pulpit, pro-
claimed in legislative halls, and enforced in courts of justice. And, in
short, let it become the political religion of the nation; and let the old
and the young, the rich and the
poor, the grave and the gay of all
sexes and tongues and colors and
conditions, sacrifice unceasingly
upon its altars.
Abraham Lincoln
Address before the Young Men's
Lyceum of Springfield, Illinois,
January 27, 1837

72.128 "If the law supposes that," said
Mr. Bumble, "the law is a ass, a
idiot."
Charles Dickens
Oliver Twist, 1838

72.129 Let a man keep the law,—any
law,—and his way will be strewn
with satisfaction.
Ralph Waldo Emerson
"Prudence," *Essays: First Series,* 1841

72.130 The mere repetition of the *Canti-
lena* [lyric melody] of the lawyers
cannot make it law.
Sir Thomas Denman, English jurist;
lord chief justice
O'Connell v. The Queen, September 4,
1844

72.131 Any laws but those we make for
ourselves are laughable.
Ralph Waldo Emerson
"Politics," *Essays: Second Series,* 1844

72.132 The law is only a memorandum.
Ralph Waldo Emerson
"Politics," *Essays: Second Series,* 1844

72.133 "Laws and principles are not for
the times when there is no temptation: they are for such moments as
this, when body and soul rise in
mutiny against their rigour; stringent are they; inviolate they shall
be. If at my individual convenience
I might break them, what would be
their worth?"
Charlotte Brontë
Jane Eyre, 1847

72.134 'T is best to make the Law our
friend.
Emma Hart Willard
Harry Guy, 1848

72.135 Law never made men a whit
more just.
Henry David Thoreau
Civil Disobedience, 1849

72.136   The law is for the protection of the weak more than the strong.
Sir William Erle, English jurist; chief justice
Reg. v. Woolley (1850), 4 Cox, C.C. 196

72.137   Ring out a slowly dying cause,
And ancient forms of party strife;
Ring in the nobler modes of life,
With sweeter manners, purer laws.
Tennyson
In Memoriam, 1850

72.138   The best use of good laws is to teach men to trample bad laws under their feet.
Wendell Phillips
Speech, April 12, 1852

72.139   "The law will admit of no rival. . . ." but I will say, that it is a jealous mistress, and requires a long and constant courtship. It is not to be won by trifling favors, but by lavish homage.
Joseph Story
The Miscellaneous Writings of Joseph Story, 1852

72.140   Are laws to be enforced simply because they were made?
Henry David Thoreau
John Brown's Body, 1859

72.141   To make laws that man cannot, and will not obey, serves to bring all law into contempt.
Elizabeth Cady Stanton
Address, 1861

72.142   Law is not a science, but is essentially empirical.
Oliver Wendell Holmes
"Codes, and the Arrangement of the Law," 5 *American Law Review* 1 (1870)

72.143   Laws are like medicines: they usually cure the disease only by setting up another that is lesser or more transient.
Otto von Bismarck
Speech in the Prussian Upper House, March 6, 1872

72.144   All law has for its object to confirm and exalt into a system the exploitation of the workers by a ruling class.
Mikhail Bakunin, *1814–1876*
Kenneth Redden, *Modern Legal Glossary,* 1983

72.145   Men would be great criminals did they need as many laws as they make.
Charles John Darling, 1st baron, English jurist
Scintillae Juris, 1877

72.146   Law is an alliance of those who have farsight and insight against the shortsighted.
Rudolf von Jhering, German jurist
Der Zweck im Recht, 1877

72.147   The life of the law has not been logic; it has been experience.
Oliver Wendell Holmes
The Common Law, 1881

72.148   The standards of the law are standards of general application. The law takes no account of the infinite varieties of temperament, intellect, and education which make the internal character of a given act so different in different men. It does not attempt to see men as God sees them. . . .
Oliver Wendell Holmes
The Common Law, 1881

72.149   God's blood! is law for man's sake made, or man

For law's sake only, to be held in bonds?
Algernon Charles Swinburne
Mary Stuart, 1881

72.150   . . . we must not be guilty of taking the law into our own hands, and converting it from what it really is to what we think it ought to be.
John Duke Coleridge, English jurist; lord chief justice, *1820–1894*
Regina v. Ramsey (1883), 1 C. & E. 126, 136

72.151   Around the ancient track marched, rank on rank,
The army of unalterable law.
George Meredith
Lucifer in Starlight, 1883

72.152   Now the law steps in, bigwigg'd, voluminous-jaw'd.
Charles Stuart Calverley, English writer, *1831–1884*
The Cock and the Bull

72.153   Laws only bind when they are in accordance with right reason, and hence with the eternal law of God.
Leo XIII, Pope
Rerum Novarum, 1891

72.154   To take Macaulay's instance, it is against the law for an apple-woman to stop up the street with her cart; it is not against the law for a miser to allow the benefactor to whom he owes his whole success to die in the poorhouse.
John Chipman Gray, American lawyer, *1839–1915*
"Some Definitions and Questions in Jurisprudence," 6 *Harvard Law Review* 21 (1893)

72.155   The attempt to guard adult man by law is a bad education for the battle of life.
William Edward Hartpole Lecky, British historian, *1838–1903*
Democracy and Liberty

72.156   No man has yet been hanged for breaking the spirit of the law.
Grover Cleveland, *1837–1908*

72.157   *Law:* Simply a matter of the length of the judge's ears.
Elbert Hubbard
Book of Epigrams, 1910

72.158   The Law! It is the arch-crime of the centuries. The path of Man is soaked with the blood it has shed. Can this great criminal determine Right? Is a revolutionist to respect such a travesty? It would mean the perpetuation of human slavery.
Alexander Berkman, Russian anarchist, *1870?–1936*
Prison Memoirs of an Anarchist, 1912

72.159   When I am sick, then I believe in law.
Anna Wickham, English poet
"Self-Analysis," *The Contemplative Quarry,* 1915

72.160   . . . no great idea in its beginning can ever be within the law. How can it be within the law? The law is stationary. The law is fixed. The law is a chariot wheel which binds us all regardless of conditions or place or time.
Emma Goldman
"Address to the Jury," *Mother Earth,* July 1917

72.161   One with the law is a majority.
Calvin Coolidge
Speech, July 27, 1920

72.162 It is perfectly proper to regard and study the law simply as a great anthropological document.
Oliver Wendell Holmes
"Law in Science and Science in Law," *Collected Legal Papers,* 1921

72.163 Law must be stable, and yet it cannot stand still.
Roscoe Pound
Introduction to the Philosophy of Law, 1922

72.164 Marriage, laws, the police, armies and navies are the mark of human incompetence.
Dora Russell, English writer
The Right to Be Happy, 1927

72.165 Law does not mean then whatever people usually do, or even what they think to be right. Certainly it does not mean what only the most enlightened individuals usually do or think right. It is the conduct which the government, whether it is a king, or a popular assembly, will compel individuals to conform to. . . .
Learned Hand
Radio address, May 14, 1933

72.166 . . . the law is not the place for the artist or the poet. The law is the calling of thinkers.
Oliver Wendell Holmes
"The Profession of the Law," *Speeches,* 1934

72.167 We must not read either law or history backwards.
Helen M. Cam, English historian
H. D. Hazeltine, G. Gapsley, and P. H. Winfield, eds., Introduction, *Selected Essays of F. W. Maitland,* 1936

72.168 Leave to live by no man's leave, underneath the Law. . . .
Rudyard Kipling, *1865–1936*
"The Old Issue"

72.169 When there is such a degree of probability as to lead to a reasonable assurance that a given conclusion ought to be and will be reduced to a judgment, we speak of that conclusion as the law.
Benjamin N. Cardozo, *1870–1938*
Kenneth Redden, *Modern Legal Glossary,* 1983

72.170 Yet law-abiding scholars write:
Law is neither wrong or right,
Law is only crimes
Punished by places and by times. . . .
W. H. Auden
"Law Like Love," 1939

72.171 It would be a narrow conception of jurisprudence to confine the notion of "laws" to what is found written on the statute books.
Felix Frankfurter
Nashville, Chattanooga and St. Louis Railway v. Browning, 310 U.S. 362, 369 (1940)

72.172 Law as it exists in the modern community may be conveniently, although perhaps not comprehensively, defined as the sum total of all those rules of conduct for which there is state sanction.
Harlan Fiske Stone, *1872–1946*
Kenneth Redden, *Modern Legal Glossary,* 1983

72.173 A man is allowed by law to be a fool, if he likes.
Arthur Lehmann Goodhart
Five Jewish Lawyers of the Common Law, 1949

72.174 A law is something which must have a moral basis, so that there is an inner compelling force for every citizen to obey.
Chaim Weizmann
Trial and Error, 1949

72.175 Law offers a guiding thread to us . . . one of purpose—and a purpose infinitely worthwhile, for in the long view it is more important that human beings should learn to get on with each other than that they should be more comfortable materially and safer physically.
Helen M. Cam, English historian
Lecture, "Law as It Looks to a Historian," Girton College, February 18, 1956

72.176 The law's final justification is in the good it does or fails to do the society of a given place and time.
Albert Camus, *1913–1960*
Laurence J. Peter, *Peter's Quotations,* 1977

72.177 Law is experience developed by reason and applied continually to further experience.
Roscoe Pound
Christian Science Monitor, April 24, 1963

72.178 Certain other societies may respect the rule of force—we respect the rule of law.
John F. Kennedy
New York Times, May 19, 1963

72.179 [Law] liberates the desire to build and subdues the desire to destroy. And if war can tear us apart, law can unite us—out of fear, or love, or reason, or all three. Law is the greatest human invention. All the rest give man mastery over his world. Law gives him mastery over himself.
Lyndon B. Johnson
Time, September 24, 1965

72.180 It is the capacity to command free assent that makes law a substitute for power. The force of legitimacy—and conversely the habit of voluntary compliance—is the foundation of the law's civilizing and liberalizing influence. Indeed . . . law in this sense is the very fabric of a free society. There is no alternative short of the millennium.
Archibald Cox, Mark De Wolfe Howe, and J. R. Wiggins
Civil Rights, the Constitution, and the Courts, 1967

72.181 One can always legislate against specific acts of human wickedness: but one can never legislate against the irrational itself.
Morton Irving Seiden, American educator; professor, Brooklyn College
A Paradox of Hate: A Study in Ritual Murder, 1967

72.182 If there isn't a law there will be.
Harold Farber
New York Times Magazine, March 17, 1968

72.183 Law is the backbone which keeps man erect.
S. C. Yuter
Bulletin of Atomic Scientists, October 1969

72.184 You have to have respect for the law. But you can't respect the law when the law is not respectable.
Ramsey Clark
Before the Senate Judiciary Committee, November 5, 1969

72.185   An Irish attorney was making the best of a rather shaky case when the judge interrupted him on a point of law. "Surely," he asked, "your clients are aware of the doctrine *de minimis non curat lex*?" "I assure you, my lord," came the suave reply, "that, in the remote and inhospitable hamlet where my clients have their humble abode, it forms the sole topic of conversation."
Walter Bryan
The Improbable Irish, 1969

72.186   I know the law. It is used to oppress those who threaten the ruling class. The judicial decree has replaced the assassin. . . . I stay with the law only because the law is maneuverable, it can be manipulated.
William M. Kunstler
Human Events, February 12, 1972

72.187   It's a terrible American weakness to believe that if you've got a problem all you have to do is pass a law. It may be important to pass the law and observe it; but even more important in the long run is the active concern of the private citizen for the values involved.
Kingman Brewster, Jr.
Dallas Times-Herald, June 15, 1972

72.188   The law is above the law, you know.
Dorothy Salisbury Davis, American writer
The Little Brothers, 1973

72.189   The contempt for law and the contempt for the human consequences of lawbreaking go from the bottom to the top of American society.
Margaret Mead
Claire Safran, "Impeachment?"
Redbook, April 1974

72.190   The law can never make us as secure as we are when we do not need it.
Alexander M. Bickel
The Morality of Consent, 1975

72.191   Law is not everything in society. . . . The public, the press, the academic community, the artists, all by their assertions and conduct inform and develop the law.
Edward H. Levi
Los Angeles Times, May 23, 1975

72.192   . . . I cannot accept the idea of law as merely repressive or punitive. It can be expressive and conducive to the development of social values.
June L. Tapp, American psychologist
Gordon Berman, "The Notion of Conspiracy Is Not Tasty to Americans," *Psychology Today,* May 1975

72.193   Unnecessary laws are bad laws, if for no other reason than they substitute legal coercion for freedom of choice.
Thomas A. Murphy, American business executive; chairman, General Motors Corporation
New York Times, January 31, 1976

72.194   The law has to encourage a kind of reasoning together. That is going to be hard for some people who don't regard the law as a reasoning device. They say use it as a weapon and go as far as you can.
Edward H. Levi
Time, December 20, 1976

72.195   Fidelity to the public requires that the laws be as plain and explicit as possible, that the less knowing may understand, and not be ensnared by them, while the artful evade their force.

Samuel Cooke
Laurence J. Peter, *Peter's Quotations,*
1977

72.196   Laws that are not enforced . . . are bad laws.

Lionel J. Castillo, American
government official; commissioner,
U.S. Immigration & Naturalization
Service
Los Angeles Herald Examiner, March
24, 1978

72.197   We've lost sight of the basic purpose of criminal law, which is to protect our fundamental rights. We look at criminal law as something that interferes with our freedom and imposes onerous duties on us, whereas the true way of looking at criminal law is as the protection of our rights to life, liberty, the security of our person and the security of our property.

Macklin Fleming, American jurist;
judge, U.S. Courts of Appeals
San Francisco Examiner & Chronicle,
July 30, 1978

72.198   Your lordships will be glad to hear that I shall present a point of law uncorrupted by any merits.

Patrick Devlin
The Judge, 1979

72.199   America is a nation of laws. . . . The law is not always an easy friend, because the law does not play favorites. But for those who seek justice in a society of responsible citizens, the law will always be an ally.

Edward I. Koch
Los Angeles Times, September 8, 1981

72.200   Lawyering is within the relatively narrow category of occupations where borderline dishonesty is fairly lucrative. In many instances, the very art of the lawyer is a sort of calculated disregard of the law or at least of ordinary notions of morality.

Eric Schnapper
Kenneth Redden, *Modern Legal
Glossary,* 1983

73. LAW AND ORDER

73.1   Fish die when they are out of water, and people die without law and order.

Talmud, *Avoda zara*

73.2   Law is a form of order, and good law must necessarily mean good order.

Aristotle
Politics, c.322 B.C.

73.3   I am of his mind that said, "Better it is to live where nothing is lawful, than where all things are lawful."
Francis Bacon
Apophthagmes, 1625

73.4   Revolt and terror pay a price. Order and law have a cost.
Carl Sandburg
The People, Yes!, 1936

73.5   Our defense is not in armaments, nor in science, nor in going underground. Our defense is in law and order.
Albert Einstein
"The Real Problem Is in the Hearts of Men," *New York Times Magazine,* June 23, 1946

73.6   In the whole history of law and order the longest step forward was taken by primitive man when, as if by common consent, the tribe sat down in a circle and allowed only one man to speak at a time.
Derek Curtis Bok, American educator
"If We Are to Act Like Free Men . . .," *Saturday Review,* February 13, 1954

73.7   The image created by the beatniks and by most of their predecessors back to the 19th century bohemians has led us to suppose that people of high originality are somehow lawless. But the truly creative man is not an outlaw but a lawmaker. Every great creative performance since the initial one has been in some measure a bringing of order out of chaos.
John W. Gardner
"Thoughts," *Think,* May–June, 1966

73.8   A man's respect for law and order exists in precise relationship to the size of his paycheck.
Adam Clayton Powell, Jr.
Keep the Faith, Baby! 1967

74. LAW ENFORCEMENT

74.1   It is not the thief who is hanged, but one who was caught stealing.
Czech proverb
H. L. Mencken, *A New Dictionary of Quotations,* 1946

74.2   Highest law, highest cross.
Latin phrase
W. Gurney Benham, *Putnam's Complete Book of Quotations, Proverbs and Household Words,* 1927

74.3   Fear is the beadle of the law.
Proverb
Thomas Fuller, *Gnomologia,* 1732

74.4   Laws can never be enforced unless fear supports them.
Sophocles
Ajax, c.450 B.C.

74.5 Nobody has a more sacred obligation to obey the law than those who make the law.
Sophocles, *496?–406 B.C.*
Laurence J. Peter, *Peter's Quotations,* 1977

74.6 If human society cannot be carried on without lawsuits, it cannot be carried on without penalties.
Aristotle, *384–322 B.C.*
W. H. Auden and Louis Kronenberger, *The Viking Book of Aphorisms,* 1962

74.7 A law observed is merely Law;
broken, it is law and executioner.
Menander
Fragments, c.300 B.C.

74.8 It becometh a law-maker not to be a law-breaker.
Francis Meres, English divine and author
Nicholas Ling, *Politeuphuia,* 1597

74.9 Let him have all the rigour of the law.
Shakespeare
2 Henry VI, I, 3, 1589–1591

74.10 It is the crime which makes the shame and not the scaffold.
Corneille
Comte de Essex, c.1650

74.11 When justice on offenders is not done,
Law, government, and commerce are o'erthrown.
Sir John Denham, English poet
Of Justice, c.1668

74.12 Xenophanes being jeered for refusing to play a forbidden game, answered. . . . "They that make laws, must keep them."
William Penn
No Cross, No Crown, 1669

74.13 The first intent of laws
Was to correct the effect, and check the cause,
And all the ends of punishment
Were only future mischiefs to prevent.
But justice intervened, when
Those engines of the law,
Instead of pinching vicious men,
Keep honest ones in awe.
Daniel Defoe
Hymn to the Pillory, 1703

74.14 . . . the *Law* shows her teeth, but dares not bite.
Edward Young, English poet,
1683–1765
Love of Fame, 1725

74.15 The atrocity of the laws prevents their execution.
de Montesquieu, *1689–1755*
W. Gurney Benham, *Putnam's Complete Book of Quotations, Proverbs and Household Words,* 1927

74.16 What is law, if those who make it Become the forwardest to break it?
James Beattie
The Wolf and the Shepherds, 1776

74.17 No man e'er felt the halter draw With good opinion of the law.
John Trumbull, American poet and jurist
M' Fingal, 1782

74.18 The execution of the laws is more important than the making of them.
Thomas Jefferson
Letter to the Abbé Arnond, 1789

74.19 He who holds no laws in awe,
He must perish by the law.
Lord Byron
"A Very Mournful Ballad on the Siege and Conquest of Alhambra,"
c.1810

74.20   Laws exist in vain for those who have not the courage and the means to defend them.
Thomas Babington Macaulay
"Burleigh and His Times," *Edinburgh Review*, April 1832

74.21   A lidless watcher of the public weal.
Tennyson
The Princess, 1847

74.22   To render a people obedient and keep them so, savage laws inefficiently enforced are less effective than mild laws enforced by an efficient administration regularly, automatically, as it were, every day and on all alike.
Alexis de Tocqueville, *1805–1859*
W. H. Auden and Louis Kronenberger, *The Viking Book of Aphorisms*, 1962

74.23   I know no method to secure the repeal of bad or obnoxious laws so effective as their stringent execution.
Ulysses S. Grant
Inaugural address, March 4, 1869

74.24   A citizen of the United States . . . is not bound to cringe to any superior, or to pray for any act of grace, as a means of enjoying all the rights and privileges enjoyed by other citizens. And when the spirit of lawlessness, mob violence, and sectional hate can be so completely repressed as to give full practical effect to this right, we shall be a happier nation, and a more prosperous one than we now are.
Joseph P. Bradley
Slaughter-House Cases, 83 U.S. (16 Wall.) 36, 112-13 (1872)

74.25   A crowded police court docket is the surest of all signs that trade is brisk and money plenty.
Mark Twain
Roughing It, 1872

74.26   After all, the eleventh commandment (thou shalt not be found out) is the only one that is virtually impossible to keep in these days.
Bertha Buxton, English writer
Jenny of the Princes, 1879

74.27   Ah, take one consideration with another
A policeman's lot is not a happy one.
W. S. Gilbert
The Pirates of Penzance, 1879

74.28   We enact many laws that manufacture criminals, and then a few that punish them.
Benjamin R. Tucker, American journalist and anarchist
Instead of a Book, 1893

74.29   The speedy arm of justice was never known to fail;
The gaol supplied the gallows, the gallows thinned the gaol,
And sundry wise precautions the sages of the law
Discreetly framed whereby they aimed to keep the rogues in awe.
John W. Smith
Selection of Leading Cases on Various Branches of the Law, 1896

74.30   Enormous offences call for a greater axe.
Sir Frederick Pollock, English jurist
The Expansion of the Common Law, 1904

74.31   Crime is contagious. If the Government becomes a lawbreaker, it breeds contempt for law; it invites

every man to become a law unto himself; it invites anarchy.
Louis D. Brandeis
Olmstead v. United States, 277 U.S. 438 (1928)

74.32   There's a lot of law at the end of a nightstick.
Grover Whalen, American law enforcement official; police commissioner, New York City, *1928–1930*
M. Francis McNamara, *2000 Famous Legal Quotations,* 1967

74.33   Criminals do not die by the hands of the law. They die by the hands of other men.
George Bernard Shaw, *1856–1950*
W. H. Auden and Louis Kronenberger, *The Viking Book of Aphorisms,* 1962

74.34   He didn't know the right people. That's all a police record means.
Raymond Chandler, *1888–1959*
Laurence J. Peter, *Peter's Quotations,* 1977

74.35   One reason for our high crime rate is that the long arm of the law is often shorthanded.
Hal Chadwick
Reader's Digest, March 1960

74.36   . . . coercion can be mental as well as physical, and . . . the blood of the accused is not the only hallmark of an unconstitutional inquisition.
Blackburn v. Alabama, 361 U.S. 199 (1960)

74.37   In the age of modern advanced technology, when the criminal can avail himself of every new invention, law-enforcement officers are denied even the simplest of electronic devices, even though they will be under the supervision of the Courts.

The result is like asking a champion boxer to fight a gorilla and insisting that the boxer abide by the Marquis of Queensbury Rules, while the gorilla is limited only by the law of the jungle.
Miles F. McDonald, American lawyer
"Law Enforcement—Have We Gone Too Far in Protecting the Accused?"
39 *New York State Bar Journal* 5 (October 1967)

74.38   America is waiting for an Attorney General who will enforce the law— and a President with the courage to demand that he do so.
Phyllis Schlafly
Safe—Not Sorry, 1967

74.39   The seeming anxiety of judges to protect every accused person from every consequence of his voluntary utterances is giving rise to myriad rules, subrules, variations and exceptions which even the most alert and sophisticated lawyers and judges are taxed to follow. Each time the judges add nuances to these rules, we make it less likely that any police officer will be able to follow the guidelines we lay down.
Warren E. Burger
Speech, reported in the *Washington Post,* June 2, 1969

74.40   If law is not made more than a policeman's nightstick, American society will be destroyed.
Arthur Goldberg
Speech, reported in the *New York Times,* June 22, 1969

74.41   Years ago, despairing citizens used to say, "There oughta be a law." There is a law. There are lots of laws. What there oughta be is severe—and equal—enforcement of the laws. In one area after another of our public

life we are seeing a reversion to that frontier phenomenon—citizens taking the law into their own hands, not to enforce it themselves, but to force the official enforcers to enforce it.
Eric Sevareid
"CBS Evening News," April 3, 1972

74.42 Who will protect the public when the police violate the law?
Ramsey Clark
Laurence J. Peter, *Peter's Quotations,* 1977

74.43 This won't be the first time I've arrested somebody and then built my case afterward.
James Garrison, district attorney, New Orleans
Laurence J. Peter, *Peter's Quotations,* 1977

74.44 I'm not *against* the police; I'm just afraid of them.
Alfred Hitchcock
Laurence J. Peter, *Peter's Quotations,* 1977

74.45 What society fails to realize is that the tension between the police and the judiciary has always been fundamental to our constitutional system. It is intentional and constitutes the real difference between a free society and a police state.
Nicholas Katzenbach
Laurence J. Peter, *Peter's Quotations,* 1977

74.46 Laws not enforced cease to be laws, and rights not defended may wither away.
Thomas E. Moriarty, American educator
Laurence J. Peter, *Peter's Quotations,* 1977

74.47 Reading isn't an occupation we encourage among police officers. We try to keep paper work down to a minimum.
Joe Orton, English playwright
Laurence J. Peter, *Peter's Quotations,* 1977

74.48 If police efficiency were an end in itself, the police would be free to put an accused on the rack. Police efficiency must yield to constitutional rights.
John Minor Wisdom, American jurist
Laurence J. Peter, *Peter's Quotations,* 1977

74.49 It is not better that all felony suspects die than that they escape. Where the suspect poses no immediate threat to the officer and none to others, the harm resulting from failure to apprehend him does not justify the use of deadly force to do so.
Byron R. White
Tennessee v. Garner, U.S. Supreme Court decision, March 27, 1985

75. LAWYERS

75.1   A lawyer must first get on, then get honor, then get honest.
Anonymous
H. L. Mencken, *A New Dictionary of Quotations,* 1946

75.2   The animals are not so stupid as is thought: they have no lawyers.
Anonymous
H. L. Mencken, *A New Dictionary of Quotations,* 1946

75.3   You can always tell a barber
By the way he parts his hair;
You can always tell a dentist
When you're in the dentist's chair;
And even a musician—
You can tell him by his touch;
You can always tell a lawyer,
But you cannot tell him much.
Anonymous
Jacob M. Braude, *Lifetime Speaker's Encyclopedia,* 1962

75.4   Who taught me first to litigate,
My neighbor and my brother hate,
And my own rights overrate?
It was my lawyer.
Anonymous
Jacob M. Braude, *Lifetime Speaker's Encyclopedia,* 1962

75.5   Now, then, all ye black guards that isn't lawyers, out ye go!
Crier at Ballinloe when ordered to clear the court by the judge

75.6   God save us from a lawyer's et cetera.
French proverb
H. L. Mencken, *A New Dictionary of Quotations,* 1946

75.7   Only painters and lawyers can change white to black.
Japanese proverb
Louis Levinson, *Bartlett's Unfamiliar Quotations,* 1971

75.8   Every business has its own best season. That is why they say June is the best month of the year for preachers. Lawyers have the other eleven.
Popular saying

75.9   It is hard to say whether the doctors of law or divinity have made the greater advances in the lucrative business of mystery.
Popular saying

75.10   Lawyers: Persons who write a 10,000 word document and call it a brief.
Popular saying

75.11   There are two kinds of lawyers: those who know the law and those who know the judge.
Popular saying

75.12　　There's no better way of exercising the imagination than the study of law.
Popular saying

75.13　　A good lawyer, an evil neighbor.
Proverb
Rosalind Fergusson, *The Facts On File Dictionary of Proverbs,* 1983

75.14　　A good lawyer must be a great liar.
Proverb
Rosalind Fergusson, *The Facts On File Dictionary of Proverbs,* 1983

75.15　　Kick an attorney downstairs and he'll stick to you for life.
Proverb
Rosalind Fergusson, *The Facts On File Dictionary of Proverbs,* 1983

75.16　　Two attorneys can live in a town, when one cannot.
Proverb
Rosalind Fergusson, *The Facts On File Dictionary of Proverbs,* 1983

75.17　　Go not for every grief to the physician, nor for every quarrel to the lawyer, nor for every thirst to the pot.
Proverb
George Herbert, *Outlandish Proverbs,* 1639

75.18　　A peasant between two lawyers is like a fish between two cats.
Spanish proverb
H. L. Menceka, *A New Dictionary of Quotations,* 1946

75.19　　Hide nothing from thy minister, physician, and lawyer.
Scottish or English proverb
John Ray, *Compleat Collection of English Proverbs,* 1670

75.20　　It's an ill cause that the lawyer thinks shame o'.
Scottish proverb
H. L. Mencken, *A New Dictionary of Quotations,* 1946

75.21　　. . . the Pharisees and lawyers rejected the counsel of God. . . .
New Testament, *Luke* 7:30

75.22　　And he said, Woe unto you also, ye lawyers! for ye lade men with burdens grievous to be borne, and ye yourselves touch not the burdens with one of your fingers.
New Testament: *Luke* 11:46

75.23　　Woe unto you, lawyers! for ye have taken away the key of knowledge: ye entered not in yourselves, and them that were entering in ye hindered.
New Testament, *Luke* 11:52

75.24　　The lawyer is always in a hurry.
Plato
Theaetetus, c.360 B.C.

75.25　　For the house of a great lawyer is assuredly the oracular seat of the whole community.
Cicero
De Oratore, 55 B.C.

75.26　　Ulysses was not beautiful, but he was eloquent.
Ovid
Ars Armatoria, c.1 B.C.

75.27　　He lets out to hire his anger and words.
Seneca,　*4 B.C.?–A.D. 65*
Hercules Furens

75.28　　A serjeant of the law, wary and wise, There was also, full rich of excellence,
Discreet he was, and of great reverence.
Chaucer
Prologue, *The Canterbury Tales,* c.1380

75.29 [The serjeant of the law.] He rode
but homely in a medley coat.
Chaucer
Prologue, *The Canterbury Tales,*
c.1380

75.30 Such poor folk as to law do go are
driven oft to curse:
But in mean while, the Lawyer
thrives,
the money in his purse.
Isabella Whitney, English poet
"The 104. Flower," *A Sweet Nosegay
or Pleasant Posye Containing a
Hundred and Ten Phylosophicall
Flowers,* 1573

75.31 For lawyers and their pleading,
They 'steem it not a straw;
They think that honest meaning
Is of itself a law.
William Byrd, English composer
"The Herdman's Happy Life,"
*Sonnets and Songs of Sadness and
Pietie, made into musicke of five
parties,* 1588

75.32 The first thing we do, let's kill all
the lawyers.
Shakespeare
2 *King Henry VI,* IV, 2, 1589–1591

75.33 Duch: Why should calamity be full
of words?
Q. Eliz: Windy attorneys to their cli-
ent woes,
Airy succeeders of intestate joys,
Poor breathing orators of miseries,
Let them have scope! though what
they will impart
Help nothing else, yet do they ease
the heart.
Shakespeare
Richard III, IV, 4, 1592–1593

75.34 Isabella: O perilous mouths,
That bear in them one and the self-
same tongue,
Either of condemnation or aproof!

Bidding the law make court'sy to
their will,
Hooking both right and wrong to the
appetite,
To follow as it draws.
Shakespeare
Measure for Measure, III, 4,
1604–1605

75.35 Few lawyers die well,
few physicians live well.
William Camden
Remains, 1605

75.36 I oft have heard him say how he ad-
mir'd
Men of your large profession, that
could speak
To every cause, and things mere con-
traries,
Till they were hoarse again, yet all be
law.
Ben Jonson
Volpone, 1605

75.37 He who loves the law dies either
mad or poor.
Thomas Middleton
The Phoenix, c.1607

75.38 Our wrangling lawyers . . . are so
litigious and busy here on earth, that
I think they will plead their clients'
causes hereafter, some of them in
hell.
Robert Burton
The Anatomy of Melancholy, 1621

75.39 He that with injury is grieved
And goes to law to be relieved,
Is sillier than a scottish chouse*
Who, when a thief has robbed his
house,
Applies himself to cunning men
To help him to his goods again.
Samuel Butler
Hudibras, 1663–1678

*Dupe

75.40   Lawyers, of whose art the basis
        Is raising feuds and splitting cases.
        Samuel Butler
        Hudibras, 1663–1678

75.41   With books and money placed for
        show
        Like nest-eggs to make clients lay,
        And for his false opinion pay.
        Samuel Butler
        Hudibras, 1663–1678

75.42   These [the lawyers] are the mounte-
        banks of
        the State,
        Who by the sleight of tongues can
        crimes create.
        Daniel Defoe
        Hymn to the Pillory, 1703

75.43   . . . very many men among us were
        bred up from their youth in the art of
        proving by words multiplied for the
        purpose that white is black, and
        black is white, according as they are
        paid.
        Jonathan Swift
        Gulliver's Travels, 1726

75.44   The toils of law, What dark and in-
        sidious men
        Have cumbrous added to perplex the
        truth,
        And lengthen simple justice into
        trade.
        James Thomson
        "Winter," *The Seasons,* 1726

75.45   These ensnare the wretched in the
        toils of law,
        Fomenting discord, and perplexing
        right,
        An iron race!
        James Thomson
        "Autumn," *The Seasons,* 1730

75.46   I know you lawyers can, with ease,
        Twist words and meanings as you
        please;

That language, by your skill made
pliant,
Will bend to favour every client;
That 'tis the fee directs the sense
To make out either side's pretence.
        John Gay, *1685–1732*
        William Andrews, *The Lawyer in
        History, Literature and Humour,* 1896

75.47   Lawyers, preachers, and tomtit's
        eggs, there are more of them hatched
        than come to perfection.
        Benjamin Franklin
        Poor Richard's Almanack, 1734

75.48   Necessity knows no law; I know
        some attorneys of the same.
        Benjamin Franklin
        Poor Richard's Almanack, 1734

75.49   Who studies ancient laws and rites,
        Tongues, arts and arms, and history,
        Must drudge, like Selden, days and
        nights,
        And in the endless labour die.
        Richard Bentley, *1662–1742*
        Who Strives to Mount Parnassus' Hill

75.50   Lawyers are always more ready to
        get a man into troubles than out of
        them.
        Oliver Goldsmith
        The Good-Natur'd Man, 1768

75.51   Boswell: But, Sir, does not affect-
        ing a warmth when you have no
        warmth, and appearing to be clearly
        of one opinion when you are in real-
        ity of another opinion, does not such
        dissimulation impair [a lawyer's]
        honesty? . . .
        Johnson: Why no, Sir. Everybody
        knows you are paid for affecting
        warmth for your client; and it is,
        therefore, properly no dissimulation:
        the moment you come from the bar,
        you resume your usual behaviour.
        Sir, a man will no more carry the ar-
        tifice of the bar into the common in-

tercourse of society, than a man who is paid for tumbling upon his hands will continue to tumble upon his hands when he should walk on his feet.

James Boswell
The Life of Samuel Johnson, 1791

75.52 ". . . he did not care to speak ill of any man behind his back, but he believed the gentleman was an attorney."

Samuel Johnson
James Boswell, *The Life of Samuel Johnson,* 1791

75.53 Then, shifting his side (as a lawyer knows how). . . .

William Cowper, *1731–1800*
The Report of an Adjudged Case

75.54 It would (to use a Yankee phrase) *puzzle a dozen Philadelphia lawyers* to unriddle the conduct of the democrats.

Anonymous
The Balance, November 15, 1803

75.55 Who calls a lawyer rogue, may find, too late,
On one of these depends his whole estate.

George Crabbe
"The Gentleman Farmer," *Tales,* 1812

75.56 I think we may class lawyers in the natural history of monsters.

John Keats, *1795–1821*
Kenneth Redden, *Modern Legal Glossary,* 1983

75.57 The New England folks have a saying that three Philadelphia lawyers are a match for the very devil himself.

Anonymous
Salem Observer, March 13, 1824

75.58 The end aim of a lawyer is duplex, first, to know, and second to appear to know—the latter brings clients and the former holds them.

Roger North, English lawyer
On the Study of Laws, 1824

75.59 It's the trade of lawyers to question everything, yield nothing, and to talk by the hour.

Thomas Jefferson, *1743–1826*
Louis Levinson, *Bartlett's Unfamiliar Quotations,* 1971

75.60 He is no lawyer who cannot take two sides.

Charles Lamb, *1775–1834*

75.61 Lawyers, I suppose, were children once.

Charles Lamb, *1775–1834*
W. H. Auden and Louis Kronenberger, *The Viking Book of Aphorisms,* 1962

75.62 He saw a lawyer killing a viper
On a dunghill hard by his own stable;
And the Devil smiled, for it put him in mind
Of Cain and his brother Abel.

Samuel Taylor Coleridge
The Devil's Thoughts, c.1834

75.63 . . . I cannot believe that a republic could subsist at the present time if the influence of lawyers in public business did not increase in proportion to the power of the people.

Alexis de Tocqueville
Democracy in America, 1835–1840

75.64 In America there are no nobles or literary men, and the people are apt to mistrust the wealthy; lawyers consequently form the highest political class and the most cultivated portion of society. . . . If I were asked where

I place the American aristocracy, I should reply without hesitation that . . . it occupies the judicial bench and the bar.

Alexis de Tocqueville
Democracy in America, 1835–1840

75.65   The more that we reflect upon all that occurs in the United States the more we shall be persuaded that the lawyers as a body form the most powerful, if not the only, counterpoise to the democratic element.

Alexis de Tocqueville
Democracy in America, 1835–1840

75.66   After twenty-five years' observation, I can give it as the condensed history of most, if not all, good lawyers, that they lived well and died poor.

Daniel Webster
Address, Charleston, South Carolina, Bar, May 10, 1847

75.67   An eminent lawyer cannot be a dishonest man.

Daniel Webster
Address, Charleston, South Carolina, Bar, May 10, 1847

75.68   And through the heat of conflict keeps the law
In calmness made.

William Wordsworth, *1770–1850*
"Character of the Happy Lawyer"

75.69   Self-defense is the clearest of all laws; and for this reason—the lawyers didn't make it.

Douglas Jerrold, English humorist and playwright, *1803–1851*
Marshall Brown, *Wit and Humor of Bench and Bar,* 1899

75.70   The sharp employ the sharp; verily, a man may be known by his attorney.

Douglas Jerrold, English humorist and playwright, *1803–1851*

75.71   Who's a great lawyer? He, who aims to say
The least his cause requires, not all he may.

William Wetmore Story
Life and Letters of Joseph Story, 1852

75.72   Most men can counsel others; few themselves.

Christopher North (psendonym of John Wilson), *1785–1854*
The Cheats

75.73   The lawyers are the cleverest men, the ministers are the most learned, and the doctors are the most sensible.

Oliver Wendell Holmes, American physician and author
The Autocrat of the Breakfast-Table, 1858

75.74   The doctor sees all the weaknesses of mankind, the lawyer all the wickedness, the theologian all the stupidity.

Arthur Schopenhauer, *1788–1860*
W. H. Auden and Louis Kronenberger, *The Viking Book of Aphorisms,* 1962

75.75   I don't want to be a doctor, and live by men's diseases; nor a minister to live by their sins; nor a lawyer to live by their quarrels.

Nathaniel Hawthorne, *1804–1864*
Remark to his mother

75.76   Whom does any body trust so implicitly as he trusts his own attorney? And yet is it not the case that the body of attorneys is supposed to be the most roguish body in existence?

Anthony Trollope
Miss Mackenzie, 1865

75.77   Weary lawyers with endless tongues.

John Greenleaf Whittier
Maud Muller, 1867

75.78   A lawyer is a learned gentleman who rescues your estate from your enemies and keeps it for himself.
> Henry Brougham, English jurist; lord chancellor, *1778–1868*
> Kenneth Redden, *Modern Legal Glossary*, 1983

75.79   All lawyers, be they knaves or fools,
Know that a seat is worth the earning,
Since Parliament's astounding rules
Vouch for their honour and their learning.
> James Edwin Thorold Rogers, English political economist
> *On the Eagerness of Lawyers to Obtain Seats in the House*, 1876

75.80   The fact that a lawyer advised such foolish conduct, does not relieve it of its foolishness. . . .
> Lucilius A. Emery, American jurist
> *Hanscom v. Marston*, 82 Me. 288, 298 (1890)

75.81   Lawyers have been known to wrest from reluctant juries triumphant verdicts of acquittal for their clients, even when those clients, as often happens, were clearly and unmistakably innocent.
> Oscar Wilde, *1854–1900*
> Kenneth Redden, *Modern Legal Glossary*, 1983

75.82   . . . a written document makes lawyers of us all. . . .
> Woodrow Wilson
> *Constitutional Government in the United States*, 1908

75.83   [*Lawyer:*] One skilled in circumvention of the law.
> Ambrose Bierce
> *The Devil's Dictionary*, 1906

75.84   "An Honest Lawyer"—book just out—
What can the author have to say?
Reprint perhaps of ancient tome—
A work of fiction anyway.
> Grace Hibbard, American writer and poet, *1870?–1911*
> "Books Received"

75.85   I don't want a lawyer to tell me what I cannot do; I hire him to tell me how to do what I want to do.
> J. P. Morgan, *1837–1913*
> Kenneth Redden, *Modern Legal Glossary*, 1983

75.86   But Benjamin [Disraeli] shied at the prospect of being buried in lawyer's chambers. "The Bar: pooh! law and bad tricks till we are forty, and then, with the most brilliant success, the prospect of gout and a coronet. Besides, to succeed as an advocate, I must be a great lawyer, and to be a great lawyer, I must give up my chance of being a great man."
> André Maurois
> *Disraeli*, 1930

75.87   The minute you read something you can't understand, you can almost be sure it was drawn up by a lawyer.
> Will Rogers, *1879–1935*
> Laurence J. Peter, *Peter's Quotations*, 1977

75.88   About half the practice of a decent lawyer consists in telling would-be clients that they are damned fools and should stop.
> Elihu Root, *1845–1937*
> Martin Mayer, *The Lawyers*, 1967

75.89   Your law may be perfect, your ability to apply it great, and yet you

cannot be a successful adviser unless your advice is followed. . . .
Louis D. Brandeis, *1856–1941*
Thomas Alpheus Mason, *Brandeis: A Free Man's Life,* 1946

75.90   Holmes divided lawyers into kitchen knives, razors, and stings. Brandeis, he said, was a sting.
Catherine Drinker Bowen
Yankee from Olympus, 1944

75.91   I shall not rest until every German sees that it is a shameful thing to be a lawyer.
Adolf Hitler, *1889–1945*
Kenneth Redden, *Modern Legal Glossary,* 1983

75.92   . . . advocates, including advocates for States, are like managers of pugilistic and election contestants in that they have a propensity for claiming everything.
Felix Frankfurter
First Iowa Hydro-Electric Cooperative v. Federal Power Commission, 328 U.S. 152, 187 (1946)

75.93   Why is there always a secret singing When a lawyer cashes in?
Why does a hearse horse snicker Hauling a lawyer away?
Carl Sandburg
"The Lawyers Know Too Much," *Complete Poems,* 1950

75.94   As to setting forth the outstanding qualities of an advocate. . . . There is no doubt that Daniel Webster named the principal quality when he said, "The power of clear statement is the great power at the bar."
John W. Davis, American educator
Letter to Eugene Gerhart, May 8, 1951

75.95   There, but for the grace of God, goes God.
Sir Winston Churchill, referring to Sir Stafford Cripps, *(1889–1952)*
Clayton Fritchey, "A Politician Must Watch His Wit," *New York Times Magazine,* July 3, 1960

75.96   The late George Haight, a giant of the Chicago bar, was once asked "What makes a good lawyer?" His short reply deserves to be remembered: "Lots of scar tissue."
George Haight, *1878–1955*
Milton B. Pollock, "Some Practical Aspects of Appellate Advocacy," *New York State Bar Bulletin,* February 1959

75.97   "Lawyers enjoy a little mystery, you know. Why, if everybody came forward and told the truth, the whole truth, and nothing but the truth straight out, we should all retire to the workhouse."
Dorothy L. Sayers
Clouds of Witness, 1956

75.98   . . . lawyers better remember they are human beings, and a human being who hasn't his periods of doubts and distresses and disappointments must be a cabbage, not a human being.
Felix Frankfurter
"Proceedings in Honor of Mr. Justice Frankfurter and Distinguished Alumni," *Occasional Pamphlet,* No. 3, Harvard Law School, 1960

75.99   A lawyer starts life giving five hundred dollars' worth of law for five dollars, and ends giving five dollars' worth for five hundred dollars.
Benjamin H. Brewster, American business executive, *1900–1961*
Laurence J. Peter, *Peter's Quotations,* 1977

75.100   Most lawyers who win a case advise their clients "We have won," and when justice has frowned upon their cause . . . "*You* have lost."
Louis Nizer
My Life in Court, 1960

75.101   . . . the Congress is predominantly a lawyers' body.
Felix Frankfurter
Callanan v. United States, 364 U.S. 587, 594 (1961)

75.102   "Old Bull" Warren at Harvard was right when he said that one didn't need brains to be a lawyer, only a cast-iron bottom.
Edward Lamb, American lawyer
No Lamb for Slaughter, 1963

75.103   In the professional sense we are all descendants of Demosthenes and Pericles. Greece had no lawyers but a person forced to appear before the jury in the Agora could have the assistance of someone to write out his speech of defense and an adviser. The classic illustration is the adviser to a beautiful girl accused of some morals offense.
Reginald Heber Smith, American lawyer
"Selected Readings on the Legal Profession," 7 *Boston Bar Journal* 1 (1963)

75.104   The trouble with lawyers is they convince themselves that their clients are right.
Charles W. Ainey, dean of the Susquehanna, Pennsylvania Bar Association
To Eugene Gerhart, August 25, 1963

75.105   Obviously, the whole purpose of a police investigation is frustrated if a suspect is entitled to have a lawyer during preliminary questioning, for any lawyer worth his fee will tell him to keep his mouth shut.
Frank S. Hogan
New York Times, December 2, 1965

75.106   The best trained, most technically skilled and ethically most responsible lawyers are reserved for the upper reaches of business and society. This leaves the least competent, least well-trained, and least ethical lawyers to the lower-income individuals.
Jerome E. Carlin, American educator
Lawyer's Ethics, 1966

75.107   When the lawyers are through, what is there left? . . . Can a mouse nibble at it and find enough to fasten a tooth in?
Carl Sandburg, *1878-1967*
Kenneth Redden, *Modern Legal Glossary,* 1983

75.108   The American Bar Association formula of a lawyer for hire specifically excludes those who most need legal help—the vast army of the poor.
William M. Kunstler
Quote, August 2, 1970

75.109   [Politics] is a beautiful fraud that has been imposed on the people for years, whose practitioners exchange gilded promises for the most valuable thing their victims own: their votes. And who benefits most? The lawyers.
Shirley Chisholm
Unbought and Unbossed, 1970

75.110   The law does not exist just for the lawyers though there are some of us who seem to think that it does. The law is for all the people and the lawyers are only its ministers.

> Robert A. Leflar, American jurist; justice, Arkansas Supreme Court
> Address, American Judicature Society, reported in *Wall Street Journal,* May 27, 1971

75.111   The public regards lawyers with great distrust. They think lawyers are smarter than the average guy but use their intelligence deviously. Well, they're wrong; usually, they are not smarter.

> F. Lee Bailey
> *Los Angeles Times,* January 9, 1972

75.112   The difference between an office lawyer and a trial lawyer is as great as between an internist and a surgeon. Both require high talents, but the specialized skills and tools are so different that they may as well be in different professions.

> Louis Nizer
> *Newsweek,* December 10, 1973

75.113   Lawyers of good education and practical competence are generally distinguished for their ability to be resourceful, orderly and dispassionate in their thinking and in their approach to problems.

> Gerald R. Ford
> Address, Georgia Bar Association, Savannah, reported in *U.S. News & World Report,* June 24, 1974

75.114   I would like to see the time come when the massive hemorrhage of some of our best talents into the [field of] law will cease. . . . Our country is already sufficiently litigation-prone and legalistic. The oversupply of lawyers not only helps

create its own demand but can get in the way of solving problems.

> David Riesman, American sociologist
> Address, American Sociological Association, Chicago, reported in the *New York Times,* August 30, 1975

75.115   [The law] is designed to protect the power and privilege of those who write the law and to ward off any values or vision that threatens it.

> Andrew Young
> *New York Times,* August 7, 1976

75.116   Lawyers are . . . operators of toll bridges across which anyone in search of justice must pass.

> Jane Bryant Quinn
> *Newsweek,* October 9, 1978

75.117   I don't think it's useful to talk about percentages when discussing lawyer competency. It depends on one's standards for competency. If the standard is that of lawyers who shouldn't be practicing at all, the incompetency rate is, maybe, five percent. If the standard is room for improvement, that would include 99 percent of all lawyers and 99.9 percent of all judges.

> Anthony G. Amsterdam, American educator
> *Los Angeles Times,* November 5, 1978

75.118   We [lawyers] shake papers at each other the way primitive tribes shake spears.

> John Jay Osborn, Jr., American lawyer
> *The Associates,* 1979

75.119   A lawyer's job is to manipulate the skeletons in other people's closets.

> Sol Stein, American publisher and writer
> *Other People,* 1979

75.120   If war is too important to be left to the generals, surely justice is too important to be left to the lawyers.
Robert McKay, American educator; dean, New York University Law School
Kenneth Redden, *Modern Legal Glossary,* 1983

75.121   It is a secret worth knowing that lawyers rarely go to law themselves.
Moses Crowell
Kenneth Redden, *Modern Legal Glossary,* 1983

75.122   How in God's name could so many lawyers get involved in something like Watergate.
John Dean
Kenneth Redden, *Modern Legal Glossary,* 1983

75.123   Apologists for the profession contend that lawyers are as honest as other men, but this is not very encouraging.
Ferdinand Lundberg, American author
Kenneth Redden, *Modern Legal Glossary,* 1983

75.124   Castles in the air are the only property you can own without the intervention of lawyers.
J. Feidor Rees, English writer

75.125   Lawyers earn a living by the sweat of their browbeating.
James Gibbons Hanneker

76. LEGAL ETIQUETTE

76.1   . . . lawyers who know how to think but have not learned how to behave are a menace and a liability not an asset to the administration of justice. . . . I suggest the necessity for civility is relevant to lawyers because they are the living exemplars—and thus teachers—every day in every case and in every court; and their worst conduct will be emulated . . . more readily than their best.
Warren E. Burger
Address, American Law Institute, Washington, D.C., reported in the *National Observer,* May 24, 1971

76.2   The lawyers' contribution to the civilizing of humanity is evidenced in the capacity of lawyers to argue furiously in the courtroom, then sit down as friends over a drink or dinner. This habit is often interpreted by the layman as a mark of their ultimate corruption. In my opinion, it is their greatest moral achievement; it is a characteristic of human tolerance that is most desperately needed at the present time.
John R. Silber, American educator; president, Boston University
Wall Street Journal, March 16, 1972

76.3   A truly qualified advocate—like every genuine professional—resembles a seamless garment, in the sense that legal knowledge, forensic skills, professional ethics, courtroom etiquette and manners are blended in the total person. There are some lawyers who scoff at the idea that manners and etiquette form any part of the necessary equipment of the courtroom advocate. Yet if one were to undertake a list of the truly great advocates of the past 100 years, I suggest he would find a common denominator: They were all intensely individualistic but each was a lawyer for whom courtroom manners were a key weapon in his arsenal. Whether engaged in the destruction of adverse witnesses or undermining damaging evidence or in final argument, the performance was characterized by coolness, poise, and graphic clarity, without shouting or ranting, without baiting witnesses, opponents or the judge.
        Warren E. Burger
        Lecture, Fordham University Law
        School, reported in the *Los Angeles
        Times,* December 28, 1973

76.4   We don't go around making jokes and doing wild things in the courtroom, letting the jury think this is a game. That doesn't mean you don't look for a little comic relief, especially on the defense side. It is like the old maxim in a rape case: If you can get laughter, you won't get a conviction. The two just don't mix.
        F. Lee Bailey, referring to his
        reputation for being flamboyant
        Los Angeles Herald Examiner,
        December 7, 1978

77. LEGAL PROCESS

77.1   Sunday is not a day for judicial or legal proceedings.
        Legal maxim

77.2   Whatever was required to be done, the Circumlocation Office was beforehand with all the public departments in the art of perceiving *HOW NOT TO DO IT.*
        Charles Dickens
        Little Dorrit, 1857

77.3   You cannot imagine the beauty of an intricate, mazy law process, embodying the doubts and subtleties of generations of men. I say, looked at that way, there is something picturesque in an Act of Parliament.
        Sir Arthur Helps, English historian
        and writer
        Friends in Council, 1847–1859

77.4   The judicial process is one of compromise, a compromise between paradoxes, between certainty and uncertainty, between the liberalism that is the exaltation of the written word and the nihilism that is destructive of regularity and order.
> Benjamin N. Cardozo, *1870–1938*
> *Selected Writings of Benjamin Nathan Cardozo,* 1947

77.5   To be effective, judicial administration must not be leaden-footed.
> Felix Frankfurter
> *Cobbledick v. United States,* 309 U.S. 323, 325 (1940)

77.6   The time has come to eliminate slow-motion justice in America. Nothing is more difficult to explain about American institutions to the intelligent inquiring layman than why a man accused of robbing a fellow citizen at the point of a gun can stall the process for two years before facing the day of punishment.
> Edward Bennett Williams
> *Salt Lake Tribune,* May 29, 1971

77.7   The law will never move as rapidly as a bullet, nor will its dispositions ever be as demolishing as a bomb. Justice should be reasoned, and reasoning takes a certain length of time.
> Edward L. Wright, American lawyer; president, American Bar Association
> *Plainview* (Texas) *Daily Herald,* July 13, 1971

77.8   There is no finality in the law any more. To move a case to trial we first have to run an obstacle course of motions. . . . Many are made merely to gain delay. They are frivolous. They are not intended to gain a legitimate remedy but as a weapon in a war of attrition to exhaust the prosecution in hope that the case will fade away, or at worst, that the prosecution will finally settle for a lesser plea.
> Frank S. Hogan
> *Los Angeles Times,* August 14, 1972

77.9   Procrastination is a sin of lawyers, trial judges, reporters, appellate judges, in brief, everyone connected with the machinery of criminal law.
> Macklin Fleming, American jurist
> *Los Angeles Times,* July 24, 1974

77.10   Whatever may have been the situation two centuries ago, or even a century ago, today's administration of justice is a highly complex and technical enterprise. What we must face up to is whether a process so intricate and complex can continue to be guided . . . by haphazard, casual and uncoordinated approaches that have characterized the administration of justice most of our 200 years.
> Warren E. Burger
> Address, American Bar Association, Seattle, Washington, reported in the *National Observer,* February 26, 1977

77.11   The harsh truth is that unless we devise substitutes for the courtroom processes, we may be on our way to a society overrun by hordes of lawyers hungry as locusts and brigades of judges never before contemplated. . . . The notion that people want black-robed judges, well-dressed lawyers and fine-paneled courtrooms as the setting to resolve their disputes is not correct. People with problems, like people with pains, want relief, and they want it as quickly and inexpensively as possible.
> Warren E. Burger
> Address, American Bar Association, New York, reported in the *Los Angeles Times,* May 28, 1977

77.12   The legal process, because of its unbridled growth, has become a cancer which threatens the vitality of our forms of capitalism and democracy.
> Laurence Silberman, American lawyer; U.S. deputy attorney general
> Kenneth Redden, *Modern Legal Glossary,* 1983

78. LEGAL PROFESSION

78.1   He that loves law will get his fill of it.
> Scottish proverb
> *Complete Collection of Scottish Proverbs,* 1721

78.2   It is a slight thing to be good according to law.
> Seneca, *4 B.C.?–A.D. 65*
> W. Gurney Benham, *Putnam's Complete Book of Quotations, Proverbs and Household Words,* 1927

78.3   He hath in great perfection the three chief qualifications of a lawyer: boldness, boldness, boldness.
> Anonymous, referring to an English judge
> *Hatton Correspondence,* c. late 16th century

78.4   I hold every man a debtor to his profession.
> Francis Bacon
> *The Elements of the Common Lawes of England,* 1630

78.5   . . . these men of Law and their confederates . . . the caterpillars of this Kingdom, who with their uncontrolled exactions and extortions, eat up the free-born people of this Nation. . . .
> Bathsua Makin, English scholar and author
> *The Malady . . . and Remedy of Vexations and Unjust Arrests and Actions,* 1646

78.6   This house, where once a lawyer dwelt,
Is now a smith's. Alas!
How rapidly the iron age
Succeeds the age of brass!
> John Erskin, *1695–1768,* alluding to the removal of a distinguished counsellor from a house in Red Lion Square, and an ironmonger becoming its occupant
> Marshall Brown, *Wit and Humor of Bench and Bar,* 1899

78.7   But what his common sense came
        short,
        He ekèd out wi' law, man.
        Robert Burns, *1759–1796*
        In the Court of Session, Edinburgh

78.8   I will not say with Lord Hale, that
        "The Law will admit of no rival" . . .
        but I will say that it is a jealous mis-
        tress, and requires a long and constant
        courtship. It is not to be won by tri-
        fling favors, but by lavish homage.
        Joseph Story
        *The Value and Importance of Legal
        Studies,* August 5, 1829

78.9   . . . daily drudgery of a precarious
        profession.
        Sir Walter Scott, *1771–1832*
        William Andrews, *The Lawyer in
        History, Literature, and Humour,* 1896

78.10   There was no great love between
        us, and it pleased Heaven to decrease
        it on further acquaintance.
        Sir Walter Scott, speaking of himself
        and the law, *1771–1832*
        "Merry Wives"

78.11   The profession of the law is the
        only aristocratic element that can be
        amalgamated without violence with
        the natural elements of democracy
        and be advantageously and perma-
        nently combined with them.
        Alexis de Tocqueville
        Democracy in America, 1835–1840

78.12   Eight points of the law:
        1. A good cause;
        2. A good purse;
        3. An honest and skillful attorney;
        4. An upright judge;
        5. Good evidence;
        6. Able counsel;

7. An upright judge;
8. Good luck
        Attributed to Charles James Fox,
        English statesman
        John Campbell, *Lives of the Lord
        Chancellors,* 1845–1847

78.13   At the top of my street* the attor-
        neys abound,
        And down at the bottom the barges
        are found;
        Fly, Honesty, fly to some safer re-
        treat,
        For there's craft in the river, and
        craft in the street.
        James Smith, English author and
        humorist, *1775–1859*
        Marshall Brown, *Wit and Humor of
        Bench and Bar,* 1882

78.14   The devil makes his Christmas-
        pies of lawyers' tongues and clerks'
        fingers.
        Thomas Adams, American clergyman
        and poet
        Sermons, 1862

78.15   YOURS OF THE 10TH RE-
        CEIVED. First of all, he has a wife
        and a baby; together they ought to
        be worth $500,000 to any man. Sec-
        ondly, he has an office in which there
        is a table worth $1.50 and three
        chairs worth, say, $1. Last of all,
        there is in one corner a large rat-
        hole, which will bear looking into.
        Respectfully,
        A. Lincoln
        Abraham Lincoln, *1809–1865*
        Letter to a New York firm inquiring
        for recommendations

78.16   It is not the saints of the world
        who chiefly give employment to our
        profession.
        Edward G. Ryan, American jurist
        Motion to Admit Miss Lavinia
        Goodell to the Bar, 1875

*Craven Street, The Strand, London

78.17   The glory of lawyers, like that of men of science, is more corporate than individual.
Oliver Wendell Holmes
Answer to Resolution of the Bar on Daniel S. Richardson, April 15, 1890

78.18   Every calling is great when greatly pursued.
Oliver Wendell Holmes
"The Law," *Speeches*, 1913

78.19   The practice of law is more than a mere trade or business, and . . . those who engage in it are the guardians of ideals and traditions to which it is right that they should from time to time dedicate themselves anew.
Hugh Patterson MacMillan, Scottish lawyer
"The Ethics of Advocacy" (address) 1916

78.20   The office of the lawyer . . . is too delicate, personal and confidential to be occupied by a corporation.
Robert H. Jackson
"Functions of the Trust Company in the Field of Law," 52 *Report of the New York State Bar Association*, 142, 144 (1929)

78.21   Was there ever such a profession as ours, anyhow? We speak of ourselves as practicing law, as teaching it, as deciding it; and not one of us can say what law means.
Benjamin N. Cardozo, *1870–1938*
Selected Writings of Benjamin Nathan Cardozo, 1947

78.22   Historically, there are three ideas involved in a profession, organization, learning, and a spirit of public service. These are essential. The remaining idea, that of gaining a livelihood, is incidental.
Roscoe Pound
"What Is a Profession," 19 *Notre Dame L.* 203, 204 (1944)

78.23   The United States is the greatest law factory the world has ever known.
Charles Evans Hughes, *1862–1948*
Laurence J. Peter, *Peter's Quotations,* 1977

78.24   The law is the only profession which records its mistakes carefully, exactly as they occurred, and yet does not identify them as mistakes. . . .
Eliot Dunlap Smith, American jurist
Louis M. Brown, "Legal Autopsy," *Journal of the American Judicial Society,* November 1954

78.25   If you think that you can think about a thing, inextricably attached to something else, without thinking of the thing it is attached to, then you have a legal mind.
Thomas Reed Powell, American educator, *1880–1955*
Laurence J. Peter, *Peter's Quotations,* 1977

78.26   Getting ahead in a big law firm means a hefty amount of evening and weekend work. . . . Wall Street lawyers still like to recall an anecdote about the late Hoyt A. Moore, a partner in Cravath, Swaine & Moore. A colleague once told Moore that the firm ought to hire more associates because the staff was overworked. "That's silly," Partner Moore replied. "No one is under pressure. There wasn't a light on when I left at 2 o'clock this morning."
Time, January 24, 1964

78.27   Our civilization must go through a period of far reaching and rapid change to survive the transition to a world that is nuclear dominated, automated, over populated and under employed; . . . An occasion may arise when, confronted by authority, the

stark choice before a profession becomes either acquiescence or the necessity to say "No." The challenge must be met on the basis of humanist principle—not self-interest. Only thus may the integrity of a profession be preserved.
A. A. Klass
"Professional Integrity and the
State," 8 *The Canadian Bar Journal* 2
(April 1965)

78.28   [Law] is not a profession at all, but rather a business service station and repair shop.
Adlai E. Stevenson, *1900–1965*
Walter Johnson and Carol Evans, *The Papers of Adlai Stevenson,* 1972

78.29   You will all remember the famous saying that war is far too serious a matter to be left to generals. We in England think that it is possibly also true that law reform is far too serious a matter to be left to the legal profession.
Leslie Scarman, English lawyer
"The Role of the Legal Profession in Law Reform," Association of the Bar of the City of New York *Record,* vol. 21, no. 1, January 1966

78.30   Edmund Burke is supposed to have said, "Law sharpens the mind by narrowing it." It seems to me that the words were meant less in praise of the profession than in warning to it. . . . To the extent that the judicial profession becomes the daily routine of deciding cases on the most secure precedents and the narrowest grounds available, the judicial mind atrophies and its perspective shrinks. What most impresses us about great jurists is not their tenacious grasp of fine points, honed almost to invisibility; it is the moment when we are suddenly made aware of the sweep

and direction of the law, and its place in the lives of men.
Irving R. Kaufman, American jurist; chief judge, U.S. Court of Appeals
Speech, Institute of Judicial Administration, August 26, 1969

78.31   Don't go into the legal profession if you want social change.
Warren E. Burger
Melvin Belli, *Los Angeles Herald-Examiner,* September 3, 1972

78.32   The practice of law in most courtrooms today is about as modern as performing surgery in a barbershop.
Gordon D. Schaber, American educator; dean, University of Pacific Law School
San Francisco Examiner, March 9, 1973

78.33   We inherit the tradition of seven or eight centuries of continuous concern for the institutions and aspirations . . . that make for a free and civilized society. It is not the age of the profession that matters . . . what matters most is that, through the centuries men of law have been persistently concerned with the resolution of disputes . . . in ways that enable society to achieve its goals with a minimum of force and maximum of reason.
Archibald Cox
New York Times, May 29, 1974

78.34   When dictators and tyrants seek to destroy the freedoms of men, their first target is the legal profession and through it the rule of law.
Leon Jaworski
Dallas Times Herald, July 5, 1974

78.35   We are coming into the Golden Age of Law. . . . It is the new breed of lawyers, the young kids fresh out of law school, who are bringing this refreshing change. In the old days it was the thing to join the "respected" Establishment law firm. Today, the reverse is true. The young attorney won't join anything unless he knows his prospective employer is involved in cost-free, diligent community and minority group activity.

Melvin Belli
San Francisco Examiner & Chronicle,
October 4, 1974

78.36   [Law is] an odd profession that presents its greatest scholarship in student-run publications.

Morton J. Horwitz, American
educator
Newsweek, September 15, 1975

78.37   If we are to achieve that more perfect system of justice, it is we lawyers, judges and professors of law . . . who must educate the public on the needs of the justice system and on how to get them. If we do not do this leadership job, it will not be done at all.

Charles S. Rhyne, president, World
Peace Through Law Center
Address to the International Lawyers
Club, reported in the *National
Observer,* October 2, 1976

78.38   No other profession is subject to the public contempt and derision that sometimes befalls lawyers. This antagonism is the bitter fruit of public incomprehension of the law itself and its dynamics. The judge is forced for the most part to reach his audience through the medium of the press whose reporting of judicial decisions is all too often inaccurate and superficial.

Irving R. Kaufman, American jurist;
chief judge, U.S. Court of Appeals
San Francisco Examiner & Chronicle,
April 17, 1977

78.39   The legal profession is a business with a tremendous collection of egos. Few people who are not strong egotistically gravitate to it. If they do, they wind up in the archives or doing tax returns, or they stay as junior partners in a law firm for the rest of their lives. To get ahead you have got to assert yourself. That's the lawyer's stock in trade.

F. Lee Bailey
U.S. News & World Report,
September 14, 1981

78.40   We may be well on our way to a society overrun by hordes of lawyers, hungry as locusts, and brigades of judges in numbers never before contemplated.

Warren E. Burger
Kenneth Redden, *Modern Legal
Glossary,* 1983

78.41   We have the heaviest concentration of lawyers on earth—one for every 500 Americans. That is three times more than in England, four times more than in Germany, 21 times more than in Japan. We have more litigation but I am not sure we have more justice. No resource of talent and training in our society, not even medical care, is more wastefully or unfairly distributed than legal skills. Ninety percent of our lawyers serve 10% of our people.

Jimmy Carter
Kenneth Redden, *Modern Legal
Glossary,* 1983

78.42   The entire legal profession—lawyers, judges, law teachers—has become so mesmerized with the stimulation of the courtroom contest that we tend to forget that we ought to be healers of conflicts. Doctors, in spite of astronomical medical costs, still retain a high degree of public confidence because they are perceived as healers. Should lawyers not be healers? Healers, not warriors? Healers, not procurers? Healers, not hired guns?

Warren E. Burger
Address, American Bar Association,
Las Vegas, reported in the *New York
Times,* February 2, 1984

78.43 Instead of resisting the trend toward popular marketing of professional services . . . [we] should encourage and shape it. The public needs the professional equivalent of Chevrolets as well as Cadillacs.

Doug Harlan, American lawyer
U.S.A. Today, February 2, 1984

78.44 The average lawyer is essentially a mechanic who works with a pen instead of a ball-peen hammer. Machinists' unions require an apprenticeship, not an advanced degree.

Bob Schmitt, American jurist
Americans for Legal Reform, Vol. 4,
No. 3, Spring 1984

78.45 Lawyers could be in space as soon as a decade after 1991, when the president foresees our sending up a manned space station. It's a hostile environment where a small dispute could become a danger to the community. People won't be able to get back to Earth to settle disputes.

Hamilton De Saussure, American
educator; professor, University of
Akron Law School,
Sacramento Bee, 1984

78.46 The key thing that makes national law firms work is synergy; with the right combination, one and one make three.

Steven Kumble, American lawyer
New York Times, October 4, 1984.

79. LEGAL SYSTEM

79.1 The law will not in its executive capacity work a wrong.

Legal maxim

79.2 Things established by law are done away with by an opposite law.

Legal maxim

79.3 We are all servants of the laws to the end that it may be possible for us to be free.

Cicero
Pro Cluentio, 66 B.C.

79.4 The gladsome light of Jurisprudence.

Sir Edward Coke
The Institutes of the Lawes of England,
Vol. 1, 1628–1641

79.5 Where there's no law there's no bread.
Benjamin Franklin
Poor Richard's Almanack, 1744

79.6 Former President Taft, after a discussion with President Hoover on the legal machinery, said: "Hoover thinks it really is machinery."
William Howard Taft, *c.1930*
Dean Acheson, *Among Friends: Letters of Dean Acheson,* 1980

79.7 Legal concepts are supernatural entities which do not have a verifiable existence except to the eyes of faith.
Felix S. Cohen, American lawyer
Transcendental Nonsense and the Functional Approach, 1935

79.8 The sacredness of human life is a formula that is good only inside a system of law.
Oliver Wendell Holmes, *1841–1935*
W. H. Auden and Louis Kronenberger, *The Viking Book of Aphorisms,* 1962

79.9 . . . bureaucracy, the rule of no one, has become the modern form of despotism.
Mary McCarthy
"The Vita Activa," *New Yorker,* October 18, 1958

79.10 . . . we have never been a tightly disciplined people and, reflecting this, our legal structure has been more relaxed than that of many other societies. If this has negative aspects, it also gives us a resiliency to tide us over and enable us to meet any crisis as it arises. We will respond slowly, but that is the nature of a democratic society.
Warren E. Burger
Speech, American Law Institute, Washington, D.C., May 19, 1970

79.11 The legal system isn't working. It is like a scarecrow in the field that doesn't scare the crows anymore because it is too beaten and tattered— and the crows are sitting on the arms and cawing their contemptuous defiance.
Edward Bennett Williams
U.S. News & World Report, September 21, 1970

79.12 The greatest weakness of our judicial system is that it has become clogged and does not function in a fluent fashion resulting in prompt determination of the guilt or innocence of those charged with crime.
Earl Warren
Speech, Johns Hopkins University, reported in the *San Francisco Examiner & Chronicle,* November 15, 1970

79.13 Man's urge for change and his need for stability have always balanced and checked each other, and our current vocabulary, which distinguishes between two factions, the progressives and the conservatives, indicates a state of affairs in which this balance has been thrown out of order. No civilization—the manmade artifact to house successive generations—would ever have been possible without a framework of stability, to provide the wherein for the flux of change. Foremost among the stabilizing factors, more enduring than customs, manners and traditions, are the legal systems that regulate our life in the world and our daily affairs with each other.
Hannah Arendt
"Civil Disobedience," *Crises of the Republic,* 1972

79.14 . . . it is quite possible to have too many laws and regulations . . . the whole legal apparatus of government may collapse from its own weight; and . . . too many laws and regulations may paralyze society so that we have a condition approximating anarchy. Too much may be the equivalent of none at all.

> Lee Loevinger, American lawyer
> Lecture, New York University,
> December 15, 1978

79.15   People in the West have acquired considerable skill in using, interpreting and manipulating law. . . . Every conflict is solved according to the letter of the law and this is considered to be the ultimate solution. If one is right from a legal point of view, nothing more is required; nobody may mention that one could still not be entirely right, call for sacrifice and selfless risk—this would simply sound absurd. Voluntary self-restraint is almost unheard of; everybody strives toward further expansion to the extreme limit of the legal frames. . . . I have spent all my life

under a Communist regime, and I will tell you that a society without any objective legal scale is a terrible one indeed. But a society with no other scale but the legal one is also less than worthy of man.

> Alexandr I. Solzhenitsyn
> Address, Harvard University,
> September 1, 1983

79.16   The law is a very mischievous system designed not to achieve but to frustrate the truth.

> Abraham Pomerantz, American
> lawyer
> Kenneth Redden, *Modern Legal
> Glossary,* 1983

79.17   [The legal culture owes an obligation to the] citizenry in general, whose attitude toward law and the legal system cannot help but be profoundly and negatively influenced by a litigation system that voraciously consumes time and money.

> Jon O. Newman, judge, U.S. Court of
> Appeals
> Cardozo lecture, 1984

---

80. LEGAL TRAINING

80.1   Much knowledge does not teach wisdom.

> Heraclitus, *6th–5th century B.C.*
> James Bryce, *Modern Democracies,*
> 1921

80.2   Books must follow sciences, and not sciences books.

> Francis Bacon, *1561–1626*
> *A Proposal for Amending the Laws of
> England*

80.3   A Little Learning *misleadeth,* and a great deal often *stupifieth* the Understanding.
> George Savile, 1st marquess of
> Halifax, English politician,
> *1633–1695*
> "False Learning," *The Complete*
> *Works of George Savile, First*
> *Marquess of Halifax,* 1912

80.4   The system of competitive examination is a sad necessity. Knowledge is wooed for her dowry, not her diviner charms.
> Charles Bowen, English jurist
> *1835–1894*
> Edward William Donoghue Manson,
> "Lecture on Education," *Builders of*
> *Our Law* 113 L.T. 356 (1902)

80.5   To know is not less than to feel.
> Oliver Wendell Holmes, *1841–1935*
> Catherine Drinker Bowen, *Yankee*
> *from Olympus,* 1944

80.6   The greatest bores in the world are the come-outers who are cock-sure of a dozen nostrums. The dogmatism of a little education is hopeless.
> Oliver Wendell Holmes, *1841–1935*
> Mark De Wolfe Howe, *Holmes-*
> *Pollock Letters,* 1946

80.7   . . . a lawyer who has not studied economics and sociology is very apt to become a public enemy.
> Louis D. Brandeis, *1856–1941*
> Samuel J. Konefsky, *The Legacy of*
> *Holmes and Brandeis,* 1956

80.8   "In university they don't tell you that the greater part of the law is learning to tolerate fools."
> Doris Lessing
> *Martha Quest,* 1952

80.9   . . . [Oliver Wendell Holmes's] father finally persuaded him when he was in college, a junior, to go and see [Ralph Waldo] Emerson. He went to see him, and there was talk about this or that. Holmes said Emerson had a beautiful voice, and, of course, Holmes had one of the most beautiful voices the Lord ever put into a throat. Emerson said to him, "Young man, have you read Plato?"
Holmes said he hadn't. "You must. You must read Plato. But you must hold him at arm's length and say, "Plato, you have delighted and edified mankind for two thousand years. What have you to say to me?"
Holmes said, "That's the lesson of independence."
So off he went and read Plato for a few months or a year, and then wrote a piece doing in Mr. Plato in one of those ephemeral literary things at Harvard. He laid this, as it were, at the feet of Mr. Emerson and awaited the next morning's mail, hoping to get a warm appreciation from Emerson. And the next day and the next and the next—no sign of life. No acknowledgement from Mr. Emerson. Holmes didn't see him again for about a year. When he saw him, this, that, and the other thing was again talked about. Emerson said, "Oh, by the way, I read your piece on Plato. Holmes, when you strike at a king, you must kill him."
> Felix Frankfurter
> Harlan Phillips, *Felix Frankfurter*
> *Reminiscences,* 1960

80.10   . . . defeat is education. It is a step to something better.
> Louis Nizer,
> *My Life in Court,* 1960

80.11   There is a story of an applicant for admission to a famous graduate school, who, when asked by the

Dean of Admissions whether he had graduated in the upper half of his college class—replied with great pride: "Sir, I belong to that section of the class which makes the upper half of the class possible."

Julius Cohen, American educator
"An Evening with Three Legal Philosophers," *Journal of Legal Education,* 1962

80.12 The idea that we should spend all our time in law school teaching people how to win instead of how to settle is very damaging in this day and age.

Michael I. Sovern, American educator; president, Columbia University
Time, April 20, 1970

80.13 Law is no longer accepted by lawyers or others as irrefutable pronouncements from on high. [Lawyers] can no longer view their profession in isolation. Science, economics, and behavioral disciplines become major determinants in the lawyer's work.

Byron R. White
Christian Science Monitor, February 24, 1971

80.14 Today, lawyers are educated and licensed as if they could eventually do everything which constitutes the practice of law. The myth of omnicompetence is precisely that—a myth. Our economic and social life is far too complex to support such a reality.

Robert W. Meserve, American lawyer; president, American Bar Association
Address, New York Bar Association, reported in the *National Observer,* February 17, 1973

80.15 . . . in spite of all the bar examinations and better law schools, we are more casual about qualifying the people we allow to act as advocates in the courtroom than we are about licensing electricians. The painful fact is that the courtrooms of America all too often have Piper-Cub advocates trying to handle the controls of Boeing 747 litigation.

Warren E. Burger
Lecture, Fordham University Law School, reported in the *Los Angeles Times,* December 28, 1973

80.16 When young men come out of law school today, they . . . should spend half their time as [Clarence] Darrow did defending clients for no recompense whatsoever. Over half of Darrow's clients never paid him. They weren't able to; they were poor. Yet he realized that you owe half your time to American society and democracy to preserve it.

Irving Stone
Los Angeles Herald-Examiner, March 15, 1974

80.17 We can't give up specialized training in the highly complex structure of law today, but we do have to return to a feeling of what the whole legal system stands for—how it relates to our own conception of the person as a human being.

Paul A. Freund, American educator; professor, Harvard Law School
U.S. News & World Report, March 25, 1974

80.18 I strongly urge that . . . no lawyer be permitted to come into the Federal court to try a case simply on a diploma from a law school or a certificate of admission to the state courts—that we require something more: a demonstration that he has

had a certain minimal experience in the trial courts of his state.
Warren E. Burger
U.S. News & World Report, March 31, 1975

80.19 One of the penalties of being a lawyer is that you don't remember things, and you don't particularly want to remember them. As a lawyer you have to force-feed your mind for your hour in court with all sorts of material you'll never ever need again, and somehow there's no room for anything else. So you get into the habit of letting everything else slide.
Archibald Cox
Publishers Weekly, March 1, 1976

80.20 Law students can learn more from knowing how to ask good questions than from studying appellate briefs. To be able to make split-second decisions, they have to feel the law in their bones.
Anthony G. Amsterdam, American educator
Time, March 14, 1977

80.21 I love teaching and there is something particularly appealing about teaching a subject that seems to deal with the lowest kind of relationships—accidents, ambulance-chasing—because you can show students that these raise the most fundamental questions about the structure of society. And if somewhere, sometime, something a law professor does hasn't a practical effect, he hasn't been a good law scholar or teacher.
Guido Calabresi, educator; professor, Yale Law School
Time, March 14, 1977

80.22 If law school graduates, like cars, could be recalled for failure to meet

commercial standards, the recall rate would be very high on those who go into courts without substantial added training. . . . We must require some form of internship before lawyers claim a right to represent clients in the trial courts.
Warren E. Burger
Address, American Bar Association, New Orleans, reported in *U.S. News & World Report,* August 21, 1978

80.23 The study of law is the search for justice, for the equitable resolution of conflict, for tolerance. The search for justice is not easy. That's why the study of law cannot and should not be easy; that is why we ask more questions than we know the answers to.
Thomas Buergenthal, American educator; dean, American University
Washington Post, August 30, 1981

80.24 There can be no question that law schools must train advocates. [Yet] the most rigorous standards of professional education are satisfied only when we teach the substance of law, and when lawyers state it as precisely as they can, being fair and clear about where their own preferences come into play.
Gerhard Gasper, American educator; dean, University of Chicago Law School
Wall Street Journal, April 13, 1982

80.25 A great many college graduates come here [to Harvard Law School] thinking of lawyers as social engineers arguing the great Constitutional issues. But as they go through here, some of these idealistic aspirations get tempered by the desire to become established, by ambition, by families and marriage. There's a certain temptation to say that the law school brings this about, when it really is an accommodation to living in society.

Archibald Cox
San Francisco Examiner & Chronicle,
June 6, 1982

80.26   To be a lawyer you have to learn to work off of precedents and to explore statutory ambiguities. But you should also understand that the law is not a disciplined set of rules. The landscape in which the law exists is changing, and so should the law school curriculum.

Charles R. Halpern, American educator; dean, City University of New York Law School at Queens College
New York Times, September 14, 1982

81. LIBERTY

81.1   Liberty is the power of doing
What is allowed by law.

Latin legal phrase
W. Gurney Benham, *Putnam's Complete Book of Quotations, Proverbs and Household Words,* 1927

81.2   Liberty is the Mistress of Mankind, she hath powerful Charms which do so dazzle us, that we find Beauties in her which perhaps are not there, as we do in other Mistresses; yet if she was not a Beauty, the World would not run mad for her. . . .

George Savile, 1st marquess of Halifax, English politician, *1633-1695*
"The Trimmer's Opinion of The Laws and Government," *The Complete Works of George Savile, First Marquess of Halifax,* 1912

81.3   Is life so dear, or peace so sweet, as to be purchased at the price of chains and slavery? Forbid it, Almighty God! I know not what course others may take, but as for me, give me liberty or give me death!

Patrick Henry, *1736-1799*
Speech, Virginia Revolutionary Council, Richmond, 1775

81.4   Corruption, the most infallible symptom of constitutional liberty.

Edward Gibbon
The Decline and Fall of the Roman Empire, 1776

81.5   What signify a few lives lost in a century or two? The tree of liberty must be refreshed from time to time with the blood of patriots and tyrants. It is its natural manure.

Thomas Jefferson
Letter to W. S. Smith, November 13, 1787

81.6   The effect of liberty to individuals is that they may do what they please: we ought to see what it will please them to do, before we risk congratulations, which may be soon turned into complaints. Prudence would dictate this in the case of separate, insulated, private men; but liberty, when men act in bodies, is *power*.
Edmund Burke
Reflections on the Revolution in France, 1790

81.7   If fields are prisons, where is Liberty?
Robert Bloomfield, English poet, *1766–1823*
The Farmer's Boy: Autumn

81.8   It is liberty alone that fits men for liberty.
William Gladstone,   *1809–1898*

81.9   [*Liberty:*] One of Imagination's most precious possessions.
Ambrose Bierce
The Devil's Dictionary, 1906

81.10   Excess of liberty contradicts itself. In short there is no such thing; there is only liberty for one and restraint for another.
Leonard T. Hobhouse, English philosopher and sociologist
Social Evolution and Political Theory, 1911

81.11   Those who won our independence believed that the final end of the State was to make men free to develop their faculties; and that in its government the deliberative forces should prevail over the arbitrary. They valued *liberty* both as an end and as a means. They believed liberty to be the secret of happiness and courage to be the secret of liberty.
Louis D. Brandeis
Whitney v. California, 274 U.S. 357, 375 (1927)

81.12   Liberty in the most literal sense is the negation of law, for law is restraint, and the absence of restraint is anarchy.
Benjamin N. Cardozo,   *1870–1938*
"The Paradoxes of Legal Science," in *Selected Writings of Benjamin Nathan Cardozo,* edited by Margaret E. Hall, 1947

81.13   What then is the spirit of liberty? I cannot define it; I can only tell you my own faith. The spirit of liberty is the spirit which is not too sure that it is right; the spirit of liberty is the spirit which seeks to understand the minds of other men and women; the spirit of liberty is the spirit which weighs their interests alongside its own without bias; the spirit of liberty remembers that not even a sparrow falls to earth unheeded; the spirit of liberty is the spirit of Him who, near two thousand years ago, taught mankind that lesson it has never learned, but has never quite forgotten; that there may be a kingdom where the least shall be heard and considered side by side with the greatest.
Learned Hand
"I Am an American Day" (speech), 1944

81.14   Liberty is too priceless to be forfeited through the zeal of an administrative agent.
Frank Murphy
Oklahoma Press Publishing Co. v. Walling, 327 U.S. 186, 219 (1946)

81.15   It is a fair summary of history to say that the safeguards of liberty have frequently been forged in controversies involving not very nice people.
Felix Frankfurter
United States v. Rabinowitz, 339 U.S. 56, 69 (1950)

81.16   We can afford no liberties with liberty itself.
> Robert H. Jackson
> *United States v. Spector,* 343 U.S. 169,
> 180 (1952)

81.17   There is no such thing as an achieved liberty; like electricity, there can be no substantial storage and it must be generated as it is enjoyed, or the lights go out.
> Robert H. Jackson
> "The Task of Maintaining our
> Liberties: The Role of the Judiciary,"
> 39 *American Bar Association Journal,*
> 961, 962 (1953)

81.18   Not every defeat of authority is a gain for individual freedom, nor every judicial rescue of a convict a victory for liberty.
> Robert H. Jackson
> "The Task of Maintaining Our
> Liberties," 39 *American Bar
> Association Journal* 964 (1953)

81.19   "The price of freedom is eternal vigilance." It was a lawyer who first used those words.
> Alfred Denning, English jurist
> *The Road to Justice,* 1955

81.20   I often wonder whether we do not rest our hopes too much upon constitutions, upon laws and upon courts. These are false hopes; believe me, these are false hopes. Liberty lies in the hearts of men and women; when it dies there, no constitution, no law, no court can save it. . . .
> Learned Hand
> Irving Dilliard, *The Spirit of Liberty,*
> 1960

81.21   What is the spirit of moderation? It is the temper which does not press a partisan advantage to its bitter end, which can understand and will respect the other side, which feels a unity between all citizens—real and not the factitious product of propaganda—which recognizes their common fate and their common aspirations—in a word, which has faith in the sacredness of the individual.
> Learned Hand
> Irving Dilliard, *The Spirit of Liberty,*
> 1960

82. LIFE

82.1   To everyone his own life is dark.
> Latin proverb
> W. Gurney Benham, *Putnam's
> Complete Book of Quotations, Proverbs
> and Household Words,* 1927

82.2   Life is like an artichoke, each day, week, month, year, gives you one little bit which you nibble off—but pre-

cious little compared with what you throw away.
Oliver Wendell Holmes
Letter from Holmes to Pollock,
January 17, 1887

82.3　Life is painting a picture, not doing a sum.
Oliver Wendell Holmes
"Class of '61," *Speeches,* 1913

82.4　. . . the world needs the flower more than the flower needs life.
Oliver Wendell Holmes
"The Use of Law Schools," *Speeches,*
1913

82.5　Life is an end in itself, and the only question as to whether it is worth living is whether you have enough of it.
Oliver Wendell Holmes
Speech, Bar Association of Boston,
Speeches, 1913

82.6　. . . all life is an experiment. Every year if not every day we have to wager our salvation upon some prophesy based upon imperfect knowledge.
Oliver Wendell Holmes, *1841–1935*
Quoted by Henry Steel Commager,
New York Times, November 20, 1985

82.7　We have to think of how to live before we can learn to die.
Richard Burdon Haldane
An Autobiography, 1929

82.8　This is life and all there is of life; to play the game, to play the cards we get; play them uncomplainingly and play them to the end. The game may not be worth the while. The stakes may not be worth the winning. But the playing of the game is the forgetting of self, and we should be game sports and play it bravely to the end.
Clarence Darrow, *1857–1938*
Arthur and Lila Weinberg, *Verdicts Out of Court,* 1963

82.9　Life has never been completely charted and as long as change is one of the great facts of life, it never will be; and law, we must always remember, is but one aspect of life.
Arthur T. Vanderbilt, American jurist
"A Report on Prelegal Education,"
New York University Law Review, vol.
25, April 1950

83.　LITIGATION

83.1　Win your lawsuit and lose your money.
Chinese proverb
Rosalind Fergusson, *The Facts On File Dictionary of Proverbs,* 1983

83.2　He'll go to law for the wagging of a straw.
English proverb
John Ray, *English Proverbs,* 1670

83.3   From litigation you can never re-
cover your losses.
Jewish folk saying
Joseph L. Baron, *A Treasury of
Jewish Quotations,* 1956

83.4   Go to law for a sheep and lose your
cow.
Proverb
Rosalind Fergusson, *The Facts On
File Dictionary of Proverbs,* 1983

83.5   He that goes to law holds a wolf by
the ear.
Proverb
Robert Burton, *The Anatomy of
Melancholy,* 1621

83.6   Law is a bottomless pit.
Proverb
Rosalind Fergusson, *The Facts On
File Dictionary of Proverbs,* 1983

83.7   Litigation . . . merely continues con-
flict and offends nature; it does not
heal.
Confucius,   *c.500 B.C.*
Joseph I. Lieberman "Confucius's
Lesson to Litigants" *The New York
Times,* July 9, 1984

83.8   You know what a ticklish thing it is
to go to law.
Plautus
Mostellaria, c.220 B.C.

83.9   As a man is friended so the law is
ended.
William Camden
Remains, 1605

83.10   Men are never wise but returning
from law.
John Wodroephe
The Spared Houres of a Soldier, 1623

83.11   The worst of law is that one suit
breeds twenty.
George Herbert,   *1593–1633*
Jacula Prudentum, 1640

83.12   A man must not go to law because
the musician keeps false time with
his foot.
Jeremy Taylor
The Worthy Communicant, 1660

83.13   The oyster is for the judge, the
shells are for the litigants.
Jean La Fontaine
Fables, 1668

83.14   That litigious pettifogger.
Anonymous
The Plain Dealer, 1677

83.15   Those who come into court to seek
justice must come with clean hands.
Sir Lloyd Kenyon, English jurist; lord
chief justice
Petrie v. Hennay, 1789

83.16   [*Litigation:*] A machine which you
go into as a pig and come out as a
sausage.
Ambrose Bierce
The Devil's Dictionary, 1906

83.17   [*Litigant:*] A person about to give
up his skin for the hope of retaining
his bone.
Ambrose Bierce
The Devil's Dictionary, 1906

83.18   [*Litigation:*] A form of hell
whereby money is transferred from
the pockets of the proletariat to that
of lawyers.
Elbert Hubbard,   *1856–1915*
Eugene E. Brussell, *Dictionary of
Quotable Definitions,* 1970

83.19   Litigation is the pursuit of practi-
cal ends, not a game of chess.
Felix Frankfurter
*Indianapolis v. Chase National Bank,
Trustee,* 314 U.S. 63, 62 S. Ct. 15, 86
L.Ed. 47, reh den 314 U.S. 714, 62 S.
Ct. 355, 356, 86 L.Ed. 569 (1941)

83.20   The tactics here employed resemble somewhat the military tactics which Marshall Foch is said to have urged on younger officers. He advised them to watch the movement of a parrot in its cage, which progresses by reaching out one claw, grasping firmly, and pausing before bringing the other claw into position—grasp, pause, grasp, pause, was his description of successful forward movement, and whatever its application to modern warfare, it is not a bad motto for constitutional litigation.
Paul A. Freund, American educator
On Understanding the Supreme Court,
1949

83.21   All litigation is inherently a clumsy, time-consuming business.
Warren E. Burger
U.S. News & World Report, December 14, 1970

83.22   We have created here in America the most litigious society in the history of mankind.
Lewis F. Powell, Jr.
Washington Post, April 12, 1973

83.23   All of us have heard the term "crisis" used frequently in the past years with reference to the courts and the process of litigation. . . . The pressures from the law explosion are severe, and the courts may not be equal to the task. Important rights may be lost. Defendants charged with crime may go free on bail, some to commit other crimes. Defendants convicted of crime may be free on bail pending delayed appeals. Business controversies may go unresolved because of the lack of a forum. Hapless plaintiffs with meritorious claims may go unpaid because of delay in trial and appellate courts.
Griffin B. Bell
Address, American Bar Association, reported in the *Washington Post,* November 30, 1977

83.24   I believe the system is out of balance. Litigation has come to be regarded as the natural order of things, as though it were the only way to go. It's not just lawyers who think this way; it's their clients too. Often people don't even seek legal counsel until a dispute has gone so far that the gladiators have to fight it out in court. Litigation should be a last resort, not a knee-jerk reflex.
Irving S. Shapiro, American lawyer, chairman, E. I. duPont de Nemours & Company
Christian Science Monitor, December 5, 1978

83.25   I have never met a litigator who did not think that he was winning the case right up to the moment when the guillotine came down.
William F. Baxter, American lawyer; assistant U.S. attorney general
Washington Post, April 18, 1982

83.26   Litigation takes the place of sex at middle age.
Gore Vidal
Kenneth Redden, *Modern Legal Glossary,* 1983

83.27   Whereas today only the progressive part of the Bar emphasizes out-of-court resolution over litigation, mediation will be the rule in space. . . .
Hamilton De Saussure, American educator; professor, University of Akron Law School
Sacramento Bee, 1984

M

84. MARRIAGE AND DIVORCE

84.1   A divorce lawyer is the man who referees the fight and winds up with the purse.
Anonymous
Leonard Louis Levinson, *Bartlett's Unfamiliar Quotations*, 1971

84.2   Consent makes marriage.
Latin legal phrase
W. Gurney Benham, *Putnam's Complete Book of Quotations, Proverbs and Household Words*, 1927

84.3   A Roman divorced from his wife, being highly blamed by his friends, who demanded, "Was she not chaste? Was she not fair? Was she not fruitful?" holding out his shoe, asked them whether it was not new and well made. "Yet," added he, "none of you can tell where it pinches me."
Plutarch,   *46?–?120*
Lives

84.4   When people understand that they *must* live together, except for a very few reasons known to the law, they learn to soften by mutual accommodation that yoke which they know they cannot shake off; they become good husbands, and good wives, from the necessity of remaining husbands and wives; for necessity is a powerful master in teaching the duties which it imposes. If it were once understood, that upon mutual disgust married persons might be legally separated, many couples, who now pass through the world with mutual comfort, with attention to their common offspring and to the moral order of civil society, might have been at this moment living in a state of mutual unkindness—in a stage of estrangement from their common offspring—and in a state of the most licentious and unreserved immorality.
Sir William Scott, English jurist
Evans v. Evans (1790), 1 Hagg. Con. Rep. 36, 37

84.5   Love, the quest; marriage, the conquest; divorce, the inquest.
Helen Rowland, American humorist
Reflections of a Bachelor Girl, 1903

84.6   Husband and wife are one, and that one is the husband.
Professor Loring
Theron G. Strong, *Joseph H. Choate,*
1917

84.7   Courtship is a republic; marriage, a monarchy; divorce, a soviet.
Helen Rowland, American humorist
"Personally Speaking," in *The Book of Diversion,* edited by F. P. Adams, D. Taylor and J. Bechdolt, 1925

84.8   . . . where divorce is allowed at all . . . society demands a specific grievance of one party against the other. . . . The fact that marriage may be a failure spiritually is seldom taken into account.
Suzanne LaFollette, American feminist and writer
"The Beginnings of Emancipation," *Concerning Women,* 1926

84.9   The claim for alimony . . . implies the assumption that a woman is economically helpless. . . .
Suzanne LaFollette, American feminist and writer
"Women and Marriage," *Concerning Women,* 1926

84.10   . . . when one hears the argument that marriage should be indissoluble for the sake of children, one cannot help wondering whether the protagonist is really such a firm friend of childhood. . . .
Suzanne LaFollette, American feminist and writer
"Women and Marriage," *Concerning Women,* 1926

84.11   Marriage, laws, the police, armies and navies are the mark of human incompetence.
Dora Russell, English writer
The Right to Be Happy, 1927

84.12   While the husband is still declared by statute to be the head of the family, he, like the King of England, is largely a figurehead.
Reginald L. Hine, American jurist
Curtis v. Ashworth, 165 Ga. 782, 787 (1928)

84.13   At the end of one millennium and nine centuries of Christianity, it remains an unshakable assumption of the law in all Christian countries and of the moral judgment of Christians everywhere that if a man and woman, entering a room together, close the door behind them, the man will come out sadder and the woman wiser.
H. L. Mencken,   *1880–1956*
Bergen Evans, *Dictionary of Quotations,* 1968

84.14   A lawyer is never entirely comfortable with a friendly divorce, any more than a good mortician wants to finish the job and then have the patient sit up on the table.
Jean Kerr, American playwright
Time, April 14, 1961

84.15   Whoever said, "Marriage is a 50–50 proposition . . ." laid the foundation for more divorce fees than any other short sentence in our language.
Who, among us, can define where "50% of the way" ends? In any given situation where two parties are desirous of achieving an end through continuous cooperation, a "50–50" fix is conducive to failure.
Austin Elliot
"Some Observations on the Attorney-Secretary Function," *Law Office Economics and Management,* November 1964

84.16   It's illegal in England to state in print that a wife can and should derive sexual pleasure from intercourse.
Bertrand Russell,   *1872–1970*
Laurence J. Peter, *Peter's Quotations,* 1977

84.17   *Holy Deadlock*
Sir Alan Patrick Herbert, English author and politician,   *1890–1971*
Title of a novel satirizing English divorce laws

---

85.   MERCY

85.1   [Mercy:] A virtue of the weak.
Anonymous
Eugene E. Brussell, ed., *Dictionary of Quotable Definitions,* 1970

85.2   Every dog is allowed one bite.
Proverb

85.3   The law is relaxed when the judge shows pity.
Publilius Syrus, Latin writer
Sententiae, c.43 B.C.

85.4   The quality of mercy is not strained,
It droppeth as the gentle rain from heaven
Upon the plain beneath:

     *   *   *

And earthly power doth then show like God's
When mercy seasons justice.
Shakespeare
The Merchant of Venice, IV, 1, 1596–1597

85.5   No ceremony that to great ones 'longs,
Not the King's crown, nor the deputed sword,
The marshal's truncheon nor the judge's robe,
Become them with one half so good a grace,
As mercy does.
Shakespeare
Measure for Measure, II, 2, 1604–1605

85.6   Yet shall I temper so
Justice with mercy.
Milton
Paradise Lost, 1667

85.7   Reason to rule, Mercy to forgive:
The first is law, the last perogative.
John Dryden
The Hind and the Panther, 1687

85.8   He only judges right who weighs, compares,
And, in the sternest sentence which his voice
Pronounces, ne'er abandons Charity.
William Wordsworth
Ecclesiastical Sonnets, 1822

85.9   We hand folks over to God's mercy, and show none ourselves.
George Eliot
Adam Bede, 1859

85.10   Gentlemen of the jury, think of his poor mother—his only mother.
Irish barrister, defending a prisoner
Marshall Brown, *Wit and Humor of Bench and Bar,* 1899

85.11   He reminds me of the man who murdered both his parents, and then, when sentence was about to be pronounced, pleaded for mercy on the grounds that he was an orphan.
Attributed to Abraham Lincoln, *1809–1865*
Franklin Pierce Adams, *FPA Book of Quotations,* 1952

85.12   If truth and justice were the rule, there would be no need for mercy.
Mendele Mocher Sforim
Di Kliatche, 1873

85.13   [*Mercy:*] An attribute beloved of detected offenders.
Ambrose Bierce
The Devil's Dictionary, 1906

85.14   I can forgive, but if you ask me to forget, you ask me to give up experience.
Louis Brandeis
Harlan Phillips, *Felix Frankfurter Reminisces,* 1960

86. MINORITIES

86.1   All, too, will bear in mind this sacred principle, that though the will of the majority is in all cases to prevail, that will, to be rightful, must be reasonable; that the minority possess their equal rights, which equal laws must protect, and to violate which would be oppression.
Thomas Jefferson
First inaugural address, 1801

86.2   Our progress in degeneracy appears to me to be pretty rapid. As a nation we began by declaring that *"all men are created equal."* We now practically read it "all men are created equal, *except negroes."* When the Know-nothings get control, it will read "all men are created equal, except negroes *and foreigners and Catholics."* When it comes to this, I shall prefer emigrating to some country where they make no pretense of loving liberty,—to Russia, for instance, where despotism can be taken pure, and without the base alloy of hypocrisy.
Abraham Lincoln
Letter to J. F. Speed, August 24, 1855

86.3   Persecution is a very easy form of virtue.
John Duke Coleridge, English jurist; lord chief justice
Reg. v. Ramsey (1883), 1 Cababe and Ellis's Q.B.D. Rep. 145

86.4   To protect those who are not able to protect themselves is a duty which every one owes to society.
> Edward Macnaghten, 1st baron,
> English jurist
> *Jenoure v. Delmege* (1890), 60 L.J.
> Rep. (N.S.) Q.B. 13

86.5   Experience tells us that sometimes, when minorities insist on their rights, they ultimately prevail.
> Robert George Kekewich, English
> jurist
> *Young v. South African &c. Syndicate*
> (1896), L.R. 2 C.D. (1896), p. 278

86.6   History teaches us that there have been but few infringements of personal liberty by the state which have not been justified. . . .in the name of righteousness and the public good, and few which have not been directed, as they are now, at politically helpless minorities.
> Harlan F. Stone
> *Minersville School District v. Gobitis,*
> 310 U.S. 586, 604 (1940)

86.7   There is room here for men of any race, of any creed, or any condition in life, but not for Protestant-Americans, or Catholic-Americans, or Jewish-Americans, nor for German-Americans, Irish-Americans, or Russian-Americans.
> Louis D. Brandeis, *1856–1941*
> Alpheus Thomas Mason, *Brandeis: A*
> *Free Man's Life,* 1946

86.8   The difference between *de jure* and *de facto* segregation is the difference between open, forthright bigotry and the shamefaced kind that works through unwritten agreements between real estate dealers, school officials, and local politicians.
> Shirley Chisholm
> *Unbought and Unbossed,* 1970

86.9   The experience of Negroes in America has been different in kind, not just in degree, from that of other ethnic groups. It is not merely the history of slavery alone but also that a whole people were marked as inferior by the law. And that mark has endured.
> Thurgood Marshall
> *University of California v. Bakke,* 438
> U.S. 265, 98 S. Ct. 2733, 57 L.Ed.2d
> 750 (1978)

---

87. MISCELLANEOUS

87.1   The act of God does no injury to any person.
> Latin legal phrase

87.2   You may not sell the cow and sup the milk.
> Proverb quoted by Edward
> Macnaghten, 1st baron, English jurist
> *Nordenfelt v. Maxim Nordenfelt Guns
> and Ammunition Co.* (1894), L.R.
> App. Cas. (1894), p. 572

87.3   Don't try to identify the tree of knowledge: Heaven forbid that we cast suspicion on any tree!
> Midrash, *Genesis Rabba*

87.4   They that once begin first to trouble the water, seldom catch the fish.
> George Jeffreys
> *Trial of William Sacheverell and others*
> (1684), 10 How. St. Tr. 92

87.5   I am by no means sure that if a man kept a tiger, and lightning broke his chain, and he got loose and did mischief, that the man who kept him would not be liable.
> Lord William Bramwell, English jurist
> *Nichols v. Marsland* (1875), L.R. 10
> Ex. 260

87.6   The farther I go west, the more convinced I am that the wise men came from the east.
> Joseph Jeckell, English lawyer and
> politician, *fl. early 18th century*
> Marshall Brown, *Wit and Humor of
> Bench and Bar,* 1899

87.7   I take it that reasonable human conduct is part of the ordinary course of things.
> Nathaniel Lindley, English jurist
> *The City of Lincoln* (1889), L.R. 15
> P.D. 18

87.8   Masterly inactivity may be prudence to one man, desperate rashness to another.
> Robert George Kekewich, English
> jurist
> *In re Liverpool Household Stores
> Association* (1890), 59 L.J. Rep. C.D.
> 618

87.9   "[Heaven is] to sit at *nisi prius* all day, and play whist all night."
> Francis Butler, English jurist; justice
> of the King's Bench
> Marshall Brown, *Wit and Humor of
> Bench and Bar,* 1899

87.10   Danger invites rescue.
> Benjamin N. Cardozo
> *Wagner v. International Ry. Co.,* 232
> N.Y. 13, 25 (1926)

87.11 The hand once set to a task may not always be withdrawn with impunity though liability would fail if it had been applied at all.
Benjamin N. Cardozo, *1928*

87.12 Nothing conduces to brevity like a caving in of the knees.
Oliver Wendell Holmes, *1841–1935*
Catherine Drinker Bowen, *Yankee from Olympus,* 1944

87.13 Every age is modern to those who are living in it.
Benjamin N. Cardozo, *1870–1938*
"Paradoxes of Legal Science,"
Selected writings of Benjamin Nathan Cardozo, 1947

87.14 The whole, though larger than any of its parts, does not necessarily obscure their separate identities.
William O. Douglas
United States v. Powers, 307 U.S. 214, 218 (1939)

87.15 I abhor averages. I like the individual case. A man may have six meals one day and none the next, making an average of three meals per day, but that is not a good way to live.
Louis D. Brandeis, *1856–1941*
A. T. Mason, *Brandeis: A Free Man's Life,* 1946

87.16 He who must search a haystack for a needle is likely to end up with the attitude that the needle is not worth the search.
Robert H. Jackson
Brown v. Allen, 344 U.S. 443, 537 (1953)

88. MONEY

88.1 Little money, little law.
Anonymous
The Parliament of Byrdes, c. 1550

88.2 She [Money] is the Sovereign Queen of all delights;
For her the Lawyer pleads, the Soldier fights.
Richard Barnfield, English poet
The Encomion of Lady Pecunia, 1598

88.3 Unnecessary laws are not good laws, but traps for money.
Thomas Hobbes
Leviathan, 1651

88.4   They who are of opinion that Money will do everything, may very well be suspected to do everything for Money.
> George Savile, 1st marquess of
> Halifax, English politician,
> *1633–1695*
> "Of Money," *The Complete Works of George Savile, First Marquess of Halifax,* 1912

88.5   But the rich man . . . is always sold to the institution which makes him rich. Absolutely speaking, the more money, the less virtue.
> Henry David Thoreau
> *Civil Disobedience,* 1849

88.6   One cannot help regretting that where money is concerned, it is so much the rule to overlook moral obligations.
> Sir Richard Malins, English jurist
> *Ellis v. Houston* (1878), L.R. 10 C.D. 240

88.7   To an imagination of any scope the most far-reaching form of power is not money, it is the command of ideas.
> Oliver Wendell Holmes
> "The Path of the Law," *Collected Legal Papers,* 1921

88.8   When a man keeps hollering, 'It's the principle of the thing,' he's talking about the money.
> Kin Hubbard (pseudonym of Frank McKinney Hubbard), American humorist, *1868–1930*
> Thad Stem, Jr. and Alan Butler, *Sam Ervin's Best Short Stories,* 1973

88.9   Men are more often bribed by their loyalties and ambitions than by money.
> Robert H. Jackson
> *United States v. Wunderlich,* 342 U.S. 98, 96 L.Ed. 113, 72 S. Ct. 154 (1951)

89. MORALS

89.1   Of what avail are empty laws if we lack principle?
> Horace
> *Odes,* 23 B.C.

89.2   Good men must not obey the laws too well.
> Ralph Waldo Emerson
> "Self-Reliance," *Essays,* 1844

89.3   Absolute morality is the regulation of conduct in such a way that pain shall not be inflicted.
> Herbert Spencer, English philosopher, *1820–1903*
> *Essays: Scientific, Political and Speculative,* 1863

89.4   This Court does not sit as a Court of morality, to inflict punishment

against those who offend against the social law.
> Sir Francis Henry Jeune, Baron St.
> Helier, English jurist
> *Evans v. Evans* (1899), L.R. Prob.
> Div. [1899], p. 202

89.5 You will see that international law is revolutionized by putting morals into it.
> Woodrow Wilson
> Address at Pueblo, 1919

89.6 Morality is simply another means of living but the saints make it an end in itself.
> Oliver Wendell Holmes, *1841–1935*
> Franklin Pierce Adams, *F.P.A. Book of Quotations,* 1952

89.7 I have often thought morality may perhaps consist solely in the courage of making a choice.
> Léon Blum
> Charles P. Curtis, Jr. and Ferris
> Greenslet, eds., *The Practical Cogitator,* 1945

89.8 You've got to have something to eat and a little love in your life before you can hold still for any damn body's sermon on how to behave.
> Billie Holiday, *1915–1959*

89.9 Morals are three-quarters manners.
> Felix Frankfurter
> Harlan Phillips, *Felix Frankfurter Reminiscences,* 1960

90. MOTIVES

90.1 The act does not constitute a criminal unless the mind is criminal.
> Latin legal phrase
> W. Gurney Benham, *Putnam's Complete Book of Quotations, Proverbs and Household Words,* 1927

90.2 Acts indicate the intention.
> Legal maxim

90.3 An act against my will is not my act.
> Legal maxim

90.4 Outward actions are a clue to hidden secrets.
> Legal maxim

90.5 *Cui bono?* [To whose good?]
> Cicero
> *Pro Sistio,* c.50 B.C.

90.6 The intention ought to be subservient to the laws, not the laws to the intention.
> Sir Edward Coke, *1552–1634*
> W. Gurney Benham, *Putnam's Complete Book of Quotations, Proverbs and Household Words,* 1927

90.7 The *end* directs and sanctifies the *means*.
Sir John Eardley Wilmot, English jurist; chief justice
Collins v. Blantern (1767), 2 Wils. Rep. 351

90.8 What passes in the mind of man is not scrutable by any human tribunal; it is only to be collected from his acts.
Sir John Willes, English jurist
King v. Shipley (1784), 3 Doug. 177

90.9 Men's feelings are as different as their faces.
Sir Nash Grose, English jurist
Good v. Elliott (1790), 3 T.R. 701

90.10 It is a principle of law, that a person intends to do that which is the natural effect of what he does.
Edward Law, Lord Ellenborough, English jurist; chief justice
Beckwith v. Wood and another (1817), 2 Starkie, 266

90.11 A man may have as bad a heart as he chooses, if his conduct is within the rules.
Oliver Wendell Holmes
The Common Law, 1881

90.12 Philosophy does not furnish motives, but it shows men that they are not fools for doing what they already want to do.
Oliver Wendell Holmes
"Natural Law," *Collected Legal Papers,* 1921

91. MURDER

91.1 Thou shalt not kill.
Old Testament, *Exodus* 20:13

91.2 The guilt of murder is the same, whether the victim be renowned or whether he be obscure.
Cicero
Pro Milone, 52 B.C.

91.3 He who slayeth one man is as guilty as if he killed the whole human race.
Muhammad
Koran, c.622

91.4 Mordre wol out, that see we day by day.
Chaucer
"The Nun's Priest's Tale," *Canterbury Tales,* c.1380

91.5 Ghost: Murder most foul, as in the best it is;
But this most foul, strange and unnatural.
Shakespeare
Hamlet, I, 5 1600–1601

91.6   The law against witches does not prove there be any; but it punishes the malice of those people that use such means to take away men's lives.
John Selden, *1584–1654*
Table-Talk, 1689

91.7   Gentlemen of the jury, the charge against the prisoner is murder, and the punishment is death; and that simple statement is sufficient to suggest the awful solemnity of the occasion which brings you and me face to face.
John Inglis
A Complete Report of the Trial of Miss Madeline Smith, 1857

91.8   Other sins only speak,
Murder cries out.
Anne Hocking, British mystery writer
Death Loves a Shining Mark, 1943

91.9   Clarissa: Oh dear, I never realized what a terrible lot of explaining one has to do in a murder!
Agatha Christie
Spider's Web, 1956

91.10   It must be true that whenever a sensational murder is committed there are people who—though they are, quite properly, of no interest to law enforcers, attorneys, or newspaper reporters—weep, lie sleepless, and realize at last that their lives have been changed by a crime in which they played no part.
Viña Delmar, American playwright
The Becker Scandal, 1968

N

92.   NATURAL LAW

92.1   Only such decrees should be issued which the majority of a community can endure.
Midrash, *Psalms*

92.2   See how people act, and that is the Law.
Talmud, *Berakhot*

92.3   What is hateful to you, do not to your fellow: that is the whole Law; all the rest is interpretation.
Hillel
Talmud, *Shabbat*

92.4   The commands of the law are conventional and have no root in nature.
Antiphon, Greek orator
Orations, c.435 B.C.

92.5   In every matter the consensus of opinion among all nations is to be regarded as the law of nature.
Cicero
Tusculanarum Disputationum, 45 B.C.

92.6   Through love every law is broken.
Chaucer
Troilus and Criseyde, 1385

92.7   Lust of love exceeds law.
John Gower
Confessio Amantis, 1393

92.8   Love has no law.
John Lydgate
"Virtues," *The Minor Poems of John Lydgate,* 1449

92.9   There are in nature certain foundations of justice, whence all civil laws are derived but as streams.
Francis Bacon
The Advancement of Learning, 1605

92.10   Oh wearisome condition of humanity!
Born under one law, to another bound.
Fulke Greville, 1st Baron Brooke,
English author and statesman
Mustapha, 1609

92.11   The first and fundamental law of Nature . . . is "to seek peace and follow it." The second, the sum of the right of Nature . . . is, "by all means we can to defend ourselves."
Thomas Hobbes
Leviathan, 1651

92.12   Law and conscience are one and the same.
> Justice Bacon, English jurist
> *Watson v. Watson* (1670), Style's Reports 56

92.13   That grounded maxim,
So rife and celebrated in the mouths
Of wisest men, that to the public good
Against the law of nature, law of nations.
> John Milton
> *Samson Agonistes,* 1671

92.14   Self-defense is nature's eldest law.
> John Dryden
> *Absalom and Achitophel,* 1681–1682

92.15   The law of heaven and earth is life for life.
> Lord Byron,   *1788–1824*
> "The Curse of Minerva"

92.16   When men are pure, laws are useless; when men are corrupt, laws are broken.
> Benjamin Disraeli
> *Contarini Fleming,* 1832

92.17   Nature's rules have no exceptions.
> Herbert Spencer
> *Social Statics,* 1851

92.18   The law of the past cannot be eluded,
The law of the present and future cannot be eluded,
The law of the living cannot be eluded—it is eternal.
> Walt Whitman
> "To Think of Time," 1855

92.19   That very law which molds a tear,
And bids it trickle from its source,
That law preserves the earth a sphere,
And guides the planets in their course.
> Samuel Rogers,   *1763–1855*
> "In a Tear"

92.20   It would not be correct to say that every moral obligation involves a legal duty; but every legal duty is founded on a moral obligation.
> John Duke Coleridge, English jurist;
> lord chief justice
> *The Queen v. Instan* (1893), L. R. 1
> Q. B. (1893), p. 453

92.21   The law that will work is merely the summing up in legislative form of the moral judgement that the community has already reached.
> Woodrow Wilson
> Address, December 20, 1915

92.22   The laws of God, the laws of man
He may keep that will and can;
Not I; let God and man decree
Laws for themselves and not for me.
> A. E. Housman
> *Last Poems,* 1922

92.23   The real law in the modern State is the multitude of little decisions made daily by millions of men.
> Walter Lippmann
> *A Preface to Morals,* 1929

92.24   The laws of the cosmos seem to be as little concerned about human felicity as the laws of the United States are concerned about human decency. Whoever set them in motion apparently had something quite different in mind—something that we cannot even guess at.
> H. L. Mencken
> *American Mercury,* March 1930

92.25   The natural law always buries its undertakers.
Heinrich Rommen, German lawyer, paraphrasing Etienne Gilson, French philosopher
Natural Law, 1947

92.26   There are no natural laws. There are only temporary habits of nature.
Alfred North Whitehead
Dialogues of Alfred North Whitehead, 1954

92.27   There is no such thing as "natural rights"; there are only adjustments of conflicting claims.
Aldous Huxley
Music at Night, 1931

92.28   The law of diminishing returns holds good in almost every part of our human universe.
Aldous Huxley
W. H. Auden and Louis Kronenberger, *The Viking Book of Aphorisms,* 1962

93.   NEED

93.1   Inability suspends the law.
Latin legal phrase
W. Gurney Benham, *Putnam's Complete Book of Quotations, Proverbs and Household Words,* 1927

93.2   No one is held bound to the impossible.
Latin legal phrase

93.3   The law does not seek to compel a man to do that which he cannot possibly perform.
Legal maxim

93.4   Need makes a wise man do evil.
Proverb
E. Gordon Duff, ed., *Salomon and Marcolphus,* 1492

93.5   Necessity has no law.
St. Augustine
Soliloquiorum: Animae ad Deum, c.410

93.6   Need has no law.
William Langland
The Vision of William Concerning Piers the Plowman, 1362–1390

93.7   It is necessity which makes laws, and force which makes them observed.
Voltaire
"Des Lois," *Dictionnaire Philosophique,* 1764

93.8   Necessity creates the law,—it super-
sedes rules; and whatever is reason-
able and just in such cases is likewise
legal.
  Sir William Scott, Lord Stowell,
  English jurist
  "The Gratitude" (1801), 3 Rob. Adm.
  Rep. 240

93.9   Law is mighty, necessity is mightier.
  Goethe, *1749–1832*
  W. Gurney Benham, *Putnam's
  Complete Book of Quotations, Proverbs
  and Household Words,* 1927

O

94. OBEDIENCE

94.1 'Tis best to keep the established laws, even to life's end.
Sophocles
Antigone, c.441 B.C.

94.2 If you cannot reconcile yourself to the law, remain in the cradle.
Pedro Calderón de la Barca,
1600–1681
La Vida es Sueño

94.3 The least of our servitudes is to the law.
Marquis de Vauvenargues, French moralist
Réflexions, 1746

94.4 A strict observance of the written laws is doubtless *one* of the high duties of a good citizen, but it is not *the highest.* The laws of necessity, of self preservation, of saving our country when in danger, are of a higher obligation. . . . To lose our country by a scrupulous adherence to written law would be to lose the law itself, with life, liberty, property and all those who are enjoying them with us; thus absurdly sacrificing the ends to the means.
Thomas Jefferson
Letter to J. B. Colvin, September 20, 1780

94.5 On great occasions every good officer must be ready to risk himself in going beyond the strict line of the law, when the public preservation requires it; his motives will be a justification.
Thomas Jefferson
Letter to W. C. Claiborne, February 3, 1807

94.6 I am beginning to think . . . that "the people have nothing to do with the laws but to obey them."
Edgar Allan Poe
"Fifty Suggestions," *Graham's Magazine,* May–June, 1845

94.7 Now these are the Laws of the Jungle, and many and mighty are they;
But the head and the hoof of the Law and the haunch and the hump is— Obey!
Rudyard Kipling
"The Law of the Jungle," *The Second Jungle Book,* 1895

94.8   No man is above the law and no man is below it; nor do we ask any man's permission when we require him to obey it. Obedience to the law is demanded as a right; not asked as a favor.
> Theodore Roosevelt
> Third annual message, December 7, 1903

94.9   Those who are too lazy and comfortable to think for themselves and be their own judges obey the laws. Others sense their own laws within them.
> Hermann Hesse
> *Demian,* 1919

94.10   Of the contrivances which mankind has devised to lift itself from savagery there are few to compare with the habit of assent, not to a factitious common will, but to the law as it is.
> Learned Hand
> "Is There a Common Will?" 28
> *Michigan Law Review* 46, 52 (1929)

94.11   It seems to me that the only law which there is any merit obeying is the one you do not agree with either because you think it is mistaken or because you think it operates against your interest; and the only law which there is any merit enforcing is the law which at least somebody would not obey if it were not enforced.
> Lord Hailsham
> *Los Angeles Times,* April 23, 1972

95.   OPINIONS

95.1   Do we admit the existence of opinion? Undoubtedly.
Then I suppose that opinion appears to you to be darker than knowledge, but lighter than ignorance?
Both; and in no small degree.
> Plato
> *The Republic,* c.370 B.C.

95.2   As many opinions as there are men; each a law to himself.
> Terence
> *Phormio,* 161 B.C.

95.3   My brothers differ from me in opinion, and they all differ from one another in the reasons of their opinion; but not withstanding their opinion, I think the plaintiff ought to recover.
> Sir John Holt, English jurist; chief justice
> *Ashby v. White* (1703), 2 Ld. Raym. 938, 950

95.4   An opinion is huddled up in conclave, perhaps by a majority of one, delivered as if unanimous, and with the silent acquiescence of lazy or

timid associates, by a crafty chief judge. . . .
Thomas Jefferson, *1743–1826*
Andrew A. Lipscomb, *The Writings of Thomas Jefferson,* 1903

95.5 Every opinion tends to become a law.
Oliver Wendell Holmes
Lochner v. New York, 198 U.S. 45, 75 (1905)

95.6 In this court dissents have gradually become majority opinions.
Felix Frankfurter
Graves v. New York ex rel. O'Keefe, 360 U.S. 466, 83 L.Ed. 927, Sup. Ct. 595 (1939)

95.7 Our opinions are at best provisional hypotheses.
Learned Hand
"Learned Hand and the Interpretation of Statutes," 60 *Harvard Law Review* 370, 393 (1947)

95.8 How I dislike writing opinions! I prefer arguments—and let someone else have the responsibility of decision.
Charles Evans Hughes, *1862–1948,* reflecting on his appointment to the World Court
Merlo Pusey, *Charles Evans Hughes,* 1951

95.9 It is true of opinions as of other compositions that those who are seeped in them, whose ears are sensitive to literary nuances, whose antennae record subtle silences, can gather from their contents meaning beyond the words.
Felix Frankfurter
" 'The Administrative Side' of Chief Justice Hughes," 63 *Harvard Law Review* 1, 2 (1949)

95.10 It is disheartening to find so much that is right in an opinion which seems to me so fundamentally wrong.
Frank Murphy
Wolf v. Colorado, 388 U.S. 25 (1949)

95.11 Lord Westbury . . . it is said, rebuffed a barrister's reliance upon an earlier opinion of his Lordship: "I can only say that I am amazed that a man of my intelligence should have been guilty of giving such an opinion." If there are other ways of gracefully and good naturedly surrendering former views to a better considered position, I invoke them all.
Robert H. Jackson
McGrath v. Kristensen, 340 U.S. 162, 177–78 (1950)

95.12 When blithe to argument I come,
Though armed with facts, and merry,
May Providence protect me from
    The fool as adversary,
Whose mind to him a kingdom is
    Where reason lacks dominion,
Who calls conviction prejudice
    And prejudice opinion.
Phyllis McGinley
"Moody Reflections," *Times Three: 1932–1960,* 1960

95.13 Chief Justice Hennessey of the Massachusetts Supreme Judicial Court in a speech related the time that an attorney rushed into the Superior Court Judge Donahue's chamber to notify the judge that the Supreme Judicial Court had affirmed one of his opinions. The acerbic judge looked up from his papers and said, "I still think I was right."
Edward F. Hennessey, American jurist
Kenneth Redden, *Modern Legal Glossary,* 1983

P

96. PLEAS

96.1 An ill plea should be well pleaded.
Proverb
H. G. Bohn, *Handbook of Proverbs,*
1855

96.2 Abr: Do you bite your thumb at us,
sir?
Sam: Is the law on our side if I say ay?
Shakespeare
Romeo and Juliet, I, 1, 1594–1595

96.3 The world is still deceived with orna-
ment.
In law, what plea so tainted and cor-
rupt
But, being seasoned with a gracious
voice,
Obscures the show of evil?
Shakespeare
The Merchant of Venice, III, 1,
1596–1597

96.4 Pleading is an exact setting forth of
the truth.
Sir Robert Atkyns, English jurist
Trial of Sir Edward Hales (1686), 11
How. St. Tr. 1243

96.5 I am sorry when any man is tripped
by a formal objection.
Justice Park, British jurist
Aked v. Stocks (1828), 4 Bing. 509

96.6 In law it is a good policy never to
plead what you need not, lest you
oblige yourself to prove what you cannot.
Abraham Lincoln
Letter to Usher F. Linder, February
20, 1848

96.7 If criminals wanted to grind justice
to a halt, they could do it by banding
together and all pleading not guilty.
It's only because we have plea-bargaining that our criminal justice system is still in motion. That doesn't say
much for the quality of justice.
Dorothy Wright Wilson, American
educator; dean, University of
Southern California Law Center
Los Angeles Times, August 11, 1974

96.8 Because of plea-bargaining, I guess
we can say, "Gee, the trains run on
time." But do we like where they are
going?
Franklin E. Zimring, American
educator; professor, University of
Chicago
Time, August 28, 1978

97. POLITICS

97.1   The Parish makes the Constable, and when the Constable is made, he governs the Parish.
> John Selden,   *1584–1654*
> *Table-Talk,* 1689

97.2   Political arguments, in the fullest sense of the word, as they concern the government of a nation, must be, and always have been, of great weight in the consideration of the Court.
> Philip Yorke, 1st earl of Hardwicke,
> English jurist; lord chancellor
> *The Earl of Chesterfield v. Janssen*
> (1750), 1 Atk. 352, *id.* 2 Ves. Sen. 153

97.3   The Constitution does not allow reasons of State to influence our judgments: God forbid it should!
> Sir William Murray, Lord Mansfield,
> English jurist; chief justice
> *Case of John Wilkes* (1770), 19 How.
> St. Tr. 1112

97.4   If I could not go to heaven but with a party, I would not go there at all.
> Thomas Jefferson
> Letter to Francis Hopkinson, March
> 13, 1789

97.5   A man full of warm, speculative, benevolence may wish his society otherwise constituted than he finds it; but a good patriot, and a true politician, always considers how he shall make the most of the existing materials of his country. A disposition to preserve, and an ability to improve, taken together, would be my standard of a statesman.
> Edmund Burke
> *Reflections on the Revolution in*
> *France,* 1790

97.6   Ministers [are] the better for being now and then a little peppered and salted.
> Unknown British politician
> Quoted by Lord Kenyon, *Holt's Case*
> (1793), 22 How. St. Tr. 1234

97.7   One cannot look too closely at and weigh in too golden scales the acts of men hot in their political excitement.
> Sir Henry Hawkins, English jurist
> *Ex parte Castioni* (1890), 60 L.J. Rep.
> (N.S.) Mag. Cas. 33

97.8   More lawyers (considering the number who play the game intensively) have been ruined by politics than by liquor, women, or the stock market.
> Arthur Garfield Hays, American
> lawyer
> *City Lawyer,* 1942

97.9   Someone asked me, as I came in, how I felt. I was reminded of a story that a fellow townsman of ours used to tell—Abraham Lincoln. They asked him how he felt once after an unsuccessful election. He said he felt like a little boy who had stubbed his toes in the dark. He said that he was too old to cry, but it hurt too much to laugh.
Adlai E. Stevenson
Life, July 23, 1965

98. POVERTY

98.1   Art thou so bare and full of wretchedness
And fear'st to die? Famine is in thy cheeks,
Need and oppression starveth in thine eyes,
Contempt and beggary hang upon thy back,
The world is not thy friend, nor the world's law;
The world affords no law to make thee rich;
Then be not poor, but break it.
Shakespeare
Romeo and Juliet, V, 1, 1594–1595

98.2   All crimes are safe but hated poverty.
This, only this, the rigid law pursues.
Samuel Johnson
"London," 1738

98.3   Poverty sets a reduced price on crime.
Sébastien Roch Nicolas Chamfort,
French writer, *1740–1794*
W. H. Auden and Louis Kronenberger, *The Viking Book of Aphorisms*, 1962

98.4   His poverty, not his will, consented to the danger.
Sir Henry Hawkins, English jurist
Thrussell v. Handyside and Co. (1888),
20 Q.B.D. 359, 364

98.5   Poverty and immorality are not synonymous.
James F. Byrnes
Edwards v. California, 314 U.S. 160,
177 (1941)

98.6   The mere state of being without funds is a neutral fact—constitutionally an irrelevance, like race, creed, or color.
Robert H. Jackson
Edwards v. California, 314 U.S. 160,
184 (1941)

98.7   Substantive and procedural law benefits and protects landlords over tenants, creditors over debtors, lenders over borrowers, and the poor are seldom among the favored parties.
John N. Turner, Canadian lawyer;
attorney general of Canada
Speech, Canadian Bar Association,
December 7, 1969

98.8   Hungry people cannot be good at learning or producing anything, except perhaps violence.
Pearl Bailey
Pearl's Kitchen, 1973

---

99. POWER

99.1   Power delegated cannot exceed that which was its origin.
Legal maxim

99.2   And he who rejoices at the destruction of human life is not fit to be entrusted with power in the world.
Lao-tzu,   *c.604?–?531 B.C.*
Tao te Ching

99.3   No power ought to be above the laws.
Cicero
Paraphrase of *De Domo Sua,* 57 B.C.

99.4   Even false becomes true when the chief says so.
Publilius Syrus, Latin writer
Maxims, 42 B.C.

99.5   . . . knowledge itself is power. . . .
Francis Bacon
Meditationes Sacrae, 1597

99.6   Bidding the law make curtsey to their will.
Shakespeare
Measure for Measure, II, 4, 1604–1605

99.7   The conscience of a people is their power.
John Dryden
The Duke of Guise, 1683

99.8   Law is but a heathen word for power.
Daniel Defoe
The History of the Kentish Petition, 1701

99.9   . . . a power over a man's subsistence amounts to a power over his will.
Alexander Hamilton
The Federalist Papers, 1787–1788

99.10   Law and arbitrary power are in eternal enmity.
Edmund Burke
Speech on the impeachment of Warren Hastings, February 15, 1788

99.11   What do I care about the law? Hain't I got the power?
Cornelius Vanderbilt,   *1794–1877*
Laurence J. Peter, *Peter's Quotations,* 1977

99.12   Power tends to corrupt and absolute power corrupts absolutely.
Lord Acton
Letter to Bishop Mandell Creighton, April 5, 1887

99.13   The prize of the general is not a bigger tent, but command.
Oliver Wendell Holmes
"Law and the Court," *Speeches,* 1913

99.14   We fear to grant power and are unwilling to recognize it when it exists.
Oliver Wendell Holmes
Tyson & Brothers v. Banton, 273 U.S. 418, 445 (1927)

99.15   I am the law.
Frank Hague, American politician; mayor, Jersey City, New Jersey, *1917–1947*
New York Times, November 11, 1937

99.16   Government of limited power need not be anemic government. Assurance that rights are secure tends to diminish fear and jealousy of strong government, and by making us feel safe to live under it makes for its better support.
Robert H. Jackson
West Virginia State Board of Education v. Barnette, 319 U.S. 624, 87 L.Ed. 1628, 63 Sup. Ct. 1178 (1943)

99.17   No one will question that this [war] power is the most dangerous one to free government in the whole catalogue of powers.
Robert H. Jackson
Woods v. Miller, 333 U.S. 138, 92 L.Ed. 596, 68 Sup. Ct. 421 (1948)

99.18   All executive power—from the reign of ancient kings to the rule of modern dictators—has the outward appearance of efficiency.
William O. Douglas
Youngstown Sheet & Tube Co. v. Sawyer, 343 U.S. 579 (1952)

99.19   . . . power is something of which I am convinced there is no innocence this side of the womb . . . .
Nadine Gordimer, South African writer

100.   PRECEDENTS

100.1   Judgment should be according to the laws, not according to the precedents.
Latin legal phrase

100.2   Don't use the conduct of a fool as a precedent.
Talmud, *Shabbat*

100.3   All things which are now regarded as of great antiquity were once new, and that which we maintain today by precedents will be among the precedents.
Tacitus
Annals, c.110

100.4   Portia: It must not be; there is no power in Venice
Can alter a decree established:
'Twill be recorded for a precedent;
And many an error by the same example
Will rush into the state.
Shakespeare
The Merchant of Venice, IV, 1, 1596–1597

100.5   Every precedent had first a commencement.
Sir Thomas Egerton, Baron Ellesmere, English jurist and statesman; lord chancellor
Case of Proclamations (1611), 2 How. St. Tr. 723, 72J

100.6   It is dangerous to make a precedent, an innovation.
Sir John Pratt, English jurist; chief justice
Layer's Case (1722), 16 How. St. Tr. 267

100.7   It is a maxim among lawyers that whatever hath been done before may be done again: and therefore they take special care to record all the decisions formerly made against common justice and the general reason of mankind. These, under the name of *precedents,* they produce as authorities to justify the most iniquitous opinions; and the judges never fail of directing accordingly.
Jonathan Swift
Gulliver's Travels, 1726

100.8   There is no magic in parchment or in wax.
William Henry Ashhurst, English jurist
Master v. Miller (1763), 4 T.R. 320

100.9   No degree of antiquity can give sanction to a usage bad in itself.
Yates and Austin, English jurists
Leach v. Three of the Kings Messengers (1765), 19 How. St. Tr. 1027

100.10   The doctrine of the law then is this: that precedents and rules must be followed, unless flatly absurd or unjust; for though their reason be not obvious at first view, yet we owe such a deference to former times as not to suppose that they acted wholly without consideration.
Sir William Blackstone
Commentaries on the Laws of England, 1765–1769

100.11   One precedent creates another. They soon accumulate and constitute law. What yesterday is fact, today is doctrine.
Junius, (pseudonym of English unidentified letter writer)
"Dedication to the English Nation,"
The Letters of Junius, 1772

100.12   Precedent, though it be evidence of law, is not law in itself.
William Murray, 1st earl of Mansfield, English jurist; chief justice
Jones v. Randall (1774), Lofft. 383, 385

100.13   To follow foolish precedents, and wink with both our eyes, is easier than to think.
William Cowper
Tirocinium, 1785

100.14 A precedent embalms a principle.
Attributed to Sir William Scott,
English jurist
Opinion, while advocate general, 1788

100.15 Every law which originated in ignorance and malice, and gratifies the passions from which it sprang, we call the wisdom of our ancestors.
Sydney Smith, English clergyman and writer
Peter Plymley's Letters, 1807

100.16 Laws are inherited like diseases.
Goethe
Faust, 1808

100.17 When a judge challenged Rufus Choate, the famous Massachusetts lawyer, to cite a precedent for his argument before the court, he replied: "I will look, your honor, and endeavor to find a precedent if you require it; though it would seem a pity that the court should lose the distinction of being the first to establish so just a rule."
Rufus Choate, *1799–1859*
Ed Bander, *The Path of the Law,* 1980

100.18 Mastering the lawless science of our law,
That codeless myriad of precedent,
That wilderness of single instances,
Through which a few, by wit or fortune led,
May beat a pathway out to wealth and fame.
Tennyson
Aylmer's Field, 1864

100.19 The acts of today may become the precedents of tomorrow.
Farrer Herschell, English jurist; lord chancellor
Speech, May 23, 1878

100.20 But as precedents survive like the clavicle in the cat, long after the use they once served is at an end, and the reason for them has been forgotten, the result of following them must often be failure and confusion from the merely logical point of view.
Oliver Wendell Holmes
"Common Carriers and the Common Law," 13 *American Law Review,* 608, 630 (1879)

100.21 The life of the law has not been logic; it has been experience.
Oliver Wendell Holmes
The Common Law, 1881

100.22 Practically . . . the law . . . is all *ex post facto.*
John Chipman Gray, American lawyer
The Nature and Sources of Law, 1909

100.23 The forms of action we have buried but they rule us from their graves.
Frederic W. Maitland
The Forms of Action at Common Law, 1909

100.24 . . . historic continuity with the past is not a duty, it is only a necessity.
Oliver Wendell Holmes
"Learning and Science," *Speeches,* 1913

100.25 There is no superstitious sanctity attaching to a precedent . . . . Courts can only maintain their authority by correcting their errors to accord with justice and the advance and progress of each age.
Walter Clark, American jurist
State v. Falkner, 1921

100.26   The repetition of a catchword can hold analysis in fetters for fifty years and more.
> Benjamin N. Cardozo
> *Mr. Justice Holmes,* 44 Harv. L. Rev. 682, 689 (March 1931)

100.27   The law, so far as it depends on learning, is indeed, as it has been called, the government of the living by the dead. To a very considerable extent no doubt it is inevitable that the living should be so governed.
> Oliver Wendell Holmes
> "Learning and Science," *Speeches,* 1934

100.28   If mankind had continued to be the slave of precedent we should still be living in the caves and subsisting on shellfish and wild berries.
> Philip Snowden, British statesman, *1864–1937*
> Laurence J. Peter, *Peter's Quotations,* 1977

100.29   The tendency to disregard precedents . . . has become so strong . . . as . . . to shake confidence in the consistency of decision and leave the courts below on an uncharted sea of doubt and difficulty without any confidence that what was said yesterday will hold good tomorrow.
> Owen J. Roberts
> *Mahnich v. Southern Steamship Co.,* 321 U.S. 96, 64 S. Ct. 455, 88 L.Ed. 561 (1944)

100.30   . . . constitutional precedents . . . have a mortality rate almost as high as their authors.
> Robert H. Jackson
> "The Task of Maintaining Our Liberties: The Role of the Judiciary" 39 *American Bar Association Journal* 962 (1953)

100.31   Every lawyer of experience comes to know (more or less unconsciously) that in the great majority of cases, the precedents are none too good as bases of prediction. Somehow or other, there are plenty of precedents to go around.
> Jerome Frank
> *Law and the Modern Mind,* 1953

100.32   An old lawyer in St. Louis made a speech sometime ago in which he said, "Do not waste your time looking up the law in advance, because you can find some Federal district court that will sustain any proposition you make."
> Sam Ervin, Jr.
> At Senate Watergate Hearings, reported in the *Dallas Times Herald,* June 20, 1973

100.33   Fred Rodell . . . once compared the law to the Killy-loo bird, a creature that he said insisted on flying backward because it didn't care where it was going but was mightily interested in where it had been.
> Fred Rodell, American educator; professor, Yale Law School
> Paraphrase in the *New York Times,* June 27, 1984

101.   PREJUDICE

101.1   It is sometimes difficult to get rid of first impressions.
Sir Lloyd Kenyon, English jurist; lord chief justice
Withnell v. Gartham (1795), 6 T.R. 396

101.2   . . . we can't abolish prejudice through laws . . .
Belva Lockwood, American lawyer and feminist, *1830–1917*
Mary Virginia Fox, *Lady for the Defense,* 1975

101.3   Deep-seated preferences cannot be argued about—you cannot argue a man into liking a glass of beer—and therefore, when differences are sufficiently far-reaching, we try to kill the other man rather than let him have his way. But that is perfectly consistent with admitting that, so far as appears, his grounds are just as good as ours.
Oliver Wendell Holmes
"Natural Law," *Collected Legal Papers,* 1921

101.4   . . . most of our so-called reasoning consists in finding arguments for going on believing as we already do.
James Harvey Robinson
The Mind in the Making, 1921

101.5   . . . we must be ever on our guard, lest we erect our prejudices into legal principles.
Louis D. Brandeis
New State Ice Co. v. Liebmann, 285 U.S. 262, 311 (1932)

101.6   . . . any man who says he is impartial about any subject on which he speaks is either ignorant or a liar. . . .
Oliver Wendell Holmes, *1841–1935*
Labor Law Journal, November 1949

101.7   Everyone is a prisoner of his own experiences. No one can eliminate prejudices—just recognize them.
Edward R. Murrow
News commentary, December 31, 1955

101.8   There are only two ways to be quite unprejudiced and impartial. One is to be completely ignorant. The other is to be completely indifferent. Bias and prejudice are attitudes to be kept in hand, not attitudes to be avoided.
Charles P. Curtis, American lawyer
A Commonplace Book, 1957

101.9   Law is a reflection and a source of prejudice. It both enforces and suggests forms of bias.
Diane B. Schulder, American lawyer and educator
"Does the Law Oppress Women?"
Sisterhood Is Powerful, edited by Robin Morgan, 1970

101.10   You've got to remember to put the law before your own prejudices.
Gerhard A. Gesell, American jurist
Los Angeles Times, June 13, 1974

102.   PRESS

102.1   Give me six lines written by the most honorable man, and I will find an excuse in them to hang him.
Cardinal Richelieu
Miramé, 1641

102.2   The press is like the air, a chartered libertine.
William Pitt
To Lord Grenville, c.1757

102.3   A writer's fame will not be the less, that he has bread, without being under the necessity of prostituting his pen to flattery or party, to get it.
Sir John Willes, English jurist
Millar v. Taylor (1768), 4 Burr. Part IV., p. 2335

102.4   Ideas are free. But while the author confines them to his study, they are like birds in a cage, which none but he can have a right to let fly: for till he thinks proper to emancipate them, they are under his own dominion.
Sir Joseph Yates, English jurist
Millar v. Taylor (1769), 4 Burr. Part IV., p. 2379

102.5   The liberty of the Press is the Palladium of all the civil, political, and religious rights of an Englishman.
Junius, (pseudonym of English unidentified letter writer)
"Dedication to the English Nation,"
The Letters of Junius, 1772

102.6   As for the freedom of the press, I will tell you what it is: the liberty of the press is that a man may print what he pleases without license. As long as it remains so, the liberty of the press is not restrained.
William Murray, 1st earl of Mansfield, English jurist; chief justice
Charge to the jury in the trial of H. W. Woodfall, 1772

102.7 Thou god of our idolatry, the Press.
William Cowper
The Progress of Error, 1782

102.8 . . . were it left to me to decide whether we should have a government without newspapers, or newspapers without a government, I should not hesitate a moment to prefer the latter.
Thomas Jefferson
Letter to Edward Carrington, January 16, 1787

102.9 The legislature of the United States shall pass no law on the subject of religion nor touching or abridging the liberty of the press.
Charles Pinckney
Resolution offered in The Constitutional Convention, 1787

102.10 A man may publish anything which twelve of his countrymen think not blamable.
Sir Lloyd Kenyon, English jurist; lord chief justice
Cuthell's Case (1799), 27 How. St. Tr. 675

102.11 Where vituperation begins, the liberty of the press ends.
Sir William Draper Best, Lord Wynford, British jurist
King v. Burdett (1820), 1 St. Tr. (n.s.) 120

102.12 No government ought to be without censors; and where the press is free none ever will.
Thomas Jefferson, *1743–1826*
Writings, 1853

102.13 I am myself a gentleman of the Press, and I bear no other scutcheon.
Benjamin Disraeli
Speech in the House of Commons, February 18, 1863

102.14 A free press stands as one of the great interpreters between the government and the people. To allow it to be fettered is to fetter ourselves.
George Sutherland, American jurist
Grosjean v. American Press Co., 297 U.S. 233, 250 (1936)

102.15 Did you ever hear anyone say "that work had better be banned because I might read it and it might be very damaging to me"?
Joseph Henry Jackson, American journalist; editor, *San Francisco Chronicle; 1894–1946*

102.16 People everywhere confuse what they read in newspapers with news.
A. J. Liebling
"A Talkative Something or Other," *New Yorker,* April 7, 1956

102.17 I won't say that the papers misquote me, but I sometimes wonder where Christianity would be today if some of those reporters had been Matthew, Mark, Luke and John.
Barry M. Goldwater
Speech, Washington, D.C., August 10, 1964

102.18 The Senator might remember that the evangelists had a more inspiring subject.
Walter Lippmann, replying to Barry M. Goldwater's speech attacking the press
Syndicated column, August 13, 1964

102.19   A free press is not a privilege but [a] necessity in a great society.
Walter Lippmann
Syndicated column, May 27, 1965

102.20   The American press is extraordinarily free and vigorous, as it should be. It should be, not because it is free of inaccuracy, oversimplification and bias, but because the alternative to that freedom is worse than those failings.
Robert Bork, American jurist; judge, U.S. Court of Appeals
New York Times, April 11, 1985

103.   PRIVACY

103.1   Public laws favor domestic privacy.
Legal maxim

103.2   The private life of a citizen ought to be within walls.
Talleyrand
Letter to M. Colomb, October 31, 1818

103.3   No rights can be dearer to a man of cultivation than exemptions from unseasonable invasions on his time by the coarse-minded and ignorant.
J. Fenimore Cooper
The American Democrat, 1838

103.4   A man has a right to pass through this world, if he wills, without having his pictures published, his business enterprises discussed, his successful experiments written up for the benefit of others, or his eccentricities commented upon, whether in handbills, circulars, catalogues, newspapers or periodicals.
Alton B. Parker, American jurist; chief justice, New York Court of Appeals
Roberson v. Rochater Folding Box Co. (1901)

103.5   I might have been a gold-fish in a glass bowl for all the privacy I got.
Saki, pseudonym of H. H. Munro
The Innocence of Reginald, 1904

103.6   The right to be alone—the most comprehensive of rights, and the right most valued by civilized men.
Louis D. Brandeis
Olmstead v. United States, 277 U.S. 438, 48 S. Ct. 564, 66 ALR 376, 72 L.Ed. 944 (1928)

103.7   It doesn't matter what you do in the bedroom as long as you don't do it in the street and frighten the horses.
Mrs. Patrick Campbell,   *1865–1940*

103.8   Civilization is the progress toward a society of privacy. The savage's whole existence is public, ruled by the laws of his tribe. Civilization is the process of setting man free from men.
Ayn Rand
The Fountainhead, 1943

103.9   The right to be let alone is indeed the beginning of all freedom.
William O. Douglas
Public Utilities Comm'n. v. Pollak, 343 U.S. 451, 467 (1952)

103.10   The Fourth Amendment and the personal rights it secures have a long history. At the very core stands the right of a man to retreat into his own home and there be free from unreasonable governmental intrusion.
Potter Stewart
New York Times, March 6, 1961

103.11   In the relationship between man and religion, the state is firmly committed to a position of neutrality.
Tom C. Clark
New York Herald Tribune, June 18, 1963

103.12   A state has no business telling a man, sitting alone in his own house, what books he may read or what films he may watch . . . Whatever may be the justifications for other statutes regulating obscenity, we do not think they reach into the privacy of one's own home.
Thurgood Marshall
Supreme Court decision, April 7, 1969

103.13   Civil laws against adultery and fornication have been on the books forever, in every country. That's not the law's business; that's God's business. He can handle it.
Thomas G. Kavanagh, American jurist; chief justice, Supreme Court of Michigan
San Francisco Examiner & Chronicle, March 5, 1978

---

104.   PROPERTY

104.1   An assignee is clothed with the rights of his principal.
Legal maxim

104.2   He who possesses land possesses also that which is above it.
Legal maxim

104.3　　He has the better title who was first in point of time.
Legal maxim

104.4　　In a case of equal right, the position of the person in possession is the better.
Legal maxim

104.5　　Possession is nine points of the law.
Legal maxim
Rosalind Fergusson, *The Facts On File Dictionary of Proverbs,* 1983

104.6　　Right is said to have commenced in possession.
Legal maxim

104.7　　For a man's house is his castle.
Sir Edward Coke
The Institutes of the Lawes of England, vol. 1, 1628–1641

104.8　　Law, in a free country, is, or ought to be, the determination of those who have property in land.
Jonathan Swift
Thoughts on Various Subjects, c.1714

104.9　　Laws are always useful to persons of property, and hurtful to those who have none.
Jean-Jacques Rousseau
Du Contrat social, 1761

104.10　　By the laws of England, every invasion of private property, be it ever so minute, is a trespass. No man can set his foot upon my ground without my licence, but he is liable to an action, though the damage be nothing.
Charles Pratt, English jurist; lord chancellor, lord chief justice
Entick v. Carrington (1765), 19 How. St. Tr. 1066

104.11　　But the most common and durable source of faction has been the various and unequal distribution of property.
James Madison
The Federalist, 1787

104.12　　Property and law are born and must die together.
Jeremy Bentham
Principles of the Civil Code, c.1843

104.13　　The highest law gives a thing to him who can use it.
Henry David Thoreau
Journal, November 9, 1852

104.14　　Property, it is theft.
Pierre Joseph Proudhon
Principle of Right, 1858

104.15　　. . . generosity is not a virtue when dealing with the property of others.
Robert M. Douglas, American jurist
Cashion v. Telegraph Co., 123 N.C. 267, 273 (1898)

104.16　　The notion that with socialized property we should have women free and a piano for everybody seems to me an empty humbug.
Oliver Wendell Holmes
"Ideas and Doubts," *Collected Legal Papers,* 1921

104.17　　The bundle of power and privileges to which we give the name of ownership is not constant through the ages. The faggots must be put together and rebound from time to time.
Benjamin N. Cardozo, *1870–1938*
"The Paradoxes of Legal Science," *Selected Writings of Benjamin N. Cardozo,* edited by Margaret Hall, 1947

104.18   The modern mystics of muscle who offer you the fraudulent alternative of "human rights" versus "property rights," as if one could exist without the other, are making a last, grotesque attempt to revive the doctrine of soul versus body.

Only a ghost can exist without material property; only a slave can work with no right to the product of his effort.
Ayn Rand
Atlas Shrugged, 1957

105. PROSECUTION

105.1   Who ever knew an honest brute at law his neighbor prosecute?
Jonathan Swift
The Logicians Refuted, c.1735

105.2   [A] plaintiff must shew that he stands on a fair ground when he calls on a Court of justice to administer relief to him.
Sir Lloyd Kenyon, English jurist; lord chief justice
Booth v. Hodgson (1795), 6 T.R. 409

105.3   Those who make the attack ought to be very well prepared to support it.
Sir Giles Rooke, English jurist
Almgill v. Pierson (1797), 2 Bos. & Pull. 104

105.4   There were no accusers; there could be no judge.
Selma Lagerlöf
The Story of Gösta Berling, 1891

105.5   One of the most reprehensible things a prosecutor can do is to attempt to put into evidence before the jury his own, and his colleagues', opinion as to the guilt of the defendants he is prosecuting.
Owen J. Roberts
United States v. Socony-Vacuum Oil Co., 310 U.S. 150, 264 (1940)

105.6   Today, the grand jury is the total captive of the prosecutor who, if he is candid, will concede that he can indict anybody, at any time, for almost anything, before any grand jury.
William J. Campbell, American jurist; judge, U.S. District Court
U.S. News & World Report, June 19, 1978

106. PROSTITUTION

106.1   Prisons are built with stones of law, brothels with bricks of religion.
William Blake, *1757–1827*
W. H. Auden and Louis
Kronenberger, *The Viking Book of Aphorisms,* 1962

106.2   . . . nothing could be more grotesquely unjust than a code of morals, reinforced by laws, which relieves men from responsibility for irregular sexual acts, and for the same acts drives women to abortion, infanticide, prostitution and self-destruction.
Suzanne LaFollette, American
feminist and writer
"Women and Marriage," *Concerning Women,* 1926

106.3   What it comes down to is this: the grocer, the butcher, the baker, the merchant, the landlord, the druggist, the liquor dealer, the policeman, the doctor, the city father and the politician—these are the people who make money out of prostitution, these are the real reapers of the wages of sin.
Polly Adler
A House Is Not a Home, 1953

106.4   At a conference on moral and social hygiene last year [1957] Earl Jowitt criticized the law against prostitution for being "based on a fiction that the man who is accosted is annoyed." He remarked that, at his "ripe old age," if he were accosted he would be "complimented."
Earl Jowitt, criticizing prostitution
law in 1957
Eugene Gerhart, *Quote It!* 1969

106.5   Prostitutes are the inevitable product of a society that places ultimate importance on money, possessions, and competition.
Jane Fonda
Thomas Kiernan, *Jane: An Intimate Biography of Jane Fonda,* 1970

106.6   It is a silly question to ask a prostitute why she does it . . . . These are the highest-paid "professional" women in America.
Gail Sheehy
Hustling, 1971

106.7   The prostitutes continue to take all the arrests, the police to suffer frustration, the lawyers to mine gold, the operators to laugh, the landowners to insist they have no responsibility, the mayor to issue press releases. The nature of the beast is, in a word, greed.
Gail Sheehy
Hustling, 1971

106.8   . . . if my business could be made legal . . . . I and women like me could make a big contribution to what Mayor Lindsay calls "Fun City," and the city and state could derive the money in taxes and licensing fees that I pay off to crooked cops and political figures.
Xaviera Hollander
The Happy Hooker, 1972

107.   PSYCHIATRY

107.1   Where the head is sick there is no law.
Proverb
B. J. Whiting and H. W. Whiting,
Proverbs, Sentences, and Proverbial Phrases: From English Writings Mainly Before 1500, 1968

107.2   Sickness has no law.
John Lydgate
Troy Book, 1420

107.3   If weakness may excuse,
What murderer, what traitor, parricide,
Incestuous, sacrilegious, but may plead it?
All wickedness is weakness.
John Milton
Samson Agonistes, 1671

107.4   Avarice, ambition, lust, etc. are species of madness.
Spinoza
Ethics, 1677

107.5   I think the law became an ass the day it let the psychiatrists get their hands on the law.
Lynn D. Compton, American lawyer; chief deputy district attorney, Los Angeles
Summation at Sirhan B. Sirhan Trial, reported in *Los Angeles Times,* April 14, 1969

108.   PUBLIC INTEREST

108.1   Whatever is injurious to the interests of the public is void, on the grounds of public policy.
Sir Nicholas Conyngham Tindal,
English jurist; chief justice
Horner v. Graves (1831), 7 Bing. 743

108.2   The trouble is that lawyers necessarily acquire the habit of assuming the law to be right . . . . As a rule, the pure lawyer seldom concerns himself about the broad aspects of public policy which may show a law to be all wrong, and such a lawyer may be oblivious to the fact that in helping to enforce the law he is helping to injure the public. Then, too, lawyers are almost always conservative. Through insisting upon the maintenance of legal rules, they become instinctively opposed to change, and thus are frequently found aiding in the assertion of legal rights under laws which have once been reasonable and fair, but which, through the process of social and business development, have become unjust and unfair without the lawyers seeing it.
Elihu Root, *1845–1937*
Philip C. Jessup, *Elihu Root,* 1938

108.3   The most important thing a lawyer can do is to become an advocate of powerless citizens. I am in favor of lawyers without clients. Lawyers should represent systems of justice. I want to create a new dimension to the legal profession. What we have now is a democracy without citizens. No one is on the public's side. All the lawyers are on the corporation's side.
Ralph Nader
Newsweek, October 3, 1969

108.4   Lawyers as a group are no more dedicated to justice or public service than a private public utility is dedicated to giving light. The profession is a public profession because it exists to satisfy a public need. But individual lawyers are members of that public profession to satisfy private personal needs.
David Melinkoff, American educator;
professor, University of California,
Los Angeles
San Francisco Examiner & Chronicle,
June 22, 1973

108.5   The President's need for complete candor and objectivity from advisors calls for great deference from the courts. However, when the privilege depends solely on the broad, undifferentiated claim of public interest in the confidentiality of such conversations, a confrontation with other values arises.

Warren E. Burger
United States v. Nixon, 418 U.S. 683
(1974) 48

108.6   I do believe our government and my profession have a positive moral and legal duty to make sure that legal services are available to the poor on an accessible, affordable, regular, dignified basis and, if necessary, free of charge. Which means that I, as a lawyer, believe that some significant part of my money, time, thought, and energy belongs—I don't give it, it *belongs*—to others, not just to me.

R. Sargent Shriver, Jr.
Washington Post, June 6, 1982

109.   PUBLIC OPINION

109.1   Laws they are not which public approbation hath not made so.

Richard Hooker
Of the Laws of Ecclesiastical Polity,
1594

109.2   The law no passion can disturb. . . . On the one hand, it is inexorable to the cries and lamentations of the prisoner; on the other, it is deaf, deaf as an adder, to the clamours of the populace.

John Adams, in defense of British
soldiers on trial after the Boston
Massacre, 1770

109.3   Public policy is a very unruly horse, and when once you get astride it you never know where it will carry you.

Sir James Burrough, English jurist
Richardson v. Mellish (1824), 2 Bing.
252

109.4   Public opinion is stronger than the Legislature, and nearly as strong as the Ten Commandments.

Charles Dudley Warner
My Summer in a Garden, 1875

109.5   Public opinion's always in advance of the law.

John Galsworthy
Windows, 1922

109.6   Compulsory unification of opinion achieves only the unanimity of the graveyard.

Robert H. Jackson
Board of Education v. Barnette, 319
U.S. 624, 641 (1943)

109.7   There are not enough jails, not enough policemen, not enough courts to enforce a law not supported by the people.

Hubert H. Humphrey
Speech, Williamsburg, Virginia, May
1, 1965

110. PUNISHMENT

110.1   Law cannot persuade, where it cannot punish.
Proverb
Rosalind Fergusson, *The Facts On File Dictionary of Proverbs,* 1983

110.2   Anyone through whom another man has been falsely punished will be barred from Heaven's Gates.
Talmud, *Shabbat*

110.3   The greatest incitement to crime is the hope of escaping punishment.
Cicero
Pro Milone, c.50 B.C.

110.4   If you did not punish crimes you would help wickedness.
Publilius Syrus, Latin writer
Sententiae, c.43 B.C.

110.5   What a slight foundation for virtue it is to be good only from fear of the law!
Seneca
De Ira, c.43

110.6   Laws do not persuade just because they threaten.
Seneca
Epistulae Morales ad Lucilium, 63–65

110.7   The rabbis said about capital cases: "We decide by a majority of one for acquittal, but only by a majority of at least two for conviction."
Rashi, Jewish legal authority
Commentaries on the Pentateuch: Exodus, c.late 11th century

110.8   Stay friend, until I put aside my beard, for that never committed treason.
Sir Thomas More
Remark to executioner, before placing his head on the block, 1535

110.9   Sicinius: He hath resisted law,
And therefore law shall scorn
him further trial
Than the severity of the public power.
Shakespeare
Coriolanus, I, 3, 1607–1608

110.10   No pain equals that of an injury inflicted under the pretense of a just punishment.
Lupercio Leonardo de Argensola,
Spanish poet and dramatist,
1559–1619
Sonetos

110.11   I went to Charing Cross to see Major General Harrison hanged, drawn, and quartered; which was done there, he looking as cheerful as any man could do in that condition.

Samuel Pepys
Diary, October 13, 1660

110.12 No Indian prince has to his palace
More followers than a thief to
th' gallows

Samuel Butler
Hudibras, 1663–1678

110.13 Men are not hang'd for stealing
Horses, but that Horses may not be
stolen.

George Savile, 1st marquess of
Halifax, English politician,
1633–1695
*The Complete Works of George Savile,
First Marquess of Halifax,* 1912

110.14 Wherever a Knave is not punished, an honest Man is laugh'd at.

George Savile, 1st marquess of
Halifax, English politician,
1633–1695
*The Complete Works of George
Saville, First Marquess of Halifax,*
1912

110.15 Hail hieroglyphic State machine,
Contrived to punish fancy in;

Daniel Defoe
Hymn to the Pillory, 1703

110.16 Whenever the offense inspires
less horror than the punishment,
the rigour of penal law is obliged to
give way to the common feelings of
mankind.

Edward Gibbon
*Decline and Fall of the Roman
Empire,* 1776

110.17 My machine will take off a head
in a twinkling, and the victim will
feel nothing but a slight sense of refreshing coolness on the neck. We
cannot make too much haste, gen-

tlemen, to allow the nation to enjoy
this advantage.

Joseph Ignace Guillotin, French
physician
To the French Assembly, 1789

110.18 Said a man ingenuously to one of
his friends: "This morning we condemned three men to death. Two of
them definitely deserved it."

Sébastien Roch Nicolas Chamfort,
French writer, *1740–1794*
W. H. Auden and Louis
Kronenberger, *The Viking Book of
Aphorisms,* 1962

110.19 An avidity to punish is always
dangerous to liberty. It leads men
to stretch, to misinterpret, and to
misapply even the best of laws. He
that would make his own liberty secure must guard even his enemy
from oppression; for if he violates
this duty he establishes a precedent
that will reach to himself.

Thomas Paine
"Dissertation on First Principles of
Government" (speech), July 7, 1795

110.20 The law doth punish man or
woman
That steals the goose from off the
common
But lets the greater felon loose
That steals the common from the
goose.

Anonymous
On the Enclosure Movement, 18th
century

110.21 The Tarpeian rock [the Roman
place of execution] is near the Capitol [the place of official distinction].

Jony-Spontini
W. Gurney Benham, *Putnam's
Complete Book of Quotations, Proverbs
and Household Words,* 1927

110.22   The tree must lie where it has fallen.
> Justice North, English jurist
> *In re Bridgewater Navigation Co., Ltd.*
> (1890), 60 L.J. Rep. (N.S.) C.D. 422

110.23   We enact many laws that manufacture criminals, and then a few that punish them.
> Benjamin R. Tucker, American
> journalist and anarchist
> *Instead of a Book,* 1893

110.24   Gentlemen of the jury, you have a solemn duty to discharge. The life of the prisoner at the bar is in your hands. You can take it—by a word. You can extinguish that life as the candle by your side was extinguished a moment ago. But it is not in your power, it is not in the power of any of us—of any one in the court or out of it,—to restore that life, when once taken, as that light has been restored.
> John Duke Coleridge, English jurist;
> lord chief justice, *1820–1894*
> Plea in a murder case during which a
> candle in the jury box went out,
> leaving the court in darkness

110.25   A community is infinitely more brutalized by the habitual employment of punishment than . . . by the occasional occurrence of crime.
> Oscar Wilde, *1854–1900*
> W. H. Auden and Louis
> Kronenberger, *The Viking Book of*
> *Aphorisms,* 1962

110.26   Corporal punishment is as humiliating for him who gives it as for him who receives it; it is ineffective besides.
> Ellen Key, Swedish writer and
> feminist
> *The Century of the Child,* 1909

110.27   . . . laws are felt only when the individual comes into conflict with them.
> Suzanne LaFollette, American
> feminist and writer
> "The Beginnings of Emancipation,"
> *Concerning Women,* 1926

110.28   The reformative effect of punishment is a belief that dies hard, chiefly, I think, because it [punishment] is so satisfying to our sadistic impulses.
> Bertrand Russell
> *Ideas That Have Harmed Mankind,*
> 1946

110.29   Punishment must be an honour. It must not only wipe out the stigma of the crime, but must be regarded as a supplementary form of education, compelling a higher devotion to the public good. The severity of the punishment must also be in keeping with the kind of obligation which has been violated, and not with the interests of public security.
> Simone Weil, French philosopher
> *L'Enracinement,* 1949; tr. as *The need*
> *for Roots,* 1952

110.30   Let us revise our views and work from the premise that all laws should be for the welfare of society as a whole and not directed at the punishment of sins.
> John Biggs, Jr., American jurist
> "Procedures for Handling the
> Mentally-Ill Offender in Some
> European Countries," *Temple Law*
> *Quarterly,* 1956

110.31   "Only lies and evil come from letting people off . . . ."
> Iris Murdoch
> *A Severed Head,* 1961

110.32   "Nothing can be right and balanced again until justice is won—the injured party has to have justice. Do you understand that? Nothing can be right, for years, for lifetimes, until that first crime is punished. Or else we'd all be animals."

> Joyce Carol Oates
> "Norman and the Killer," *Upon the Sweeping Flood and Other Stories,* 1965

110.33   This Court inescapably has the duty, as the ultimate arbiter of the meaning of our Constitution, to say whether, when individuals condemned to death stand before our Bar, "moral concepts" require us to hold that the law has progressed to the point where we should declare that the punishment of death, like punishments on the rack, the screw, and the wheel, is no longer morally tolerable in our society.

> William J. Brennan, Jr.
> *Gregg v. Georgia,* 428 U.S. 153, 96 St. Ct. 2909, 49 L.Ed.2d 859 (1976)

R

111. RAPE

111.1   History, sacred and profane, and the common experience of mankind teach that women of the character shown in this case are prone to make false accusations both of rape and of insult upon the slightest provocation or without even provocation, for ulterior purposes.

James E. Horton, American jurist
Memorandum granting a new trial in
the Scottsboro case, June 22, 1933

111.2   In no state can a man be accused of raping his wife. How can any man steal what already belongs to him?

Susan Griffin, American poet
Ramparts, September 1971

111.3   Rape is a culturally fostered means of suppressing women. Legally we say we deplore it, but mythically we romanticize and perpetuate it, and privately we excuse and overlook it . . . .

Victoria Billings, American journalist
"Sex: We Need Another Revolution,"
The Womansbook, 1974

111.4   [Rape] is the only crime in which the victim becomes the accused and, in reality, it is she who must prove her good reputation, her mental soundness, and her impeccable propriety.

Freda Adler, American educator
Sisters in Crime, 1975

267

112. REASON

112.1 What is inconsistent with and contrary to reason is not permitted in law.
Legal maxim

112.2 A man without reason is a beast in season.
Proverb
John Ray, *English Proverbs,* 1678

112.3 Law governs man, reason the law.
Proverb
Rosalind Fergusson, *The Facts On File Dictionary of Proverbs,* 1983

112.4 Reason lies between the spur and the bridle.
Proverb
George Herbert, *Outlandish Proverbs,* 1640

112.5 Reason is the wise man's guide, example the fool's.
Welsh proverb

112.6 The law of things is a law of universal reason, but most men live as if they had a wisdom of their own.
Heraclitus
Cosmic Fragments, c.500 B.C.

112.7 The law is reason free from passion.
Aristotle
Politics, c.322 B.C.

112.8 Law is nothing else but right reason, calling us imperiously to our duty, and prohibiting every violation of it.
Cicero
Orationes Philippicae, c.60 B.C.

112.9 Reason is the mistress and queen of all things.
Cicero
Tusculanae Disputationes, 45 B.C.

112.10 That which natural reason has established amongst all men is called the law of nations.
Gaius, Roman jurist, *130–180*
Institutes

112.11 Law is a regulation in accord with reason, issued by a lawful superior for the common good.
Thomas Aquinas
Summa Theologica, c.1258–1260

112.12 Every why hath a wherefore.
Shakespeare
The Comedy of Errors, II, 2, 1592–1593

112.13 . . . for like reason doth make like law . . . .
Sir Edward Coke
The Institutes of the Lawes of England, vol. 1, 1628–1641

112.14 How long soever it hath continued, if it be against reason, it is of
no force in law.
Sir Edward Coke
The Institutes of the Lawes of England,
vol. 1, 1628–1641

112.15 Reason is the life of the law; nay,
the common law itself is nothing
else but reason.
Sir Edward Coke
The Institutes of the Lawes of England,
vol. 1, 1628–1641

112.16 Reason is but choosing.
John Milton
Areopagitica, 1644

112.17 The law of England is, at best,
but the reason of Parliament.
John Milton
Eikonoclastes, 1649

112.18 Men never wish ardently for
what they only wish for from reason.
La Rochefoucauld
Maximes, 1665

112.19 God so commanded, and left that
command
Sole daughter of his voice; the rest
we live
Law to ourselves, our reason is our
law.
John Milton
Paradise Lost, 1667

112.20 'Tis more than reason that goes
to persuasion.
Quoted by Thomas Twisden, English
jurist
Manby v. Scott (1672), 1 Levinz. 4; 2
Sm. L.C. (8th Ed.) 462

112.21 In vain thy Reason finer webs shall
draw,
Entangle justice in her net of law,
And right, too rigid, harden into
wrong,
Still for the strong too weak, the
weak too strong.
Alexander Pope
An Essay on Man, 1732

112.22 If you will not hear reason,
She will surely rap your knuckles.
Benjamin Franklin
Poor Richard's Almanack, 1757

112.23 Within the brain's most secret cells
A certain Lord Chief Justice dwells
Of sovereign power, whom one and
all,
With common voice, we Reason
call.
Charles Churchill, English poet and
satirist
The Ghost, 1762–1763

112.24 Passion and prejudice govern the
world; only under the name of reason.
John Wesley
Letter to Joseph Benson, October 5,
1770

112.25 Reason and free enquiry are the
only effectual agents against error.
Thomas Jefferson
Notes on the State of Virginia,
c.1781–1783

112.26 I told [John Marshall] it was law
logic—an artificial system of reasoning, exclusively used in the
courts of justice, but good for nothing anywhere else.
John Quincy Adams
Clifton Fadiman and Charles van
Doran, *The American Treasury,*
1455–1955, 1955

112.27   Reason alone can make the laws obligatory and lasting.
Honoré Sabriel Riquetti, comte de Mirabeau, *1749–1791*
W. Gurney Benham, *Putnam's Complete Book of Quotations, Proverbs and Household Words*, 1927

112.28   Reason is founded on the evidence of our senses.
Percy Bysshe Shelley
Queen Mab, notes, 1813

112.29   Reason is nothing but the analysis of belief.
Franz Schubert
Diary, March 27, 1824

112.30   Doth not the idiot eat? Doth not the idiot drink? Doth not the idiot know his father and mother? . . . Think you he does this for nothing? He does it all because he is a man, and because, however imperfectly, he exercises his reason.
William H. Seward
Freeman Case, 1846

112.31   Reason is only a tool.
Nietzsche
Beyond Good and Evil, 1886

112.32   I can stand brute force, but brute reason is quite unbearable. There is something unfair about its use. It is hitting below the intellect.
Oscar Wilde
The Picture of Dorian Gray, 1891

112.33   The life of reason is no fair reproduction of the universe, but the expression of man alone.
George Santayana
The Life of Reason, 1901

112.34   A page of history is worth a volume of logic.
Oliver Wendell Holmes
New York Trust Co. v. Eisner, 256 U.S. 345 (1921)

112.35   If we would guide by the light of reason, we must let our minds be bold.
Louis D. Brandeis
New State Ice Co. v. Liebmann, 285 U.S. 262 (1932)

112.36   Indeed, nothing is so likely to lead us astray as an abject reliance upon canons of any sort; so much the whole history of verbal interpretation teaches, if it teaches anything.
Learned Hand
Van Vranken v. Helvering, 313 U.S. 585, 61 S. Ct. 1095, 85 L.Ed. 1541 (1940)

112.37   . . . two and two will always make four, despite reports of presidents and financial advisers who insist on stretching it into five.
Louis D. Brandeis, *1856–1941*
Alpheus Thomas Mason, *Brandeis: A Free Man's Life,* 1946

112.38   The eternal struggle in the law between constancy and change is largely a struggle between history and reason, between past reason and present needs.
Felix Frankfurter
Mr. Justice Holmes and the Supreme Court, 1961

112.39   Ever since Kant divorced reason from reality, his intellectual descendants have been diligently widening the breach.
Ayn Rand
"The Cashing-In: The Student 'Rebellion'", *The New Left,* 1968

113. RELIGION

113.1   He that is void of fear, may soon be just; And no religion binds men to be traitors.
Ben Jonson
Catiline, 1611

113.2   He that seemeth to be religious, and bridleth not his tongue, his religion is vain.
John Lisle, English jurist
Hewet's Case (1658), 5 How. St. Tr. 894

113.3   Fanatic fools, that in those twilight times,
With wild religion cloaked the worst of crimes!
John Langhorne
The Country Justice, c.1766

113.4   I for one would never be a party, unless the law were clear, to saying to any man who put forward his views on those most sacred things, that he should be branded as apparently criminal because he differed from the majority of mankind in his religious views or convictions on the subject of religion. If that were so, we should get into ages and times which, thank God, we do not live in, when people were put to death for opinions and beliefs which now almost all of us believe to be true.
John Duke Coleridge, English jurist; lord chief justice
Reg. v. Bradlaugh and others (1883), 15 Cox, C.C. 230

113.5   If nowhere else, in the relation between Church and State, "good fences make good neighbors."
Felix Frankfurter
McCollum v. Board of Education, 333 U.S. 203, 232 (1948)

113.6   . . . in our country are evangelists and zealots of many different political, economic and religious persuasions whose fanatical conviction is that all thought is divinely classified into two kinds—that which is their own and that which is false and dangerous.
Robert H. Jackson
American Communication Assn. v. Douds, 339 U.S. 382, 438 (1950)

113.7   The day that this country ceases to be free for irreligion, it will cease to be free for religion.
Robert H. Jackson
Zorach v. Clausor, 1952

113.8   The hazards of churches supporting government are hardly less in their potential than the hazards

of governments supporting churches. . . . We cannot ignore the instances in history when church support of government led to the kind of involvement we seek to avoid.
Warren E. Burger
Walz v. Tax Commission, 397 U.S. 664, 90 S. Ct. 1409, 25 L.Ed.2d 697 (1970)

113.9 Just as the right to speak and the right to refrain from speaking are complementary components of a broader concept of individual freedom of mind, so also the individual's freedom to choose his own creed is the counterpart of his right to refrain from accepting the creed established by the majority. At one time it was thought that this right merely proscribed the preference of one Christian sect over another, but would not require equal respect for the conscience of the infidel, the atheist, or the adherent of a non-Christian faith such as Mohammedism or Judaism.

But when the underlying principle has been examined in the crucible of litigation, the Court has unambiguously concluded that the individual freedom of conscience protected by the First Amendment embraces the right to select any religious faith or none at all.
John Paul Stevens
Wallace v. Jaffree, No. 83–812 (1985)

114. REVENGE

114.1 If a man has caused the loss of a gentleman's eye, his eye one shall cause to be lost.
Hammurabi's Code 1792–1750 B.C.

114.2 The law forbids revenge.
Adapted from *Abot de Rabbi Nathan*

114.3 Revenge is a kind of wild justice, which the more man's nature runs to, the more ought law to weed it out . . . .
Francis Bacon
"Of Revenge," *Essayes,* 1625

114.4 An injured friend is the bitterest of foes.
Thomas Jefferson
French Treaties opinion, April 28, 1793

114.5 Cases were decided in the chambers of a six-shooter instead of a supreme court.
Thomas Babington Macaulay
"Burleigh," *Essays,* 1832

114.6 Wisdom has taught us to be calm and meek,

To take one blow, and turn the other
cheek;
It is not written what a man shall do,
If the rude caitiff smite the other too!
Oliver Wendell Holmes, American
physician and author
"Non-Resistance," *The Works of
Oliver Wendell Holmes: The Poetical
Works,* 1877

114.7 The avenger of blood . . . would
now be himself punished as a criminal for taking the law into his own
hands.
E. B. Taylor, English anthropologist
Anthropology, 1881

114.8 The instinct for retribution is part
of the nature of man, and channeling
that instinct in the administration of
criminal justice serves an important
purpose in promoting the stability of
a society governed by law.
Potter Stewart
Gregg v. Georgia, 428 U.S. 153, 96 St.
Ct. 2909, 49 L.Ed.2d 859 (1976)

115. RIGHTS

115.1 Rights are lost by disuse.
Latin legal phrase

115.2 The laws assist those who are vigi-
lant, not those who sleep over their
rights.
Legal maxim

115.3 When a greater right belongs to a
man, the lesser right ought to be included.
Legal maxim

115.4 Old rights must remain: it would
be very unreasonable if it should be
otherwise.
Sir Joseph Yates, English jurist
Mayor, &c. of Colchester v. Seaber
(1765), 3 Burr. Part IV. (1872)

115.5 We hold these truths to be self-evident, that all men are created equal,
that they are endowed by their Creator with certain unalienable Rights,
that among these are Life, Liberty
and the pursuit of Happiness. That
to secure these rights, Governments
are instituted among Men, deriving
their just powers from the consent of
the governed. That whenever any
Form of Government becomes destructive of those ends, it is the Right
of the People to alter or abolish it,
and to institute a new Government,
laying its foundation on such principles and organizing its power in such
form, as to them shall seem most

likely to effect their Safety and Happiness.

Thomas Jefferson
Declaration of Independence, 1776

115.6 [B]ear in mind this sacred principle, that though the will of the majority is in all cases to prevail, that will, to be rightful, must be reasonable; that the minority possess their equal rights, which equal laws must protect, and to violate which would be oppression.

Thomas Jefferson
First inaugural address, March 4, 1801

115.7 Human beings have *rights,* because they are *moral* beings: the rights of *all* men grow out of their moral nature; and as all men have the same moral nature, they have essentially the same rights.

Angelina Grimké, American
abolitionist
Letters to Catherine Beecher, ed. by
Isaac Knapp, 1836

115.8 I recognize no rights but *human* rights—I know nothing of men's rights and women's rights . . . .

Angelina Grimké, American
abolitionist
Letters to Catherine Beecher, ed. by
Isaac Knapp, 1836

115.9 Of course this is pure fiction, and fiction always is a poor ground for changing substantial rights.

Oliver Wendell Holmes
Haddock v. Haddock, 201 U.S. 562,
26 S. Ct. 525, 50 L.Ed. 867 (1906)

115.10 Most rights are qualified.

Oliver Wendell Holmes
American Bank and Trust Co. v.
Federal Reserve Bank of Atlanta,
Georgia, 256 U.S. 350, 41 S. Ct. 499,
25 ALR 971, 65 L.Ed. 983 (1921)

115.11 Such words as "right" are a constant solicitation to fallacy.

Oliver Wendell Holmes
Jackman v. Rosenbaum Co., 260 U.S.
22, 31 (1922)

115.12 . . . peaceable assembly for lawful discussion cannot be made a crime.

De Jonge v. Oregon, 299 U.S. 353
(1937)

115.13 The right to participate in the choice of representatives for Congress includes . . . the right to cast a ballot and to have it counted at the general election whether for the successful candidate or not.

Harlan F. Stone
United States v. Classic, 313 U.S. 299,
85 L.Ed. 1368, 61 Sup. Ct. 1031
(1941)

115.14 It was not by accident or coincidence that the rights to freedom in speech and press were coupled in a single guaranty with the rights of the people peaceably to assemble and to petition for redress of grievances. All these, though not identical, are inseparable. They are cognate rights, and therefore are united in the first Article's assurance.

Wiley B. Rutledge
Thomas v. Collins, 323 U.S. 516,
89 L.Ed. 430, 65 Sup. Ct. 315 (1944)

115.15 In these days, it is doubtful that any child may reasonably be expected to succeed in life if he is denied the opportunity of an education. Such an opportunity, where the State has undertaken to provide it, is a right which must be made available to all on equal terms.

Earl Warren
Brown v. Board of Education of
Topeka, 347 U.S. 483, 74 S. Ct. 686,
98 L.Ed. 873 (1954)

115.16 Prior to any questioning, the person must be warned that he has a right to remain silent, that any statement he does make may be used as evidence against him, and that he has a right to the presence of an attorney, either retained or appointed.
Earl Warren
Miranda v. Arizona, 384 U.S. 436, 86 S. Ct. 1602, 16 L.Ed.2d 694 (1966)

116. RULE OF LAW

116.1 Right is the rule of law, and law is declaratory of right.
Aphorism
Benjamin Whichcote, *Moral and Religious Aphorisms,* 1753

116.2 Therefore he who bids the law rule may be deemed to bid God and Reason alone rule, but he who bids man rule adds an element of the beast; for desire is a wild beast, and passion perverts the minds of rulers, even when they are the best of men.
Aristotle
Politics, c.322 B.C.

116.3 Even habitual disobedience in some things is consistent with the rule of law: it is certain that only a minority of motorists observe the statutory speed limit on a clear road, but England is not therefore in a state of anarchy.
Sir Frederick Pollock, English jurist
Mark De Wolfe Howe, *Holmes-Pollock Letters,* 1946

116.4 Great states, able to defend *themselves,* do not entrust matters of life and death to a head count of states that can do neither. The "sovereign equality of all states" is an illusion. A universal "rule of Law" can neither be formulated in a manner acceptable to people with different concepts of law nor enforced under present conditions except by war.
Dorothy Thompson
"The Discrepancy Between Democratic Ideals and Realities,"
Ladies Home Journal, October 1960

116.5 The first step in the direction of a world rule of law is the recognition that peace no longer is an unobtainable ideal but a necessary condition of continued human existence.
Margaret Mead
New York Times Magazine,
November 26, 1961

116.6 What the rule of law means for Englishmen, what due process of law means to Americans, is inseparably bound up with our traditional no-

tions of Magna Carta. Whether all that has been read into the document is historically or legally sound, is not of the first importance; every historian knows that belief itself is a historical fact, and that legend and myth cannot be left out of account in tracing the sequence of cause and effect.
> Helen M. Cam, English historian
> "Magna Carta-Event or Document?"
> (lecture), July 7, 1967

116.7   The rule of law can be wiped out in one misguided, however well-intentioned generation. And if that should happen, it could take a century of striving and ordeal to restore it, and then only at the cost of the lives of many good men and women.
> William T. Gossett, American lawyer; president, American Bar Association
> Speech, American Bar Association, August 11, 1969

116.8   Too often, practitioners of the law are simply journeymen of legal practice . . . not creators of legal justice and do not, in fact, understand, the philosophical bases of law, its ultimate goals, or its importance . . . in a democratic society . . . . It should be the role of universities to constantly explore the possibilities of improving the rule of law, of constantly studying the extension of the rule of law, of constantly working for the universalization of the basic principles

which lead to an international conformity of basic law. It should be the role of universities to study the extension of law to other areas of human disputes and arguments and violence, so as to substitute basic principles and rational procedures for prejudice and violence.
> Robert John Henle, American educator; president, Georgetown University
> Vital Speeches, October 15, 1972

116.9   [Rule of law] places restraints on individuals and on governments alike. This is a delicate, a fragile balance to maintain. It is fragile because it is sustained only by an ideal that requires each person in society, by an exercise of free will, to accept and abide the restraints of a structure of laws.
> Warren E. Burger
> Address, Law Day Service, St. John's Cathedral, Jacksonville, Florida, June 15, 1973

116.10   Woman throughout the ages has been mistress to the law, as man has been its master . . . . The controversy between rule of law and rule of men was never relevant to women—because, along with juveniles, imbeciles, and other classes of legal nonpersons, they had no access to law except through men.
> Freda Adler, American educator
> Sisters in Crime, 1975

S

117. SELF-INCRIMINATION

117.1   No one need accuse himself except before God.
> Latin legal phrase
> W. Gurney Benham, *Putnam's Complete Book of Quotations, Proverbs and Household Words,* 1927

117.2   A man may not accuse himself of a crime.
> Talmud, *Yevamot*

117.3   No man is bound to accuse himself.
> John Selden, *1584–1654*
> *Table-Talk,* 1689

117.4   I hope your Worship will not be angry; . . . am I obliged to accuse myself?
> Daniel Defoe
> *The Behavior of Servants,* 1724

117.5   . . . nor shall any person . . . be compelled in any Criminal Case to be a witness against himself. . . .
> Constitution of the United States,
> Fifth Amendment, 1791

117.6   The Fifth Amendment is an old friend and a good friend. It is one of the great landmarks in men's struggle to be free of tyranny, to be decent and civilized.
> William O. Douglas
> *An Almanac of Liberty,* 1954

117.7   This constitutional protection must not be interpreted in a hostile or niggardly spirit. Too many, even those who should be better advised, view this privilege as a shelter for wrongdoers. They too readily assume that those who invoke it are either guilty of a crime or commit perjury in claiming the privilege. Such a view does scant honor to the patriots who sponsored the Bill of Rights as a condition to acceptance of the Constitution by the ratifying States. The founders of the Nation were not naive or disregardful of the interests of justice. . . .
> Felix Frankfurter
> *Ullman v. United States,* 350 U.S. 422,
> 100 L.Ed. 511, 76 Sup. Ct. 497 (1956)

117.8   The critical point is that the Constitution places the right of silence *beyond the reach of government.*
> William O. Douglas
> *Ullman v. United States,* 350 U.S. 422,
> 100 L.Ed. 511, 76 Sup. Ct. 497 (1956)

117.9   There is no requirement that police stop a person who enters a police
station and states that he wishes to
confess a crime, or a person who
calls the police to offer a confession
. . . Volunteered statements of any

kind are not barred by the Fifth
Amendment . . . .
Earl Warren
Miranda v. Arizona, 384 U.S. 436, 86
S. Ct. 1602, 16 L.Ed.2d 694 (1966)

---

118.   SENTENCES

118.1   From a foolish judge, a quick sen-
tence.
Proverb
Rosalind Fergusson, *The Facts On
File Dictionary of Proverbs,* 1983

118.2   No! No! Sentence first—Verdict
afterwards.
Lewis Carroll
Alice's Adventures in Wonderland,
1865

118.3   You only have so many options
when you sentence. You can put a
defendant on probation, order him
to be put on work-release and go to a
half-way house, or send him to an
institution. But what it comes right
down to is that there is no alternative
that's any good. I guess you could
call it a judge's dilemma.
Charles W. Halleck, American jurist;
judge, Superior Court of the District
of Columbia
Washington Post, October 9, 1971

118.4   I think a judge's education is very
imperfect when it comes to the sentencing process.
Edward M. Davis, American law
enforcement official; chief of police,
Los Angeles
Interview, *Human Events,* March 22,
1975

118.5   The toughest part of this job is
sentencing. I've lost all kinds of sleep
over sentences. I find it dreadful.
Malcolm Muir, American jurist;
judge, U.S. District Court
San Francisco Examiner & Chronicle,
March 8, 1981

119. SEVERITY

119.1   In a thousand pounds of law,
there's not an ounce of love.
Proverb
Rosalind Fergusson, *The Facts On
File Dictionary of Proverbs,* 1983

119.2   In making laws, severity; in ad-
ministering laws, clemency.
Chinese proverb
William Scarborough, *Chinese
Proverbs,* 1875

119.3   There is a point beyond which
even justice becomes unjust.
Sophocles
Electra, c.409 B.C.

119.4   Rigorous law is often rigorous in-
justice.
Terence,   *c.185–159 B.C.*
The Self-Tormentor, 163 B.C.

119.5   It is hard, but the law is so written.
Ulpian,   *c.2nd–3rd century*
W. Gurney Benham, *Putnam's
Complete Book of Quotations, Proverbs
and Household Words,* 1927

119.6   It is better that a judge should lean
on the side of compassion than severity.
Cervantes
Don Quixote, 1605

119.7   Is not this a lamentable thing, that
of the skin of an innocent lamb
should be made parchment? That
parchment, being scribbled o'er,
should undo a man?
Shakespeare
2 Henry VI, IV, 2, 1589–1591

119.8   Lucio:
He arrests him on it;
And follows close the rigour of the
statute,
To make him an example.
Shakespeare
Measure for Measure, I, 4, 1604–1605

119.9   The bloody book of law
You shall yourself read in the bitter
letter
After your own sense.
Shakespeare
Othello, I, 3, 1604–1605

119.10   The law is blind and speaks in general terms;
She cannot pity where occasion
serves.
Thomas May, English poet and
playwright
The Heir, 1620

119.11   At Halifax the law so sharpe doth
deale,
That who so more than thirteen
pence doth steale,

They have a jyn that wondrous
quick and well,
Sends thieves all headless into
heaven or hell.
John Taylor, English journalist and
pamphleteer
Halifax Law, 1630

119.12   Extremity of law is extremity of
wrong.
John Clarke, English clergyman
Paroemiologia Anglo-Latina, 1639

119.13   I oft have heard of Lydford Law,
How in the morn they hang and
draw,
And sit in judgment after.
William Browne, English poet
Lydford Castle, 1644

119.14   Thwackman was for doing jus-
tice, and leaving mercy to Heaven.
Henry Fielding
Tom Jones, 1749

119.15   Ambiguity lurks in generality
and may thus become an instrument of severity.
Felix Frankfurter
McComb v. Jacksonville Paper Co.,
336 U.S. 187, 197 (1949)

119.16   All laws are an attempt to domes-
ticate the natural ferocity of the
species. We can't stop murder, but
we can make it tougher to get away
with it. We can't stop a banker from
stealing the widow's money, but we
can make it harder for him to steal
it.
John W. Gardner
San Francisco Examiner, July 3, 1974

120.   SIN

120.1   The law grows of sin, and chastises
it.
Proverb
Rosalind Fergusson, *The Facts On
File Dictionary of Proverbs,* 1983

120.2   The law groweth of sin, and doth
punish it.
John Florio
Firste Fruites, 1578

120.3   Law can discover sin, but not re-
move.
John Milton
Paradise Lost, 1667

120.4   As the aim of the law is not to
punish sins, but is to prevent certain
external results . . . .
Oliver Wendell Holmes
Commonwealth v. Kennedy, 170 Mass.
18, 20 (1897)

120.5   I may hate the sin but never the sinner.
> Clarence Darrow, *1857–1938*
> Irving Stone, *Clarence Darrow for the Defense,* 1941

120.6   Sin . . . has been made not only ugly but passé. People are no longer sinful, they are only immature or un-der privileged or frightened or, more particularly, sick.
> Phyllis McGinley
> "In Defense of Sin," *The Province of the Heart,* 1959

120.7   Is it wise constantly to advertise the fact that the wages of sin are often very high?
> Lord Hartley Shawcross, English lawyer
> *New York Times,* June 19, 1963

121. SLANDER

121.1   Done to death by slanderous tongues,
Was the Hero that here lies.
> Shakespeare
> *Much Ado About Nothing,* III, 1, 1598–1599

121.2   Slander,
Whose whisper o'er the world's diameter,
As level as the cannon to his blank,
Transports his poison'd shot.
> Shakespeare
> *Hamlet,* IV, 1, 1600–1601

121.3   Hurl your calumnies boldly;
Something is sure to stick.
> Francis Bacon
> *De Augmentis Scientiarum,* 1623

121.4   I hate the man who builds his name
On ruins of another's fame.
> John Gay
> *Fables,* 1727

121.5   Squint-eyed Slander.
> James Beattie, *1735–1803*
> *The Judgment of Paris*

121.6   Slander, the foulest whelp of sin.
> Robert Pollock, Scottish poet
> *Course of Time,* 1827

122. SOCIETY

122.1   I am of a mind that said, "Better is it to live where nothing is lawful, than where all things are lawful."
Francis Bacon
Of Church Controversies, 1589

122.2   One of the eternal conflicts out of which life is made up is that between the effort of every man to get the most he can for his services, and that of society, disguised under the name of capital, to get his services for the least possible return.
Oliver Wendell Holmes
Vegelahn v. Guntner, 167 Mass. 92, 1081, 44 N.E. 1077 (1896)

122.3   Our laws make law impossible; our liberties destroy all freedom; our property is organized robbery; our wisdom is administered by inexperienced dupes, our power wielded by cowards and weaklings, and our honor false in all its points. I am an enemy of the existing order for good reasons.
George Bernard Shaw
Preface, *Major Barbara,* 1905

122.4   I say that all society is founded on the death of men. Certainly the romance of the past is.
Oliver Wendell Holmes
Letter to Doctor Wu, September 6, 1925

122.5   Civilization is nothing else but the attempt to reduce force to being the last resort.
Ortega y Gasset,   *1883–1955*
W. H. Auden and Louis Kronenberger, *The Viking Book of Aphorisms,* 1962

123. SPEECH

123.1   An unprincipled orator subverts the laws.
Latin phrase
W. Gurney Benham, *Putnam's Complete Book of Quotations, Proverbs and Household Words,* 1927

123.2   . . . every man speaks more virtuously than he either thinks or acts.
Francis Bacon
The Advancement of Learning, 1605

123.3   Liberty of speech inviteth and provoketh liberty to be used again, and so bringeth much to a man's knowledge.
Francis Bacon
The Advancement of Learning, 1605

123.4   Give me the liberty to know, to utter, and to argue freely according to conscience, above all liberties.
John Milton
Areopagitica, 1644

123.5   I disapprove of what you say, but I will defend to the death your right to say it.
Attributed to Voltaire, *1694–1778*
Bartlett's Familiar Quotations, 15 ed., 1980

123.6   Only the suppressed word is dangerous.
Ludwig Boerne, German writer
An Kundigurg der Wage, 1818

123.7   If all mankind minus one were of one opinion and only one person were of the contrary opinion, mankind would be no more justified in silencing that person than he, if he had the power, would be justified in silencing mankind . . . . If the opinion is right, they are deprived of the opportunity of exchanging error for truth; if wrong, they lose, what is almost as great a benefit, the clearer perception and livelier impression of truth, produced by its collision with error.
John Stuart Mill
On Liberty, 1859

123.8   The most stringent protection of free speech would not protect a man from falsely shouting fire in a theater and causing a panic.
Oliver Wendell Holmes
Schenck v. United States, 249 U.S. 47, 52, 63 L.Ed. 470, 473, 39 S. Ct. 247 (1919)

123.9   The question in every case is whether the words are used in such circumstances and are of such a nature as to create a clear and present danger.
Oliver Wendell Holmes
Schenck v. United States, 249 U.S. 47, 52, 63 L.Ed. 470, 473, 39 S. Ct. 247 (1919)

123.10 Eloquence may set fire to reason.
Oliver Wendell Holmes
Gitlow v. New York, 268 U.S. 652, 673
(1925)

123.11 If there be time to expose
through discussion the falsehood
and fallacies, to avert the evil by the
process of education, the remedy to
be applied is more speech, not enforced silence.
Louis D. Brandeis
Whitney v. California, 274 U.S. 357,
377 (1927)

123.12 I . . . probably take the extremest
view in favor of free speech, (in
which, in the abstract, I have no
very enthusiastic belief, though I
hope I would die for it). . . .
Oliver Wendell Holmes, *1841–1935*
Mark De Wolfe Howe, *Holmes-
Pollock Letters,* 1946

123.13 It must never be forgotten, however, that the Bill of Rights was the
child of the Enlightenment. Back of
the guarantee of free speech lay
faith in the power of an appeal to
reason by all the peaceful means for
gaining access to the mind . . . . But
utterance in a context of violence
can lose its significance as an appeal to reason and become part of
an instrument of force. Such utterance was not meant to be sheltered
by the Constitution.
Felix Frankfurter
*Milk Wagon Drivers Union of Chicago
v. Meadowmoor Dairies,* 312 U.S. 287,
293 (1941)

123.14 Free speech is not to be regulated
like diseased cattle and impure butter. The audience . . . that hissed
yesterday may applaud today, even
for the same performance.
William O. Douglas
Kingsley Books, Inc. v. Brown, 354
U.S. 436, 447 (1957)

123.15 . . . I had rather take my chance
that some traitors will escape detec-
tion than spread abroad a spirit of
general suspicion and distrust,
which accepts rumor and gossip in
place of undismayed and unintimi-
dated inquiry. I believe that that
community is already in process of
dissolution where each man begins
to eye his neighbor as a possible
enemy, where non-conformity with
the accepted creed, political as well
as religious, is a mark of disaffection; where denunciation, without
specification or backing, takes the
place of evidence; where orthodoxy
chokes freedom of dissent; where
faith in the eventual supremacy of
reason has become so timid that we
dare not enter our convictions in
the open lists, to win or lose.
Learned Hand
Irving Dilliard, *The Spirit of Liberty,*
1960

123.16 . . . a municipality may not em-
power its licensing officials to roam
essentially at will, dispensing or
withholding permission to speak,
assemble, picket, or parade, according to their own opinions regarding
the potential effect of the activity in
question on the "welfare," "decency," or "morals" of the community.
Potter Stewart
Shuttlesworth v. Birmingham, 394 U.S.
147, 89 S. Ct. 935, 22 L.Ed.2d 162
(1969)

123.17 Free speech carries with it some
freedom to listen.
Warren E. Burger
*Richmond Newspapers, Inc. v.
Virginia,* 488 U.S. 555, 100 S. Ct.
2814, 65 L.Ed.2d 973 (1980)

124. STATE

124.1 Many laws in a state are a bad sign.
Italian proverb
W. Gurney Benham, *Putnam's Complete Book of Quotations, Proverbs and Household Words,* 1927

124.2 For this is the bond of men in cities, that all shall rightly preserve the laws.
Euripides
Supplices, c.420 B.C.

124.3 I see that the State in which the law is above the rulers . . . has salvation.
Plato, *428–c.348 B.C.*
Laws

124.4 The more corrupt the state, the more numerous the laws.
Tacitus
Annals, c.116

124.5 The principal foundations of all states are good laws and good aims; and there cannot be good laws where there are not good aims.
Machiavelli
The Prince, 1532

124.6 Whatever the state permits, it commands.
Sixtus V, pope, *1520–1590*

124.7 A state, useful and valuable as the contrivance is, is the inferior contrivance of man; and from his native dignity derives all its acquired importance. . . . Let a state be considered as subordinate to the people: But let everything else be subordinate to the state.
James Wilson
Chisholm v. Georgia, 2 U.S. (2 Dall.) 419, 455 (1793)

124.8 By a state I mean, a complete body of free persons united together for their common benefit, to enjoy peaceably what is their own, and to do justice to others.
James Wilson
Chisholm v. Georgia, 2 U.S. (2 Dall.) 419, 455 (1793)

124.9 Rights that depend on the sufferance of the State are of uncertain tenure . . . .
Suzanne LaFollette, American feminist and writer
"What Is to Be Done," *Concerning Women,* 1926

125.   SUCCESS

125.1   A man may be reputed an able man this year, and yet be a beggar the next: it is a misfortune that happens to many men, and his former reputation will signify nothing.
Sir John Holt, English jurist; chief justice
Reg. v. Swendsen (1702), 14 How. St. Tr. 596

125.2   Always bear in mind that your own resolution to succeed is more important than any other one thing.
Abraham Lincoln
Letter to Isham Reavis, November 5, 1855

125.3   But I refused to be defeated by the shadow of a bygone day.
Sir Edward Clarke, English lawyer
The Story of My Life, 1923

125.4   . . . no man is unsuccessful who has plenty to do. So long as one can honestly perform his share of the world's work he enjoys the only success it is possible for anybody to achieve.
Joseph H. Choate,   *1832–1917*
Theron G. Strong, *Joseph H. Choate,* 1917

125.5   Fulfillment may fall short of expectation.
Benjamin N. Cardozo
Walton Water Co. v. Village of Walton, 238 N.Y. 46, 50 (1924)

125.6   Reputation and learning are akin to capital assets, like the good will of an old partnership. . . . For many, they are the only tools with which to hew a pathway to success.
Benjamin N. Cardozo
Welch v. Helvering, 290 U.S. 111, 115–16 (1933)

125.7   Good and bad come mingled always. The long-time winner is the man who is not unreasonably discouraged by persistent streaks of ill fortune nor at other times made reckless with the thought that he is fortune's darling. He keeps a cool head and trusts in the mathematics of probability, or as often said, the law of averages.
Roy A. Redfield, American lawyer
Factors of Growth in a Law Practice, 1962

126. SUITS

126.1   A piece of paper blown by the wind into a law-court may in the end only be drawn out again by two oxen.
Chinese proverb
S. G. Champion, *Racial Proverbs*, 1938

126.2   Winning a cat you lose a cow.
Chinese proverb
William Scarborough, *Chinese Proverbs*, 1875

126.3   Win your lawsuits and lose your money.
Chinese proverb
William Scarborough, *Chinese Proverbs*, 1875

126.4   One goes to court with one lawsuit and comes home with two.
Danish proverb
H. L. Mencken, *A New Dictionary of Quotations*, 1946

126.5   I'll make him water his horse at Highgate [I'll sue him and make him take a journey to London].
English proverb
John Ray, *English Proverbs*, 1678

126.6   If you've a good case, try to compromise; if a bad one, take it to court.
French proverb
H. L. Mencken, *A New Dictionary of Quotations*, 1946

126.7   May you have a lawsuit in which you know you are in the right.
Gypsy curse
W. H. Auden and Louis Kronenberger, *The Viking Book of Aphorisms*, 1962

126.8   A lawsuit is a fruit-tree planted in a lawyer's garden.
Italian proverb
H. L. Mencken, *A New Dictionary of Quotations*, 1946

126.9   Lawsuits consume time, and money, and rest, and friends.
Proverb
Rosalind Fergusson, *The Facts On File Dictionary of Proverbs*, 1983

126.10   Sue a beggar and get a louse.
Proverb
John Clarke, *Paroemiologia Anglo-Latina*, 1639

126.11   A happy death is better than a lawsuit.
Spanish proverb
H. L. Mencken, *A New Dictionary of Quotations*, 1946

126.12   I can try a lawsuit as well as other men, but the most important thing is to prevent lawsuits.
Confucius
Analects, c.500 B.C.

126.13 We should make it our aim that there may be no lawsuits at all.
Confucius, *c.500 B.C.*
Joseph I. Lieberman, "Confucius's Lesson to Litigants," *New York Times,* July 9, 1984

126.14 [Hippodamus] maintained that there are three subjects of lawsuits—insult, injury and homicide.
Aristotle
Poetics, c.340 B.C.

126.15 Suits at court are like winter nights, long and wearisome.
Thomas Deloney, English ballad writer and pamphleteer
Jack of Newbury, 1597

126.16 To go to law is for two persons to kindle a fire, at their own cost, to warm others and singe themselves to cinders.
Owen Felltham, English writer
Resolves, 1623

126.17 For 'tis a low, newspaper, humdrum, lawsuit Country.
Lord Byron
Don Juan, 1819–1824

126.18 [*Court fool:*] The plaintiff.
Ambrose Bierce
The Devil's Dictionary, 1906

126.19 Fairness and honesty are finding it increasingly hard to prevail in a judicial system clogged with frivolous suits.
William B. Spann, Jr., American lawyer; president, American Bar Association
Wall Street Journal, June 20, 1978

126.20 If a lawyer is worth his salt, has done his investigation on the suit, talked to the experts, and has grounds to believe his client's claims, he should proceed fullsteam ahead with the law suit. This will be a deterrent to any lawyer with an ounce of brains to stop filing any frivolous suits.
Ivan E. Barris, American lawyer; vice president, Michigan Bar Association
Los Angeles Times, August 27, 1978

126.21 Lawsuits help insure that Americans have a good life. We protect our rights by litigating if anyone attempts to trample on them. We have always been like that. One of the Colonial flags included a rattlesnake with the legend, "Don't Tread On Me." That's the American mind of today as expressed by lawyers.
Melvin Belli
Interview, *U.S. News & World Report,* September 20, 1982

127. SUPREME COURT

127.1   Like all human institutions, the Supreme Court must earn reverence through the test of truth.
Felix Frankfurter
"Mr. Justice Holmes and the Constitution," 41 *Harvard Law Review* (1927)

127.2   No matter whether th' constitution follows th' flag or not, th' supreme court follows th' illiction returns.
Finley Peter Dunne, *1867–1936*
Edward J. Bander, ed., *Mr. Dooley on the Choice of Law,* 1963

127.3   . . . on a question of public policy it is no disrespect to the Supreme Court to say that the majority of the Court were mistaken. There is no reason why five gentlemen of the Supreme Court should know better what public policy demands than five gentlemen of Congress.
Louis D. Brandeis, *1856–1941*
Alpheus Thomas Mason, *Brandeis: A Free Man's Life,* 1946

127.4   Civil liberties had their origin and must find their ultimate guaranty in the faith of the people. If that faith should be lost, five or nine men in Washington could not long supply its want.
Robert H. Jackson
Douglas v. Jeannette, 319 U.S. 157, 182 (1943)

127.5   This Court is forever adding new stories to the temples of constitutional law, and the temples have a way of collapsing when one story too many is added.
Robert H. Jackson
Douglas v. Jeannette, 319 U.S. 157, 181 (1943)

127.6   The people can change Congress but only God can change the Supreme Court.
George W. Norris, *1861–1944*
Laurence J. Peter, *Peter's Quotations,* 1977

127.7   We want a Supreme Court which will do justice under the Constitution—not over it. In our courts we want a government of laws and not of men.
Franklin Delano Roosevelt, *1882–1945*
Laurence J. Peter, *Peter's Quotations,* 1977

127.8   By the very nature of the functions of the Supreme Court, each member of it is subject only to his own sense of the trusteeship of what are perhaps the most revered traditions in our national system.
Felix Frankfurter
" 'The Administrative Side' of Chief Justice Hughes," 63 *Harvard Law Review,* 1, 2 (1949)

127.9   One is entitled to say without qualification that the correlation between prior judicial experience and fitness for the functions of the Supreme Court is zero.
Felix Frankfurter
"Supreme Court in the Mirror of Justice," 105 *University of Pennsylvania Law Review* (1957)

127.10   The difficulty in modification of the Constitution makes the Supreme Court a very powerful body in shaping the course of our civilization. In dealing with the constitutional guarantees of human dignity, it often has the application of the national conscience in its keeping. It is a sort of diplomatic priesthood.
F. D. G. Ribble
167 *Washington and Lee Law Review* (1957)

127.11   Whenever you put a man on the Supreme Court he ceases to be your friend.
Harry S. Truman
New York Times, 1959

127.12   It is nine men, nine very human men, participating in a process that can be impressive or disturbing, grave or funny. And contrary to the general impression, the process is more visible than most of what goes on in government.
Anthony Lewis
"Nine Very Human Men," *New York Times Magazine,* January 17, 1965

127.13   The criticism of the Court that is, perhaps, most frequently heard and that pretty well encompasses all other ones is that the Court is too political. This criticism is misguided or well-taken, depending on what is meant by it. If it means that the Court should make no decisions that can in any sense be deemed political, but should follow some certain body of rules called Constitutional Law, the answer is that The Law as so conceived is a myth, it does not exist, and hence the Court, in order to function at all, must make law rather than simply follow it. Therefore, it must make what are bound to be, in a sense, political decisions.
But if the criticism means that the Court's occasions and modes of policymaking should be different from those of the elected organs of government, then the criticism is well-taken. It means, then, not that this has been a political court but that it has in some instances been wrongly political, that it has been political after the fashion of a legislature or an executive rather than a court.
Alexander M. Bickel
"Is the Warren Court Too 'Political'?" *New York Times Magazine,* September 25, 1966

127.14   I have no objection to nine aging gentlemen appointed for life interpreting the law; but I would deprive them of the last word . . . .
Robert M. Hutchins, president, Center for the Study of Democratic Institutions
Interview, *Los Angeles Times,* June 17, 1969

127.15   It is not likely ever, with human nature as it is, for nine men to agree always on the most important and controversial issues of life. If it ever comes to such a pass I would say that the Supreme Court will have lost its strength and will no longer be a real force in the affairs of our country.

Earl Warren
New York Times, June 23, 1969

127.16   The vision of America held and defined by the Warren Court was the noblest and most honorable of them all—a vision of justice in its ultimate form, the form of freedom. It may not have been perfect . . . . But it dared to turn from darkness to face the sun.

Archibald MacLeish
New York Post, October 14, 1969

127.17   . . . there are a lot of mediocre judges and people and lawyers, and they are entitled to a little representation [on the U.S. Supreme Court], aren't they? We can't have all Brandeises, Frankfurters, and Cardozos and stuff like that there.

Roman L. Hruska, American politician; U.S. senator, Nebraska
Address, U.S. Senate, reported in the
New York Times, March 17, 1970

127.18   I can't get alarmed when [the Supreme Court] overrules a prior decision, especially if it is 5–4. Who is to say that five men 10 years ago were right whereas five men looking the other direction today are wrong.

Harry A. Blackmun
Interview, *Los Angeles Herald-Examiner,* April 20, 1970

127.19   One of the first things I was taught when I went through law school was that we should have predictability in our laws. What has happened is that the Supreme Court has too often destroyed predictability . . . because of its assumption of the legislative authority.

James L. Buckley
Washington Post, January 10, 1971

127.20   The Court is the creature of the litigation the lawyers bring to it.

Earl Warren
Interview, *Washington Post,* March 15, 1971

127.21   . . . the primary role of the Court is to decide cases. From the decision of cases, of course, some changes develop. But to try to create or substantially change civil or criminal procedure, for example, by judicial decision is the worst possible way to do it. The Supreme Court is simply not equipped to do that job properly.

Warren E. Burger
Address, American Law Institute, Washington, D.C., reported in the
National Observer, May 24, 1971

127.22   I go onto the Court with deep personal misgivings whether I'll like it. In fact, I rather suppose I won't . . . . But the Supreme Court has a very special place in the life and attitude of any lawyer of my age . . . . For those of my generation, it is a revered institution, the pinnacle of our profession.

Lewis F. Powell, Jr.
Interview, *Washington Post,* October 24, 1971

127.23   At least, my role in presenting the foreign policy statement will have the merit which John G. Johnson found in staying at the bar instead of accepting President Cleveland's offer of a place on the Supreme Court. "I would rather talk to the damned fools," he said, "than listen to them."

Dean Acheson, *1893–1971*
Among Friends: Letters of Dean Acheson, 1980

127.24   I feel about the future of the United States whenever the president starts out on his travels the way the marshal of the Supreme Court feels about the law when he opens a session of the court. You will recall that he ends up his liturgy by saying, "God save the United States for the Court is now sitting."
Dean Acheson, *1893–1971*
Among Friends: Letters of Dean Acheson, 1980

127.25   The Supreme Court is becoming a wholly owned subsidiary of the rich and powerful, instead of the impartial and compassionate tribunal it has been.
Arthur M. Schlesinger, Jr.
New York Times, October 24, 1972

127.26   A man might be a very great liberal in political life and he might be equally as conservative in judicial process because they are entirely different. You see, in the political process, the legislative bodies have the oversight, within Constitutional limits, of everything in their jurisdiction . . . . But the Court is not a self-starter in that respect. It can never reach out and grab any issue and bring it into court and decide it, no matter how strongly it may feel about the condition it's confronted with.
Earl Warren
New York Times, December 20, 1972

127.27   We [on the Supreme Court] never have the hours and the moments to put our feet on the window sills and reflect a bit.
Harry A. Blackmun
San Francisco Examiner, February 13, 1973

127.28   The first opinion the Court ever filed had a dissenting opinion. Dissent is a tradition of this court . . . . When someone is writing for the Court, he is hoping to get eight others to agree with him, so many of the majority opinions are rather stultified.
William O. Douglas
Interview, *New York Times,* October 29, 1973

127.29   The Court's great power is its ability to educate, to provide moral leadership.
William O. Douglas
Interview, *Time,* November 12, 1973

127.30   I think it's so easy, because of the pressures here [on the Court] and the demands on our time, for us [justices] to stay in our ivory tower and not get out. I think we are too confined at times. It doesn't seem to me that we should hit the political circuit, but it's good to hear the voices of America from a different podium than the rostrum before us.
Harry A. Blackmun
Interview, *New York Times,* July 14, 1975

127.31   The history of the U.S. Supreme Court clearly demonstrates that the justices of the Court invariably decide cases on the basis of their own values—their own prejudices, their own economics, their own sociology, their own morals, their own theology, their own philosophy . . . . When a majority of the Court was pro-business, it struck down laws fixing minimum wages. When a majority of the Court was pro-labor, it struck down laws restricting picketing and boycotting. When a majority of the Court was libertarian, it struck down anti-pornography laws. When a majority of the Court embraced anti-Negro and anti-Japanese prejudices, it ruled against black and yellow people.

> Professor Virgil C. Blum, American educator; professor, Marquette University
> Speech, *Vital Speeches,* December 15, 1975

127.32   I have been told that there is no precedent for admitting a woman to practice in the Supreme Court of the United States. The glory of each generation is to make its own precedents. As there was none for Eve in the Garden of Eden, so there need be none for her daughters on entering the colleges, the church, or the courts.

> Belva Lockwood, American lawyer and feminist
> Mary Virginia Fox, *Lady for the Defense,* 1975

127.33   Taft, when he became solicitor general, wrote a letter back to his father in Cincinnati saying rather plaintively that when he rose in the Supreme Court to make a speech, "[the judges] . . . think that is a good chance to read all the letters that have been waiting for some time, to eat lunch . . . and to devote their attention to correcting proof and other matters . . . . However, I expect to get a good deal of practice addressing a lot of mummies."

> Archibald Cox
> *The Role of the Supreme Court in American Government,* 1976

127.34   The Court is . . . perhaps one of the last citadels of jealously preserved individualism. For the most part, we function as nine, small independent law firms.

> Lewis F. Powell, Jr.
> *Los Angeles Times,* July 9, 1978

127.35   I do not believe it is the function of the judiciary to step in and change the law because the times have changed. I do well understand the difference between legislating and judging. As a judge, it is not my function to develop public policy.

> Sandra Day O'Connor
> *Washington Post,* September 10, 1981

127.36   The vast majority of the filings [before the U.S. Supreme Court] are from lawyers who have never been there. They have no intuitive sense of what's worthy, and no one to tell them. So they go to the big court . . . . There's also an ego factor. A lawyer wants a moment of glory.

> A. E. Howard, American educator; professor, University of Virginia
> *Washington Post,* September 24, 1982

127.37   . . . the proper role of the judiciary is one of interpreting and applying the law, not making it. . . .

> Sandra Day O'Connor, at her confirmation hearing
> *New York Times,* February 23, 1984

127.38   The Court's only armor is the cloak of public trust; its sole ammunition, the collective hopes of our society.

> Irving R. Kaufman, American jurist
> "Keeping Politics Out of the Court,"
> *New York Times* December 9, 1984

T

128. TAXATION

128.1   To tax and to please, no more than to love and be wise, is not given to men.
> Edmund Burke, *1729–1797*
> 36 *Harvard Business Review* 1,
> January–February, 1958

128.2   . . . the power to tax involves the power to destroy; . . .
> John Marshall
> *M'Culloch v. Maryland,* 17 U.S. (4 Wheat.) 316, 431 (1819)

128.3   Of all debts men are least willing to pay the taxes.
> Ralph Waldo Emerson
> "History," *Essays,* 1830–1840

128.4   The liberty of the citizen to do as he likes so long as he does not interfere with the liberty of others to do the same, which has been a shibboleth for some well-known writers, is interfered with . . . by every state or municipal institution which takes his money for purposes thought desirable, whether he likes it or not.
> Oliver Wendell Holmes
> *Lochner v. New York,* 198 U.S. 45, 49 L.Ed. 937, 25 Sup. Ct. 539 (1905)

128.5   . . . even the fixing of a tariff rate must be moral.
> Ida Tarbell, American writer
> *The Tariff in Our Times,* 1906

128.6   Taxes are what we pay for civilized society . . . .
> Oliver Wendell Holmes
> *Compania General de Tabacos de Filipinas v. Collector of Internal Revenue,* 275 U.S. 87, 100 (1927)

128.7   The power to tax is not the power to destroy while this Court sits.
> Oliver Wendell Holmes
> *Panhandle Oil Co. v. Knox,* 277 U.S. 233 (1928)

128.8   Death and taxes and childbirth! There's never any convenient time for any of them!
> Margaret Mitchell
> *Gone with the Wind,* 1936

128.9   The physical power to get the money does not seem to me a test of the right to tax. Might does not make right even in taxation.
> Robert H. Jackson
> *International Harvester Company v. Wisconsin Department of Taxation,* 322 U.S. 435, 450 (1944)

128.10　I'm a middle-bracket person with a
　　　　middle-bracket spouse
　　　　And we live together gaily in a mid-
　　　　dle-bracket house.
　　　　We've a fair-to-middlin' family; we
　　　　take the middle view;
　　　　So we're manna sent from heaven
　　　　to internal revenue.
　　　　Phyllis McGinley
　　　　"The Chosen Peoples," *Times Three:*
　　　　1932–1960, 1960

128.11　No one has ever suggested that
　　　　tax exemption has converted librar-
　　　　ies, art galleries, or hospitals into

arms of the state . . . There is no
genuine nexus between tax exemption and establishment of religion.
　　Warren E. Burger
　　Walz v. Tax Commission, 397 U.S.
　　664, 90 S. Ct. 1409, 25 L.Ed.2d 697
　　(1970)

128.12　Behind every man who achieves
　　　　success
　　　　Stand a mother, a wife and the IRS.
　　　　Ethel Jacobson, American literary
　　　　critic
　　　　Reader's Digest, April 1973

129.　TESTIMONY

129.1　A man's death-trap may be be-
　　　　tween his teeth.
　　　　Jewish folk saying
　　　　Joseph L. Baron, *A Treasury of*
　　　　Jewish Quotations, 1956

129.2　Half an answer also tells you
　　　　something.
　　　　Jewish folk saying
　　　　Joseph L. Baron, *A Treasury of*
　　　　Jewish Quotations, 1956

129.3　No answer is a type of answer.
　　　　Jewish folk saying
　　　　Joseph L. Baron, *A Treasury of*
　　　　Jewish Quotations, 1956

129.4　Thou shalt not bear false witness
　　　　against thy neighbor.
　　　　Old Testament, *Exodus,* 20:13

129.5　If one man says, "You're a don-
　　　　key," don't mind; if two say so, be
　　　　worried; if three say so, get a saddle.
　　　　Midrash, *Genesis Rabba*

129.6　Judge a man only by his own
　　　　deeds and words; the opinions of
　　　　others can be false.
　　　　Talmud

129.7　An oath [in court] is worthless if it
　　　　affirms the impossible: for instance,
　　　　that you saw a camel fly.
　　　　Talmud, *Shebrioth*

129.8 Ingenuity is one thing, and simple testimony another, and plain truth, I take it, needs no flowers of speech.
Sir James Mansfield, English jurist; chief justice
Wilkes v. Wood (1763), 19 How. St. Tr. 1176

129.9 Every man is bound to leave a story better than he found it.
Mary Augusta Ward, English social worker
Robert Elsmer, 1888

129.10 Remember that the eyes of God and of her Majesty's police court are upon you.
London "beak" [magistrate] to a witness who was about to take the oath
Marshall Brown, *Wit and Humor of Bench and Bar,* 1899

129.11 Sir Rowland: You must know better than I do, Inspector, how very rarely two people's account of the same thing agrees. In fact, if three people were to agree exactly, I should regard it as suspicious. Very suspicious, indeed.
Agatha Christie
Spider's Web, 1956

129.12 The plaque at the front of the courtroom, high on the wall, was permanent and yet its words were new each time Jack read them, read them half against his will, his eyes moving restlessly forward and up to them while testimony droned on: *Conscience Speaks the Truth.*
Joyce Carol Oates
Do with Me What You Will, 1970

130. THOUGHT

130.1 The thought of man shall not be tried, for the devil himself knoweth not the thought of man.
Chief Justice Brian
Great Britain Yearbooks, 17 Edward IV, 1444

130.2 If there be any among us who would wish to dissolve this Union or to change its republican form, let them stand as monuments of the safety with which error of opinion may be tolerated where reason is left free to combat it.
Thomas Jefferson
First inaugural address, March 4, 1801

130.3 A man is bound to be parochial in his practice . . . . But his thinking should be cosmopolitan and detached. He should be able to criticize what he reveres and loves.
Oliver Wendell Holmes
"John Marshall," *Speeches,* 1913

130.4   If there is any principle of the Constitution that more imperatively calls for attachment than any other it is the principle of free thought—not free thought for those who agree with us but freedom for the thought we hate.
Oliver Wendell Holmes
United States v. Schwimmer, 279 U.S. 644, 654, 73 L.Ed. 889, 893, 49 S. Ct. 448 (1929)

130.5   We can have intellectual individualism and the rich cultural diversities that we owe to exceptional minds only at the price of occasional eccentricity and abnormal attitudes.
Robert H. Jackson
Board of Education v. Barnette, 319 U.S. 624, 641–42 (1943)

130.6   There is no such crime as a crime of thought; there are only crimes of action.
Clarence Darrow,   *1857–1938*
Arthur Weinberg, ed., *Attorney for the Damned,* 1957

130.7   Freedom of speech and freedom of action are meaningless without freedom to think. And there is no freedom of thought without doubt.
Bergen Evans
The Natural History of Nonsense, 1946

131.   TORTS

131.1   No man should take advantage of his own wrong.
Legal maxim

131.2   Strife produces strife, and injury produces injury.
Legal maxim

131.3   It makes no difference whether a good man has defrauded a bad man or a bad man defrauded a good man, or whether a good or bad man has committed adultery: the law can look only to the amount of damage done.
Aristotle
Nicomachean Ethics, c.340 B.C.

131.4   But it is the first function of the law to see that no one shall injure another unless provoked by some wrong.
Cicero
De Officiis, 45–44 B.C.

131.5 The construction of the law does no injury.
Sir Edward Coke, *1552–1634*
W. Gurney Benham, *Putnam's Complete Book of Quotations, Proverbs and Household Words,* 1927

131.6 The law is an equal dispenser of justice, and leaves none without a remedy, for his right, without his own laches.
Justice Vaughn
Tustian v. Roper (1670), Jones's (Sir Thos.) Rep. 32

131.7 It is a vain thing to imagine a right without a remedy; for want of right and want of remedy are reciprocal.
Sir John Holt, English jurist; chief justice
Ashby v. White (1703), 2 Raym. 953

131.8 God forbid that the rights of the innocent should be lost and destroyed by the offence of individuals.
Sir John Eardley Wilmot, English jurist; chief justice
Mayor etc. of Colchester v. Seaber (1765), 3 Burr. Part IV. (1871)

131.9 Better that an individual should suffer an injury than that the public should suffer an inconvenience.
Justice Ashhurst, English jurist
Russell v. The Mayor of Devon (1788), 1 T.R. 673

131.10 What a man does in his closet ought not to affect the rights of third persons.
Sir Lloyd Kenyon, English jurist; lord chief justice
Outram v. Morewood (1793), 5 T.R. 123

131.11 The public can have no rights springing from injustice to others.
Sir John Romilly, English jurist
Walker v. Ware, Hadham, etc. Rail. Co. (1866), 12 Jur. (n.s.) 18

131.12 That great principle of the common law which declares that it is your duty so to use and exercise your own rights as not to cause injury to other people.
Sir Charles James Watkin Williams, English jurist
Gray v. North-Eastern Rail. Co. (1883), 48 L.T.R. (n.s.) 905

131.13 A nuisance may be merely a right thing in the wrong place, like a pig in the parlor instead of the barnyard.
George Sutherland, American jurist
Euclid v. Ambler Co., 272 U.S. 365, 388 (1926)

---

132.   TRIALS

132.1   A benefit may be conferred, but not a disability imposed, on a man in his absence.
Talmud, *Eruvin*

132.2   No man can be declared guilty in his absence [from the courtroom].
Talmud, *Ketubot*

132.3   A man confesses guilt by avoiding trial.
Publilius Syrus, Latin writer
Sententiae, c.43 B.C.

132.4   It is abominable to convict a man behind his back.
Sir John Holt, English jurist; chief justice
The Queen v. Dyer (1703), 6 Mod. 41

132.5   All trial is the investigation of something doubtful.
Samuel Johnson, *1709–1784*
Eugene Brussell, *Dictionary of Quotable Definitions,* 1970

132.6   The charge is prepar'd, the lawyers are met,
The judges all ranged,—a terrible show!
John Gay
Beggar's Opera, 1728

132.7   [*Trial:*] A formal inquiry designed to prove and put upon record the blameless characters of judges, advocates and jurors.
Ambrose Bierce
The Devil's Dictionary, 1906

132.8   Only a very foolish lawyer will dare guess the outcome of a jury trial.
Jerome Frank
Law and the Modern Mind, 1930

132.9   A trial is still ordeal by battle. For the broadsword there is the weight of evidence; for the battle-axe the force of logic: for the sharp spear, the blazing gleam of truth; for the rapier, the quick and flashing knife of wit.
Lloyd Paul Stryker, American lawyer
Quoted in reports of his death, June 22, 1955

132.10   In criminal trials a state can no more discriminate on account of poverty than on account of religion, race or color.
Hugo Black
Griffin v. Illinois, 351 U.S. 12, 19, 100 L.Ed. 891, 899, 76 S. Ct. 585, 55 ALR2d 1055 (1956)

132.11   In our own lifetime we have seen how essential fair trials are to civilization. The establishment of the modern dictatorships was not the result of a failure of democracy: it was due to a failure of law. There is no "trying" choice between fair trials and free speech, because free speech itself will die if there are no fair trials. For that matter it is almost always the first victim.

> Arthur L. Goodhart, American
> educator
> "Fair Trial and Contempt of Court in
> England," 4 *New York Law Journal* 1
> (June 25, 1964)

132.12 This idea of a fair trial has been the greatest contribution made to civilization by our Anglo-American polity.

> Arthur L. Goodhart, American
> educator
> "Fair Trial and Contempt of Court in
> England," 4 *New York Law Journal* 1
> (June 25, 1964)

132.13 Guilt or innocence become irrelevant in the criminal trial as we flounder in a morass of artificial rules, poorly conceived and often impossible of application. Like the hapless centipede on the flypaper, our efforts to extricate ourselves from this self-imposed dilemma will, if we keep it up, soon have all of us immobilized.

> Warren E. Burger
> Speech, reported in the *Washington
> Post,* May 26, 1969

132.14 I would rather see the law moving toward the day when we could scientifically determine innocence or guilt, instead of having to play the theater that is the trial to see if innocence or guilt can be proved by the cunning of prosecution or defense.

> F. Lee Bailey
> *New York Times Magazine,*
> September 20, 1970

132.15 Those who think the information brought out at a criminal trial is the truth, the whole truth and nothing but the truth are fools. Prosecuting or defending a case is nothing more than getting to those people who will talk for your side, who will say what you want said. . . . I use the law to frustrate the law. But I didn't set up the ground rules.

> F. Lee Bailey
> *New York Times Magazine,*
> September 20, 1970

132.16 An incompetent attorney can delay a trial for years or months. A competent attorney can delay one even longer.

> Evelle J. Younger, American lawyer;
> attorney general, California
> *Los Angeles Times,* March 3, 1971

132.17 The criminal trial today is less a test of guilt or innocence than a competition in which the knowledge of the rules, gamesmanship, and, above all, self-control is likely to decide the outcome; a kind of showjumping contest in which the rider for the prosecution must clear every obstacle to succeed.

> Robert Mark, English law
> enforcement official; commissioner,
> London Metropolitan Police
> *Washington Post,* November 23, 1971

132.18 I'll tell you what my daddy told me after my first trial. I asked him, "How did I do?" He paused and said, "You've got to guard against speaking more clearly than you think."

> Howard H. Baker, Jr.
> Interview, *Washington Post,* June 24,
> 1973

132.19 The institution of trial by jury is almost 1000 years old. But it may not last another 50 unless we can show the public that it is an efficient tool for the administration of justice.

    Irving Kaufman, American jurist
    Reader's Digest, September 1973

132.20   [Preparation] is the be-all of good trial work. Everything else—felicity of expression, improvisational brilliance—is a satellite around the sun. Thorough preparation is that sun.

    Louis Nizer
    Newsweek, December 11, 1973

132.21   Public participation—as in the jury trial—is the cornerstone in the administration of justice and vital to our system of law.

    June L. Tapp, American psychologist
    Gordon Bermant, "The Notion of Conspiracy Is Not Tasty to Americans," *Psychology Today,* May 1975

132.22   Law is not justice and a trial is not a scientific inquiry into truth. A trial is the resolution of a dispute.

    Edison Haines
    Laurence J. Peter, *Peter's Quotations,* 1977

132.23   To work effectively, it is important that society's criminal process "satisfy the appearance of justice," . . . and the appearance of justice can best be provided by allowing people to observe it.

    Warren E. Burger
    Richmond Newspapers, Inc. v. Virginia, 488 U.S. 555, 100 S. Ct. 2814, 65 L.Ed.2d 973 (1980)

132.24   It is not the bad lawyers who are screwing up the justice system in this country—it's the good lawyers. If you have two competent lawyers on opposite sides, a trial that should take three days could easily last six months.

    Art Buchwald
    Kenneth Redden, *Modern Legal Glossary,* 1983

133.　TRUTH

133.1   The thing is true, according to the law of Medes and Persians, which altereth not.

    Old Testament, *Daniel* 6:12

133.2   What is truth? said jesting Pilate; and would not stay for an answer.

    Francis Bacon, *1561–1626*
    "Of Truth" *Essayes*

133.3   Truth is the same in all persuasions.

George Jeffreys
Titus Oates' Case (1685), 10 How. St.
Tr. 1262

133.4   It is error alone which needs the support of government. Truth can stand by itself.

Thomas Jefferson
Notes on the State of Virginia,
c.1781–1783

133.5   The greater the truth, the greater the libel.

William Murray, 1st earl of
Mansfield, English jurist; chief justice
Presiding in 1784, over the king's
bench, probably quoting a legal
maxim

133.6   And, finally, that truth is great and will prevail if left to herself; that she is the proper and sufficient antagonist to error, and has nothing to fear from the conflict unless by human interposition disarmed of her natural weapons, free argument and debate; errors ceasing to be dangerous when it is permitted freely to contradict them.

Thomas Jefferson
Virginia Act for Religious Freedom,
1786

133.7   Presumption means nothing more than, as stated by *Lord Mansfield,* the weighing of probabilities, and deciding, by the powers of common sense, on which side the truth is.

Sir William Draper Best, Lord
Wynford, British jurist; chief justice
King v. Burdett (1820), 1 St. Tr. (n.s.)
114

133.8   It was a wise saying, that the farthest way about was often the nearest way home.

John Mitford, Lord Redesdale,
English jurist
Corporation of Ludlow v. Greenhouse
(1827), 1 Bligh, New Rep. 49

133.9   Truth, like all other good things, may be loved unwisely—may be pursued too keenly—may cost too much.

Sir James Lewis Knight-Bruce,
English jurist
Pearse v. Pearse (1846), 1 De Gex &
Sm. 28, 29

133.10   The lawyer's truth is not Truth, but consistency or a consistent.

Henry David Thoreau
Civil Disobedience, 1849

133.11   Truth is always in harmony with herself, and is not concerned chiefly to reveal the justice that may consist with wrong doings.

Henry David Thoreau
Civil Disobedience, 1849

133.12   Truth and falsehood, it has been well said, are not always opposed to each other like black and white, but oftentimes, and by design, are made to resemble each other so as to be hardly distinguishable; just as the counterfeit thing is counterfeit because it resembles the genuine thing.

Sir Anthony Cleasby, English jurist
Johnson v. Emerson (1871), L.R. 6 Ex.
Ca. 357

133.13   But O the truth, the truth! The many eyes
That look on it! the diverse things they see.

George Meredith
"The Ballad of Fair Ladies in
Revolt," c.1887

133.14   I used to say, when I was young, that truth was the majority vote of that nation that could lick all others.
> Oliver Wendell Holmes
> "Natural Law," *Collected Legal Papers,* 1920

133.15   No poet ever interpreted nature as freely as a lawyer interprets the truth.
> Jean Giraudoux, *1882–1944*
> Laurence J. Peter, *Peter's Quotations,* 1977

133.16   To present the truth is difficult in any case and particularly so in relation to industry, which is constantly in a state of adjustment to its changing environment and opportunities. With respect to help in avoiding mistakes and troubles, I have learned that the positive approach to difficulty is often the more effective. As a caddy once remarked to me, "Good golf is what you do, sir—not what you don't do!"
> Erwin Haskell Schell, Jr., American psychiatrist
> *The Million Dollar Lecture and Letters to Former Students,* 1952

133.17   For the trouble with lying and deceiving is that their efficiency depends entirely upon a clear notion of the truth that the liar and deceiver wishes to hide. In this sense, truth, even if it does not prevail in public, possesses an ineradicable primacy over all falsehoods.
> Hannah Arendt
> "Lying in Politics," *Crises of the Republic,* 1972

133.18   All sides in a trial want to hide at least some of the truth. The defendant wants to hide the truth because he's generally guilty. The defense attorney's job is to make sure the jury does not arrive at that truth. The prosecution is perfectly happy to have the truth of guilt come out, but it, too, has a truth to hide: it wants to make sure the process by which the evidence was obtained is not truthfully presented because, as often as not, that process will raise questions.
> Alan M. Dershowitz
> Interview, *U.S. News & World Report,* August 9, 1982

134. TYRANNY

134.1   The more by law, the less by right.
Danish proverb
H. L. Mencken, *A New Dictionary of Quotations,* 1946

134.2   [A king] is above his laws.
Proverb
"Jack Cade's Proclamation," in James Gairdner, *Three Fifteenth-Century Chronicles* (1460), Camden Society Publications: London, 1838

134.3   The purpose of law is to prevent the strong always having their way.
Ovid,   *43 B.C.–?A.D. 17*
Fasti, c.8

134.4   Wherever Law ends, Tyranny begins.
John Locke
Second Treatise of Government, 1690

134.5   The voice of nations and the course of things
Allow that laws superior are to kings.
Daniel Defoe
The True-Born Englishman, 1701

134.6   There is no crueler tyranny than that which is perpetuated under the shield of law and in the name of justice.
de Montesquieu,   *1689–1755*
Laurence J. Peter, *Peter's Quotations,* 1977

134.7   God forbid, my lords, that there should be a power in this country of measuring the civil rights of the subject by his moral character, or by any other rule but the fixed laws of the land! . . . Unlimited power is apt to corrupt the minds of those who possess it; and this I know, my lords, that where law ends, tyranny begins!
William Pitt
"The English Constitution," Speech, delivered in the House of Lords in reply to Lord Mansfield in the Case of Wilkes, January 9, 1770

134.8   One law for the lion and ox is oppression.
William Blake
The Marriage of Heaven and Hell, 1790

134.9   O Paddy dear, an' did ye hear the news that's goin' round?
The shamrock is by law forbid to grow on Irish ground!
No more St. Patrick's Day we'll keep, his color can't be seen,
For there's a cruel law agin the wearin' o' the Green!
Anonymous
"The Wearing O' the Green," c.1795

134.10   For they're hangin' men an' women
          there for wearin' o' the Green.
          Anonymous
          "The Wearing O' the Green," c.1795

134.11   The Law is the true embodiment
          Of everything that's excellent.
          It has no kind of fault or flaw,
          And I, my lords, embody the Law.
          Sir W. S. Gilbert
          Iolanthe, 1882

134.12   A crown and justice? Night and day
          Shall first be yoked together.
          Algernon Charles Swinburne
          Marino Faliero, 1885

134.13   Legality and oppression are not
          unknown to run hand in hand.
          Sir Henry Hawkins, Baron Brampton,
          English jurist
          *Roberts v. Jones; Willey v. Great
          Northern Railway Co.* (1891), L.R. 2
          Q.B. (1891)

134.14   The testimony of centuries, in
          governments of varying kinds over
          populations of different races and
          beliefs, stood as proof that physical
          and mental torture and coercion
          had brought about the tragically
          unjust sacrifices of some who were
          the noblest and most useful of their
          generations.
          Hugo Black
          Chambers v. Florida, 309 U.S. 227, 84
          L.Ed. 716, 60 Sup. Ct. 472 (1940)

134.15   . . . it is from petty tyrannies that
          large ones take root and grow. This
          fact can be no more plain than
          when they are imposed on the most
          basic rights of all. Seedlings planted
          in that soil grow great and, growing,
          break down the foundations of lib-
          erty. . . .
          Wiley B. Rutledge
          Thomas v. Collins, 323 U.S. 516, 89
          L.Ed. 430, 65 Sup. Ct. 315 (1944)

U

135. USURY

135.1   Usury is murder.
Hebrew proverb

135.2   To borrow upon Usury bringeth
on Beggary.
Proverb
Thomas Fuller, *Gnomologia,* 1732

135.3   The usurer is as deaf as a door-
nail.
Thomas Wilson
A Discourse upon Usury, 1572

135.4   These eyght thynges are rare times
seene . . . an old usurer without
money. . . .
John Florio
Firste Fruites, 1578

135.5   A legal thief, a bloodless murderer,
A fiend incarnate, a false usurer.
Joseph Hall, English clergyman;
bishop of Norwich
Virgidemarium, IV, 1598

135.6   Usurers live by the fall of young
heirs, as swine by the dropping of
acorns.
George Wilkins
The Miseries of Inforst Mariage, 1607

135.7   To speak of a usurer at the table
mars the wine.
George Herbert
Jacula Prudentum, 1640

135.8   There are three forms of usury: interest on money, rent of land and
houses, and profit in exchange. Whoever is in receipt of any of these is a
usurer.
Benjamin R. Tucker
Instead of a Book, 1893

135.9   Man was lost if he went to a usu-
rer, for the interest ran faster than a
tiger upon him. . . .
Pearl S. Buck
"The Frill," *First Wife and Other
Stories,* 1933

V

136.   VICTIMS

136.1 There's no weapon that slays
Its victim so surely (if well aimed) as
  praise.
Edward Robert Bulwer-Lytton, earl
of Lytton
Lucile, 1860

136.2 As someday it may happen that a
victim must be found, I've got a
little list—I've got a little list.
Of society offenders who might well
  be under ground,
And who never would be missed—
who never would be missed.
Sir W. S. Gilbert
The Mikado, 1885

136.3 The first thing to be done by a bi-
ographer in estimating character is to
examine the stubs of the victim's
cheque books.
Silas Weir Mitchell, *1829-1891*
Harvey William Cushing, *Life of Sir
William Osler,* 1925

136.4 The rain it raineth on the just
And also on the unjust fella:
But chiefly on the just, because
The unjust steals the just's umbrella.
Charles Bowen
Thad Stem, Jr. and Alan Butler, *Sam
Ervin's Best Short Stories,* 1973

136.5 Do you think there could be some-
thing like victims without crimes?
Rosellen Brown, American writer
"A Letter to Ismael in the Grave,"
Street Games, 1974

W

137. WAR

137.1 Where drums beat, laws are silent.
Proverb
Rosalind Fergusson, *The Facts On File Dictionary of Proverbs,* 1983

137.2 But we fight for our lives and our laws.
Old Testament, 1 *Maccabees* 3:21

137.3 Go, tell the Spartans, thou who passest by,
That here obedient to their laws we lie.
Simonides of Ceos, *556–c.468 B.C.*
J. M. Cohen and M. J. Cohen, *The Penguin Dictionary of Quotations,* 1960

137.4 The law speaks too softly to be heard amid the din of arms.
Caius Marius, *c.157–86 B.C.*
"Caius Marius" Plutarch, *Lives*

137.5 Hotspur: The arms are fair,
When the intent of bearing them is just.
Shakespeare
I *Henry IV,* V, 2, 1597–1598

137.6 Religious cannons, civil laws are cruel;
Then what should war be?
Shakespeare
Timon of Athens, 1607–1608

137.7 Force and fraud are in war the two cardinal virtues.
Thomas Hobbes
Leviathan, 1651

137.8 Who overcomes by force hath overcome but half his foe.
John Milton
Paradise Lost, 1667

137.9 Force first made conquest, and that conquest law.
Alexander Pope
An Essay on Man, 1733

137.10 One to destroy, is murder by the law,
And gibbets keep the lifted hand in awe;
To murder thousands takes a specious name,
War's glorious art, and gives immortal fame.
Edward Young, *1683–1765*
Love of Fame

137.11　Ez fer war, I call it murder—
　　　　Ther you hev it plain and flat;
　　　I don't want to go no further
　　　　Than my testyment fer that.
　　　　　Of James Russell Lowell
　　　　　The Biglow Papers, 1848

137.12　Follow law, and forms of law, as
　　　far as convenient.
　　　　　Abraham Lincoln
　　　　　Instructions to Ulysses S. Grant,
　　　　　October 21, 1862

137.13　A bayonet in the hands of one
　　　man is no better than in the hand of
　　　another. It is the bayonet that is evil
　　　and all of its fruits are bad.
　　　　　Clarence Darrow
　　　　　Resist Not Evil, 1903

137.14　And lo, there dawns another, swift
　　　　and stern,
　　　When on the wheels of wrath, by
　　　　Justice' token,

Breaker of God's own Peace, you
shall in turn
Yourself be broken.
　　Sir Owen Seaman, English humorist
　　and author
　　"To the German Kaiser," *Punch,*
　　August 19, 1914

137.15　The appalling thing about war is
　　that it kills all love of truth.
　　　Georg Brandes
　　　Letter to Georges Clemenceau, March
　　　1915

137.16　If men recognize no law superior
　　to their desires, then they must fight
　　when their desires collide.
　　　R. H. Tawney
　　　Laurence J. Peter, *Peter's Quotations,*
　　　1977

137.17　You cannot shake hands with a
　　clenched fist.
　　　Indira Gandhi,　*1917–1984*

138.　WITNESSES

138.1　Woe to the dough that the baker
　　testifies against.
　　　Babylonian Talmud, *Pesahim*

138.2　A witness may not act as a judge.
　　　Talmud, *Bava Qamma*

138.3　These are ineligible to serve as
　　judges or witnesses: a gambler, a
　　usurer, and a dealer in forbidden
　　produce.
　　　Talmud, *Sanhedrin*

138.4 One eye-witness is worth more than ten who tell what they have heard.
Plautus, *c.254–184 B.C.*
Truculentus

138.5 The innocent man on trial fears fortune, but not a witness.
Publilius Syrus, Latin writer
Sententiae, c.43 B.C.

138.6 Witnesses, not hired in any honest fashion, sell their perjuries.
Ovid, *43 B.C.–?A.D. 18*
Amores

138.7 Witnesses may lie, either be mistaken themselves, or wickedly intend to deceive others . . . but . . . circumstances cannot lie.
Richard Mounteney, Irish jurist
Annesley v. Lord Anglesea (1743), 17 How. St. Tr. 1430

138.8 . . . the lawyer's vacation is the space between the question put to a witness and his answer!
Rufus Choate, *1799–1859*
Samuel Gilman Brown, *The Works of Rufus Choate,* 1862

138.9 We better know there is a fire whence we see much smoke rising than we could know it by one or two witnesses swearing to it. The witnesses may commit perjury, but the smoke cannot.
Abraham Lincoln
Unsent letter to J. R. Underwood and Henry Grider, October 26, 1864

138.10 Wherever a man commits a crime, God finds a witness. . . . Every secret crime has its reporter.
Ralph Waldo Emerson
"Natural Religion," *Essays,* c.1875

138.11 And summed it so well that it came to far more
Than the witnesses ever had said!
Lewis Carroll
The Hunting of the Snark, 1876

138.12 There is an old story of blind men trying to describe an elephant. One felt the elephant's leg and declared that the creature was like a tree, another felt the enormous side and said the elephant was like a wall, while a third, feeling the tail, was positive the animal was like a rope. Each man had a notion of reality that was limited by the number and kind of attributes he had perceived.
Wayne C. Minnick, American educator
The Art of Persuasion, 1957

139. WOMEN

139.1   Men make laws, women make manners.
Guibert, French writer, *18th century*
W. Gurney Benham, *Putnam's Complete Book of Quotations, Proverbs and Household Words,* 1927

139.2   . . . there is no country in the world where there is so much boasting of the "chivalrous" treatment she enjoys . . . . In short, indulgence is given her as a substitute for justice.
Harriet Martineau, American writer
"Women," *Society in America,* 1837

139.3   . . . all laws which prevent women from occupying such a station in society as her conscience shall dictate, or which place her in a position inferior to that of man, are contrary to the great precept of nature, and therefore of no force or authority.
Elizabeth Cady Stanton
History of Woman Suffrage, 1881

139.4   . . . such laws as conflict, in any way, with the true and substantial happiness of women, are contrary to the great precept of nature and of no validity, for this is "superior in obligation to any other."
Elizabeth Cady Stanton
History of Woman Suffrage, 1881

139.5   Thus far women have been the mere echoes of men. Our laws and constitutions, our creeds and codes, and the customs of social life are all of masculine origin. The true woman is as yet a dream of the future.
Elizabeth Cady Stanton
Speech, International Council of Women, 1888

139.6   Women are one-half of the world but until a century ago . . . it was a man's world. The laws were man's laws, the government a man's government, the country a man's country . . . . The man's world must become a man's and a woman's world. Why are we afraid? It is the next step forward on the path to the sunrise, and the sun is rising over a new heaven and a new earth.
Martha Thomas, American educator
Address, North American Woman Suffrage Association, 1908

139.7   Nature gave women too much power; the law gives them too little.
Will Henry, American political adviser and columnist, *1890–1970*
Readers Digest, August 1971

139.8   It's hard for a mere man to believe that women don't have equal rights.
Dwight D. Eisenhower
Speech, August 7, 1957

139.9 It is horrible to listen to men in black togas having discussions about your morals, your cystitis, your feelings, your womb, the way you straddled your legs.
Gigliola Pierobon, Italian feminist
"Gazette News: Abortion in Italy,"
Ms., October 1973

139.10 . . . classifications based on sex, like classification based on race, alienage, or national origin, are inher-

ently suspect, and must therefore be subjected to strict judicial scrutiny.
Frontiero v. Richardson, 411 U.S. 677 (1973)

139.11 The Constitution requires that Congress treat similarly situated persons similarly, not that it engage in gestures of superficial equality.
William H. Rehnquist
Rostker v. Goldberg, June 25, 1981

140.   WORDS

140.1 The thought hath good lips and the quill a good tongue.
Italian proverb
W. Gurney Benham, *Putnam's Complete Book of Quotations, Proverbs and Household Words,* 1927

140.2 Then words came like a fall of winter snow.
Homer
Iliad, c.8th century B.C.

140.3 Usage, in which lies the decision, the law, and the norm of speech.
Horace
Ars Poetica, 13 B.C.

140.4 All laws are promulgated for this end: that every man may know his duty; and therefore the plainest and

most obvious sense of the words is that which must be put on them.
Sir Thomas More
Utopia, 1516

140.5 The heaviest thing that is, is one Et cetera.
John Florio
Firste Fruites, 1578

140.6 A word must become a friend or you will not understand it. Perhaps you do well to be cool and detached when you are seeking information, but I remind you of the wife who complained, "When I ask John if he loves me, he thinks I am asking for information."
Sir Edward Coke
Case of Swans (1592) 7 Rep. 15, 17

140.7   There must be no departure from the words of the law.
Sir Edward Coke, *1552–1634*
W. Gurney Benham, *Putnam's Complete Book of Quotations, Proverbs and Household Words,* 1927

140.8   We can judge of the intent of the parties only by their words.
Sir John Powell, English jurist
Idle v. Cooke (1704), 2 Raym. 1149

140.9   Words pass from men lightly.
Sir John Eardley Wilmot, English jurist; chief justice
Pillans v. Van Mierop (1764), 3 Burr. Part IV. 1671

140.10   Most of the disputes in the world arise from words.
William Murray, 1st earl of Mansfield, English jurist; chief justice
Morgan v. Jones (1773), Lofft. 177

140.11   We seek to find peace of mind in the word, the formula, the ritual. The hope is an illusion.
Benjamin N. Cardozo
The Growth of the Law, 1924

140.12   In the case at bar, also, the logic of words should yield to the logic of realities.
Louis D. Brandeis
Di Santo v. Pennsylvania, 273 U.S. 34, 47 S. Ct. 267, 71 L.Ed. 524 (1927)

140.13   Words after all are symbols, and the significance of the symbols varies with the knowledge and experience of the mind receiving them.
Benjamin N. Cardozo
Cooper v. Dasher, 290 U.S. 106, 54 S. Ct. 6, 78 L.Ed. 203 (1933)

140.14   We live by symbols, and what shall be symbolized by any image of the sight depends upon the mind of him who sees it.
Oliver Wendell Holmes
"John Marshall," *Speeches,* 1934

140.15   . . . words acquire scope and function from the history of events which they summarize.
Felix Frankfurter
Phelps Dodge Corporation v. National Labor Relations Board, 313 U.S. 177, 61 S. Ct. 845, 133 ALR 1217, 85 L.Ed. 1271 (1941)

140.16   Words, especially those of a constitution, are not to be read with such stultifying narrowness.
Harlan F. Stone
United States v. Classic, 313 U.S. 299, 85 L.Ed. 1368, 61 Sup. Ct. 1031 (1941)

140.17   There is no surer way to misread any document than to read it literally.
Learned Hand
Guiseppi v. Walling, 324 U.S. 244, 65 S. Ct. 605, 89 L.Ed. 921 (1944)

140.18   In law also the emphasis makes the song.
Felix Frankfurter
Bethlehem Co. v. State Board, 330 U.S. 767, 780 (1947)

140.19   Law has always been unintelligible, and I might say that perhaps it ought to be. And I will tell you why, because I don't want to deal in paradoxes. It ought to be unintelligible because it ought to be in words— and words are utterly inadequate to deal with the fantastically multiform occasions which come up in human life . . . .
Learned Hand
"Thou Shalt Not Ration Justice," *Brief Case,* November 4, 1951

140.20   Many words have no legal meaning. Others have a legal meaning very unlike their ordinary meaning. For example, the word "daffy-down-dilly." It is a criminal libel to

call a lawyer a "daffy-down-dilly." Ha! Yes, I advise you never to do such a thing. No, I certainly advise you *never* to do it.
Dorothy L. Sayers
Unnatural Death, 1955

140.21   A word may denote to an advocate something which he wished an audience to understand; yet it may have connotations which will produce an antagonistic impression. The result is ambiguity leading to misunderstanding of meaning. In 1954 Secretary of Defense Charles Wilson was the victim of such connotative ambiguity. Discussing the plight of unemployed workers while in Detroit, he expressed the opinion that they should show more initiative in seeking reemployment, and concluded by saying, "Personally, I like bird dogs better than kennel-fed dogs . . . bird dogs like to go out and hunt around for food, but the kennel-dogs just sit on their haunches and yelp."
Wayne C. Minnick, American educator
The Art of Persuasion, 1957

SELECTIVE BIBLIOGRAPHY

Adams, Franklin Pierce. *FPA's Book of Quotations*. New York: Funk and Wagnalls, 1952.

Andrews, William, ed. *The Lawyer in History, Literature, and Humour*. London: Wm. Andrews and Co., 1896.

Auden, W.H., ed., and Louis Kronenberger. *The Viking Book of Aphorisms: A Personal Selection*. New York: Viking Press, 1962, 1966.

Baron, Joseph L., ed. *A Treasury of Jewish Quotations*. South Brunswick, N.J.: A.S. Barnes and Co., 1956, 1965.

Bartlett, John. *Familiar Quotations: A Collection of Passages, Phrases and Proverbs Traced to Their Sources in Ancient and Modern Literature*. Boston: Little, Brown and Company, 1948.

Benham, W. Gurney. *Putnam's Complete Book of Quotations, Proverbs and Household Words*. New York: G.P. Putnam's Sons, 1927.

Braude, Jacob M. *Lifetime Speaker's Encyclopedia*, vol. 2. Englewood Cliffs, N.J.: Prentice Hall, 1962.

Broom, Herbert. *A Selection of Legal Maxims*. Philadelphia: T. & J.W. Johnson & Co., 1868.

Brown, Marshall. *Wit & Humor of Bench and Bar*. Chicago: T.M. Flood & Co., 1899.

Brussell, Eugene E., ed. *Dictionary of Quotable Definitions*. Englewood Cliffs, N.J.: Prentice Hall, 1970.

Cohen, J.M., and M.J. Cohen. *The Penguin Dictionary of Quotations*. New York: Allen Lane/Viking Press, 1960, 1977.

Collison, Robert and Mary. *The Dictionary of Foreign Quotations*. New York: Facts On File, 1980.

Cook, Paul C. *A Treasury of Legal Quotations Selected by Paul C. Cook*. New York: Vantage Press, 1961.

Cushman, Robert F. *Leading Constitutional Decisions*. Englewood Cliffs, N.J.: Prentice-Hall, 1977.

Edelhart, Mike, and James Tinen. *America the Quotable*. New York: Facts On File, 1983.

Evans, Bergen. *Dictionary of Quotations.* New York: Delacorte Press, 1969.

Fadiman, Clifton, and Charles Van Doren. *The American Treasury, 1455–1955.* New York: Harper and Brothers, 1955.

Fergusson, Rosalind. *The Facts On File Dictionary of Proverbs.* New York: Facts On File, 1983.

Gerhart, Eugene. *Quote It? Memorable Legal Quotations.* New York: Clark Boardman Co.; Albany: Sage Hill Publishers, 1969.

Harnsberger, Caroline Thomas. *Treasury of Presidential Quotations.* Chicago: Follet Publishing Co., 1964.

Katz, Marjorie, and Jean Arbeiter. *Pegs to Hang Ideas On.* New York: M. Evans and Co., 1973.

Kenin, Richard, and Justin Wintle, eds. *The Dictionary of Biographical Quotation.* New York: Alfred A. Knopf, 1968.

McNamara, M. Francis. *Ragbag of Legal Quotations Compiled by Francis McNamara.* New York: Matthew Bender and Co., 1960.

———. *2000 Famous Legal Quotations.* Rochester, N.Y.: Aqueduct Books, 1967.

MacDonald, William, ed. *Select Documents Illustrative of the History of the United States, 1776–1861.* New York and London: Macmillan Co., 1911.

Mencken, H.L., ed. *A New Dictionary of Quotations on Historical Principles from Ancient and Modern Sources.* New York: Alfred A. Knopf, 1946.

Moncreiff, F.C. *Wit and Wisdom of the Bench and Bar.* London, Paris, and New York: Cassel, Peter, Golpin and Co., 1882.

Norton-Kyshe, James William. *The Dictionary of Legal Quotations.* London: Sweet and Maxwell, 1904.

The Oxford Dictionary of Quotations. 3rd edition. New York: Oxford University Press, 1979.

Partnow, Elaine. *The Quotable Woman: 1800–On.* Garden City, N.Y.: Anchor Press, 1978.

———. *The Quotable Woman: From Eve to 1799.* New York: Facts On File, 1985.

Peter, Laurence J. *Peter's Quotations: Ideas for Our Times.* New York: William Morrow Co., 1977.

Reader's Digest Press editors. *Reader's Digest Treasury of Modern Quotations.* New York: Thomas Y. Crowell Co., 1975.

Rosten, Leo. *Leo Rosten's Treasury of Jewish Quotations.* New York: McGraw-Hill, 1972.

Seldes, George, ed. *The Great Quotations.* Secaucus, N.J.: Citadel Press, 1960, 1966, 1983.

Simpson, James B. *Contemporary Quotations: A Treasury of Notable Quotes Since 1950.* New York: Thomas Y. Crowell, 1964.

Stem, Thad, Jr., and Alan Butler. *Senator Sam Ervin's Best Stories.* Dunham, N.C.: Moore Publishing Co., 1973.

Stevenson, Burton. *Home Book of Proverbs, Maxims & Familiar Phrases.* New York: Macmillan Co., 1948.

Walsh, William S. *International Encyclopedia of Prose and Poetical Quotations.* New York: Holt, Rinehart and Winston, 1951.

Whiting, Bartlett Jere, and Helen Wescott Whiting. *Proverbs, Sentences, and Proverbial Phrases: From English Writings Mainly Before 1500.* Cambridge, Mass.: Belknap Press, Harvard University Press, 1968.

Index of Subjects

Index of Subjects

Index of Authors

Index of Authors